LAST MANN STANDING

by

ANTHONY MANN

TROUSER PRESS

©Anthony Mann 2010

Cover Design by: Tim Harvey
Typesetting and "Colouring-In of Cover": Tim Harvey

Published by Trouser Press.

First published 2010.

British Library Cataloguing-in-Publication Data
A catalogue record for this book is available from the
British Library

ISBN
97809516501-6-5

Printed and bound by
J F Print, Sparkford, Somerset

ACKNOWLEDGEMENTS

Firstly, I thank my wife, Maureen who gave up hours of watching "Eastenders" in order to type this tome.

My thanks to all those who told and sent me jokes, especially Peter Richards who, via e-mail, unerringly brightened up many a dull morning with a witty quip or jolly joke.

Finally, my thanks, as always, to the Press for stories in their newspapers. Not only have they provided a basis for comment in this book, they have also provided us with a means of wrapping the vegetable peelings to go into our newly acquired kitchen recycling caddy.

PREFACE

Welcome to the antidote to all that is politically correct. Packed full of views, observations, anecdotes and jokes, there is hopefully something for everyone. Long words, such as "pulchritudinous" and "disestablishmentarianism" for the educated, the highbrow and those who shop at Waitrose, and short words like "a" and "the" for those who shop at Asda. Not to be forgotten - for this is a very "inclusive" book - there are also three-syllable words for the work-shy, who come upon them by default, and the taxpayers' generosity. Words like "ben-e-fit"!

This is an England in decline and whilst I cannot guarantee that by reading this book the country's standards will rise, I think one can say with some certainty that a few blood pressures will.

This page is reserved for all those readers who wish to draw their own conclusions.....

CONTENTS

CHAPTER ONE

Middle England Never Complains,
It Merely Queues In Sainsbury's

Well, hello there once more, nice to see you again. It is you, isn't it? If not, you've got a double. Anyway, life is still a mixture of continuity and surprise – continuity in that despite all the grumblers, the BBC television licence is the best £140 odd quids' worth I will ever spend per annum. I'd pay that just for Radio 4. It's also nice to know that every couple of months there will be a new series of "I'm Sorry I Haven't A Clue" and "Just A Minute" which will always be presented by Nicholas Parsons – until he dies, anyway! Continuity in that "Strictly Come Dancing" will always bring forth Britain's innate ability to support and nurture the underdog. We all remember where we were when John Sargeant resigned. I was in the loo – a memorable moment in itself. Someone once said to me, "You always remember where you were the day John F. Kennedy was assassinated". You should have seen the chap's face when I replied, "So, he's dead, is he?" Continuity in that towns with any aspirations of grandeur will always possess a Mount Pleasant and that wherever you travel there will always be a poster adorning a lamp post advertising a Persian rug sale nearby. Continuity in that despite all options available in preserves, pickles and glue, one always reverts to Tiptree Jams, Branston and Evo-Stick.

Surprise in the expectation that after decades of cease fire, broken before the ink has dried on the words "cease" and "fire", the Palestinians and Israelis could ever be persuaded to enact a lasting, peaceful settlement. All the time there are still survivors on both sides, they will continue to bomb the hell out of each other. And when you see it on the TV screen you really do wonder what the heck they are fighting over. Johnny Journalist reporting from yet another sand dune, with the towns appearing to have been built from Godforsaken blocks of sand (or should that be Allah-forsaken?). I mean, the scenery is so drab. Not once have I sat there on the settee, eating a Pot Noodle, and thought, "Mmmm, d'you know, that looks ever so much like Guildford". It never seems the sort of place where anyone would lazily stretch his or her arms in contentment and exclaim, "Oh, what a lovely day. Let's pack a picnic and fire up the Micra", and then trundle off to Gaza's equivalent of the New Forest. I wonder if they have any areas of outstanding natural beauty, like the South Downs, for instance?

There was a lovely letter on Teletext which read, "It is all very well for the Vatican to condemn the violence in Gaza, but they cannot see that such killings are the inevitable outcome when 'beliefs' based on no more than blind faith are allowed to triumph over common sense. When will the world grow up and rid itself of this silly and dangerous reliance on religion and let us all move on". I couldn't have put that better myself. In fact, I haven't. The interesting aspect of this letter is that the writer resides on Merseyside! Exactly. It's so unusual to find someone in the north-west so erudite and readable, without any mention of the whinging, self-loathing and maudlin which usually permeates through Johnny Northerner's scribings. You know, on reflection, I'm not at all sure that he's actually from the north-west. I'm beginning to suspect that he or she originally hailed from either Haslemere or Godalming.

I've just arrived in Hoddesdon to give a talk to a ladies' club. If you've just arrived in Hoddesdon, please give me a wave as Hertfordshire can be a very lonely place. At 5 pm I turned on the News and almost immediately switched off. I pressed the button once more at 5.09 pm and again the subject under discussion was Prince Harry's description of some Pakistani chappie whom he knew as a "Paki". So? It's no different from a Welshman being Taffy, or Jock the Scot, or Paddy the Irishman. Don't some people get touchy? I am English, obviously (never did accept the Welsh contribution from my father). Some people describe themselves as British, but that's a slightly diluted handle. After all, as we all know, any fool can be British but it takes a lot more breeding to be English. But never mind. A Turk is from Turkey, a Dane is

2

from Denmark, Italians are Wops, anyone with a slightly swarthy appearance is a Dago, or if wearing a high viz jacket – a Day-Glo. But moving on, if from the West Country you'd be a Swede Basher, and from Norfolk, or north Somerset, an in-bred. And do they mind? Of course not, though residents of West Surrey will always be known as "proper" people! Sadly, East Surrey has Redhill in it.

While I think of it, doesn't David Barby, the antiques chappie on "Bargain Hunt", remind you of the lion in the original Wizard of Oz? And also, doesn't Neil Sedaka remind you of Bernie Winters? No? Well, they do me. Also, while I think of it, I've just returned from Sainsbury's – they are out of ham and egg pie – or Gala pie as it is sometimes known.

The festive period turned up one or two gems that wouldn't seem out of place on the first of April. M&S, Boots, Peacocks and Debenhams in the seaside town of Great Yarmouth displayed 6'6" cardboard police constables strategically placed to deter shoplifters. These "deterrents" were free for up to ten days – thought Christmas had twelve – but if stores wished to use them for a longer period, then they had to pay for them. Now there's a surprise. With our sense of British humour, however, shoppers started having their photographs taken alongside them, with some desperate housewives wishing to take them home, citing their preference for the strong, silent type. Ho, ho! The manager of Debenhams said that from outside the store the cardboard cut-outs looked "very realistic". Well, if he meant the policemen didn't actually stop anyone, arrest a thief, or make a determined, seasoned shoplifter think twice, then he was right. It was all very realistic.

The above story concluded, of course, with a paragraph about an unemployed chap, one Shaun Johnson, who walked into his local Job Centre where he was advised that if he wanted more than his Job Seeker's Allowance, then he ought to shoplift instead. This advice was given to him by one of the Job Centre counter staff, along with the cautionary advice that he should not steal more than £100 worth of goods, as over that amount, it tends to land you with a court appearance. Nice to learn that staff at the Job Centre are so knowledgeable about such matters.

Just getting back to the police for a minute, I read with some degree of concern that Sussex Police Farce is spending £10,000 of council taxpayers' lolly in providing Indian head massages for its call centre staff. Their Chief Constable, Martin Richards, stated that it was an "appropriate use of resources and a good way to relieve stress among workers facing pressurised situations". He added that this was "nothing new in organisations where staff was employed in call handling work. We recognise that our hard working staff can be sitting in set positions at their desks for long periods, taking calls and dealing with a variety of challenging issues. This service is a way of relieving the pressure". Fine, but it should be paid for by the individual if they feel it's necessary, not by the poor sod that foots their wages. Which reminds me, I did laugh, not out loud you understand, more of an understated snigger, when I learned that a woman rang 999 to complain that she couldn't get through to the "Strictly Come Dancing" voting line, as it was continually engaged. A certain amount of class about that, I felt.

Fortunately, "Skating On Ice" and "Masterchef" both return this week so my fix is sated. In a couple of years time we'll probably be watching "Masterchef On Ice", and "Dancing on Aga". Well, they do have to milk everything, don't they?

By the way, whatever happened to Siamese twins? We now have conjoined ones instead. Was I in the loo, yet again, when this change took place? I wonder how heavily the axe would have fallen on any broadcaster's neck should they have slipped on one of the many PC banana skins. Having recently had both twins die for one mother-to-be, we now learn of another case. This time one body, two heads. Despite all medical advice, the mother refuses to have a termination and wants them to be "given a chance". Somebody I know said that being female, if this happened to her, she would be horrified to have been told what she was carrying and would want it "out of her body asap". Read on, of course, and we learn (why am I not surprised?) that the bearer of this child/children is a Catholic and that well-worn path of acceptance is being trodden once more. It is, apparently, a "gift from God". I think it's more likely to be a gift from the taxpayer, if it survives. Still, as they say – two heads are better than one!

Has anyone thought ahead? What happens if these twins grow up and take part on a "Celebrity Mastermind"? Can you imagine John Humphries, or his successor, asking, "What is the capital of Scotland?" In unison, one mouth expletes "Glasgow", while the other bleats out "Edinburgh". Whose answer is he going to accept? What happens if it/they are good footballers and are signed by Manchester United? They are always going to have two chances of heading for goal. It's a very unlevel playing field (the spell check does not like the word "unlevel" and suggests "uneven", but I suggest "unlevel" is more appropriate, so I'm leaving it as it is!!). I can remember when the old saying read, "Get a head, get a hat". It'll soon be replaced with "Get a head, get another one"!

Appropriate joke:
Two mates chatting, one says, "I hear you are having sex with your girlfriend's twin. How do you tell them apart?" "Oh, that's easy", replied the mate, "his name's Nigel and he's got a moustache!"

What do you mean, it's too early in the book for you to have to start thinking so deeply.

I've just scanned the news. It says that a suicidal twin has killed her sister by mistake. Okay, enough.

Christmas can be kind and it can also be very cruel. I encountered both aspects over the festive period. Kind in that all Nick Park's wonderful "Wallace & Gromit" films could be enjoyed on a daily basis, cruelty raising its very ugly heads in the shape of what could only be described as the "Daily Express's" festive joke, that of placing photographs of both the Pope and

5

Peter Tatchell jowl by jowl. Hideous in the extreme to be confronted by one, but by both is a torture even the Japanese haven't yet used to good effect in one of their game shows. The newspaper article was headed, "Gay Rights Group accuse the Pope of spreading fear!" It could so easily have read, "Pope accuses gay rights group of spreading Aids" – well, I thought it was funny. Which reminds me of a joke:

Gay Tom goes into the doctor's surgery and has some tests carried out. The doctor comes back and says, "Tom, I'm not going to beat about the bush – you have Aids". Tom is devastated. "But doc, what can I do?" "Eat twenty curried sausages, thirty sprouts drenched in a curried sauce, ten jalapeno peppers, three tins of baked beans, a box of figs, half a box of bran flakes and top it off with a gallon of prune juice". Tom looks bewildered. "Will it cure me, doc?" "No", he replies, "but it should leave you with a better understanding of what your arse is for!"

Interesting to note that whilst we give fortunes in aid to people living in far off places, namely squalor, who will never return the favour in a million years because we are British, our heritage sites and museums are suffering from a lack of funding. What other country in this world would allow such iconic monuments as Hadrian's Wall to be on the "at risk" structure list. It shows the arrogance of British governments, past, present and probably future, hell bent on saving the world whilst abandoning our history. Still, as long as they delude themselves into believing that they are world leaders, nothing will change. Not content with foreign aid, we now, of course, free foreign prisoners early due to overcrowding in British jails. We then pay them compensation for the inconvenience. You couldn't make it up, could you? Why is our hard earned tax being given to offenders from abroad? Apparently just under £370,000 has been gifted to these bastards. Me? I'd let them rot in a prison scenario not encountered since Newgate. Bread, water and slop outs. No TV, no radio, no exercise, just the endless drudge until the sentence is completed in full and then they'd be returned to their country of origin.

Human rights? Oh, no. Sorry, you lost them the day you erred. The Howard League for Penal Reform has a lot to answer for.

The annual farce of awarding gongs went about its sordid business by handing out a KCB to the Permanent Secretary, one Nicholas Macpherson. Apparently, it's in recognition of his "extraordinary work in response to the crisis in the financial services industry". He was also involved in the nationalisation of "Northern Rock". Wasn't this Eton-educated chappie just doing the job for which he was no doubt paid very handsomely, or have I missed something? There's a chap called Lewis Hamilton who is involved in off-road driving, apparently, becoming an MBE. Was that for winning something or merely moving abroad? If medals are to be given away, then one candidate who should be awarded something is a lady called Barbara Jagger. She is about to retire from her job as a receptionist at a vet's practice in Keighley, Yorks. Over a 24-year period she has looked after over 4,000 cats and dogs. Miss Jagger has also cared for unwanted and injured squirrels, owls, seagulls, goats, pigs, sheep and donkeys. Now, that's what I call a trooper.

There's the story of young Eddie, the Queen's offspring, provoking a day or two's emotions, with pictures of him appearing to hit a dog with a stick, published in all the tabloids. The RSPCA are going to be working hard, apparently, to establish whether a full enquiry should be played out. Now, if there is, and Eddie is found guilty, he could be fined or even sent to prison, though I won't be holding my breath. The other err-apparent is none other than that saviour of Liverpool and England, Stephen Gerrard, who it is alleged hit some chap in a nightclub. He and two others will appear later this month at North Sefton Magistrates Court. Doesn't sound overly salubrious, does it, though it's probably quite upmarket for the north-west.

Huntingdon Life Sciences, the laboratory company who experiment on animals under the guise of bio-medical research, must be feeling pretty pleased with themselves this morning. Four animal rights extremists, or heroes, dependent on your view, are facing up to fourteen years behind bars for blackmailing companies who supplied HLS. Given that successive governments support the legal experimentation on live animals, I am not surprised those who feel so much anger take the measures that they do. Anyone knowingly involved in this practice should be ashamed of their contribution, for they are all as guilty as the one wielding the literal death sentence.

If these tests are so necessary and so humane, surely we should be seeing them screened on prime time TV. Maybe a BBC documentary on a day in the life of an animal, which has had no say in its abuse, mutilation and ultimate fate. Perhaps then the public may feel slightly less comfortable and the journalists who condemn these activists will realise just who the real criminals are. But then, advances in science (by whatever means) are designed to make money and that really is the name of the testing game – bastards!

I see that a huntsman – or should that be huntsperson – died recently after being thrown from his horse and breaking his neck. Either his horse was anti-fox hunting or there is a god.

Just occasionally, common sense prevails, but at what cost? A market trader who had been convicted for the most heinous crime of selling fruit and vegetables in Imperial measures celebrated after further charges against her were dropped. Known as the "Metric Martyr" Janet Devers, aged 64, gained a criminal record last year and was forced to pay almost £5,000 in costs for selling goods on her stall in pounds and ounces, rather than the Euro kilo. At the last minute of the latest hearing, Hackney Council did a U-turn, stating that it was not in the public interest to pursue the case, a case which has so far cost the tax payer £30,000. This lady is now planning to appeal against her original convictions. The Innovations Secretary (didn't know we had one), John Denham, stated last year that these cases were "not in the public interest". Wouldn't you just love to know what his department does, when it's not making statements like this? And isn't it a pity that the statements don't filter down to local council level in a much shorter time and at less cost.

Well, we've gone and done it! We've been to the RSPCA in Chobham and acquired another dog. After twenty-one months of being without a four-pawed companion, we've selected the new family member. As I write these notes with my write hand (for those north of Rickmansworth the second spelling of "write" is a play on words) my left is stroking him under the chin and around his neck. He is a dog who requires a lot of attention and affection. Go back five weeks to the Saturday before Christmas. Maureen and I arrived at the RSPCA at around 11 am, with a view to assess those who generally do not look too dissimilar from convicts on Death Row, the only difference being that these little fellows haven't done an awful lot wrong. We walked past runs containing all types dogs we didn't really want – Rottweilers, Ridgebacks, Alsatian cross, huge-headed Mastiff cross, Staffies, English Bulls, cross-bulls, all sorts of bulls..... and so on. Dogs whose perceived aggression led you to knowing the type of human wastage that would want something so aggressive at the end of a studded collar and lead. And if not the dog, then certainly their wife!

We espied several hopefuls before passing what appeared to be an empty run. As if trying to attract our attention, a collie came bounding forward from its inner sanctuary, sat by the mesh, raised his paw and said to us, "I'll take you". Well, his eyes did anyway. It is the old adage that the dog picks its new owner. And it definitely appeared to be a two-way verdict. The information slip told us that his name was Ben and that he was a four-year-old collie-cross. An initial walk with the lead, and then a free run in the enclosure convinced us that Ben would be just the ticket. These days you cannot take a dog home with you , unlike days past when on the two occasions we have purchased RSPCA dogs, they have both come home with us straight away. Two dogs, twenty-eight years of pleasure between them, and that's what I like about mongrels, they usually outlast their pedigree counterparts. Morgan, our first, was abandoned on the Hog's

Back due to having epileptic fits, which we didn't know about at the time of purchase. They actually died out over the ensuing years and he lived to the age of 14. He was a cross something-retriever, with a lovely nature, and could tell us of my parents' impending arrival when they had only just reached the outskirts of our village. (Not that Ash Vale is really a village any more, but no one likes referring to their home area as an urban sprawl). We acquired Cassie, our second dog, at the age of approximately two and she died 21 months ago at the grand old age of eighteen. Being an ex-motor trader, old habits die-hard and we were able to write her back at £5 per year. As she cost £50, she'd paid her debt by the time she was twelve! You could tell she was an ex-motor trader's dog, as her back legs weren't in line with the front. She was the canine version of a "cut and shut". But we loved her. In the last year, Cassie had a few problems "down below", so after she had gone we didn't get another dog straight away, we just got new carpet instead!

Twenty-one months on, and the pangs of that wagging tail and the greeting not being there tend to get to you. And as Maureen is now working part-time and I'm spending more time at home, we thought "why not?" Prices have gone up now, of course. A mongrel is £120, and a pedigree £140. You also have to have a home visit, which I agree with. This duly went ahead and having passed our vetting stage, we were allowed to collect Ben. All the relevant vaccinations were completed and castration was carried out. That's Ben, not me as I was done years ago! We picked him up on the Saturday after Christmas, having handed over the fee and another £100 for food, bedding and toys. Maureen looked up collies on a doggie web site and came to the conclusion that Ben is related to the Smooth Hair Collie. He appears to have most of the credentials, being mainly a black and white sheepdog, but with tan in all the right places to make him a tri-coloured collie, plus the obligatory white ruff around his neck. He doesn't have any paperwork giving his ancestry, which is good, nor did the RSPCA proclaim him to be a pedigree, which as I said earlier would have cost us £20 more – which is also good! But he looks as English as you or me.

The first night home Ben sniffed around the house, worked his way around the garden and appeared to like playing catch-and-fetch with either a quoit or ball. Two golden rules were written in stone. One, Ben was not to be allowed upstairs. Two, Ben would not get up on the armchairs or settee. The first rule lasted until bedtime on the first night. Having made sure he was aware of the position of his newly acquired bed, which was laid in the front hall so that he had access to the kitchen and his water bowl, he didn't find it easy to settle. In fact, he didn't settle to the point that he only became content when we took the bed upstairs and placed it outside our bedroom. He knows not to enter either of the three bedrooms, although he stands with his paws in the manner of an athlete, taking advantage of every inch of the gripper as the starting line before the hop, skip and jump. He is prone, however, to chewing pants, socks and tights. There is probably a canine name for this fetish. In human terms he would be classified "a pervert"! So, we've noticed that whilst he stands steadfast by the door of our bedroom while we're around, you daren't inadvertently leave it open as he sneaks in and removes said items and chews them on his bed, though he doesn't attempt to try and hide them when you come into sight. In fact, he appears to be quite proud of his find.

Rule number two was broken during an evening's television when we realised that there were three of us watching "Masterchef" from the same settee. Maureen, sitting tight against the left arm, me tight against the right, Ben lying on his back, head cradled by me, blithely stroking quite subconsciously his tummy. It was only the sound of his contentment being louder than the outspoken overtones of John Torode that brought it home to us, that quite without our knowledge he had sloped up, twisted round and lay spread-eagled in the manner of an Aldershot prostitute, the tickling of his tummy, however, being the closest of contact! I later rang our daughter and described Ben, as he sat next to me being patted and stroked throughout the telephone conversation. "Dad", she exclaimed at length, "what you've got is another grandchild – but one you really like!" Ouch!

It comes as no surprise that Prince Edward has been cleared of animal cruelty. The RSPCA stated that there was insufficient evidence for a prosecution to take place. It doesn't go unnoticed, of course, that the Queen is Patron of the RSPCA. Wouldn't want to upset the forelock tugging, I suspect. I saw the same photographs as everyone else and the poor, black Lab does appear to be cowering as Eddy hovers above with his shepherd's crook in what could only be described as an aggressive stance. What a pity nobody took a video. Perhaps they did, and were got at – who knows.

That highly paid organisation, the Royal Family, is still going through it on yet another front. Young Harry. Now I have more sympathy with this fellow, already having gained two stars from me for showing total disregard for royal protocol by wearing a Nazi uniform to a party (shows imagination). He then describes an army colleague as a "Paki". As I said, the news of such awfulness took up several minutes of current affairs programmes, but now that the dust is settling, it appears that he is to be reprimanded by his commanding officer. He will, of course, escape a formal enquiry as no complaint has been received from the victim (paid off, probably!) It goes on to explain that the reprimanding will be in the form of a dressing down and possibly a refresher course on race relations. Oh, no, not a refresher course!! Have you ever heard anything so ludicrous? That self-serving pious group of humourless scrotes, otherwise known as the Equality and Human Rights Commission will wish to be satisfied that he is properly punished. I really do hope that Harry, who seems quite normal for a Royal, tells them all to bugger off. Just a thought, but can you imagine the furore if he had described his mate as a black bastard? Someone I know once said that if they ever bought a brown Labrador, they would call him Nigger, just for the hell of it. As he said, if it was good enough for Guy Gibson, of Dam Busters fame, it was good enough for him.

Hot on the trail of this little race debacle, or breath of fresh air, comes the news that Carol Thatcher has been dropped from the "One Show" on BBC because she referred to some tennis player as a Golliwog. The remark was made in private, after the recording had been concluded. As you can imagine, she has no supporters. Not only criticism made of her choice of description by Adrian Chiles and Jo Brand, who were also in the Green Room, but everybody who works for the Beeb seems to have got in on the act. Are they all so frightened of their jobs? Phrases like "using a word like that should be unacceptable at any time", "she was in the Green Room of a national television station, which I would hardly call private", "we are considering her future as a matter of urgency" and "her position on the One Show is no longer tenable". I am just so glad that she has no intention of apologising. Ms. T has just gone up several notches in my estimation – good girl, stick with individuality of thought and don't let the bastards grind you down.

It would be reassuring to think that it was "that time of the year", but it just never ceases, i.e. April Fool's Day. It's the "potty time" when names have to be changed or dropped in order to placate some namby-pamby do-gooder, or one of our many religious cults. Firstly, we have the case of a headmistress who has banned the use of the word "school" from her, well, school! This is due to her fear that children will stop attending classes. Staff has been informed that they now work at a "place of learning" and the pupils are to wear slippers, not shoes. The head, a Ms. Kingdon, (why no surprises that she is a Ms?) stated that the word "school" could have "negative images for children and parents in the deprived suburbs of Sheffield". There are no bells for lessons, and no door is locked. According to our Ms, Watercliffe Meadows, is where you "start from scratch and create a new type of learning experience". Experience? It's a school, not a shopping mall. Our lady of learning then goes on to say, "We wanted to de-institutionalise the place and bring the school closer to real life". It makes you wonder which real life planet people like Ms. K inhabits. Still, I am sure all of her pupils will attain 110% success rate. After all, success is mandatory – at least in the results, if not the knowledge.

Right, a clutch of school jokes of a sniggering, lavatorial nature:

A teacher asks her class, "If there are five birds sitting on

a fence, and you shoot one of them, how many will be left?"
She calls on little Harry, who replies
"None, they would all fly away with the first gun shot".
The teacher replies, "The correct answer is four, but I like your thinking".
Little Harry then says, "I have a question for you Miss Rogers. There are three women sitting on a bench eating ice cream: one is delicately licking the sides of the triple scoop of ice cream, the second is gobbling down the top and sucking on the cone, the third is biting off the top of the ice cream – which one is married?"
The teacher, blushing a great deal, replies, "Well, I suppose the one who has gobbled down the top and sucked the cone".
To which little Harry replies, "The correct answer is 'the one with the wedding ring on', but I like your thinking!"

Time for another? Oh, okay.

The following day at the same school (I'm just setting the scene).

Miss Rogers says to her class, "Today we are going to learn multi-syllable words. Does anyone have an example of a multi-syllable word?"
Harry sticks up his hand. "Yes, Miss Rogers, mas-tur-bate".
Miss Rogers smiles and says, "Well, Harry, that's a real mouthful".
To which Little Harry replies, "No, Miss Rogers, you're thinking of a blow job".

And it wasn't long after this that Miss Rogers and another female teacher had to take a group of primary school infants on a field trip to Cheltenham Races to see and learn about thoroughbred horses. When it was time to take the children to the toilet it was decided that the girls would go with one teacher and the boys would go with Miss Rogers. She was waiting outside the men's toilet when one of the boys came out and told her that none of them could reach the urinals. Having no choice

she went inside, helped the boys with their u⌐
hoisting them up, one by one, holding th⌐
direct the flow away from their clothes.
couldn't help but notice that he was unusua⌐
Trying not to show that she was staring, Miss Rogе⌐
must be in Year 4?" "No, love", came the reply, "I'm riding ⌐
Arrow in the 2.15".

What a hoot and what a day out it must have been for Miss Rogers! Whilst she was taking her brood back to the coach for their return to school, two men stood talking. One said to the other, "You know, I reckon school days were the best of my life". "You reckon?" said his mate. "Yeah, playing football till just before lessons commenced, having a fag behind the rubbish bins, fondling the girls behind the bike shed, you know, I really do miss being a caretaker"!

The next story concerns the money wasted by that institutional cancer, the Health and Safety Movement. Police officers in Lancashire have not been able to move portable speed indicators until they have attended seminars on what type of ladder should be used and how to assemble and disassemble same. They then have to learn how to walk up and back down those very same ladders. Not exactly the length of a fire engine ladder, are they? These bastions of danger are two-step, portable, bright aluminium chappies that we all possess, care of Home Base, B & Q, etc. Forty-five employees of the service have had to waste their time on this costly exercise. Who are these arses that concoct yet more obstacles to fly in the face of common sense?

As a child, I always felt sympathy, and not a little sadness, at the plight of the dodo. It all seemed such bad luck to have come within 300 years of now and still become extinct at a time when humanity was becoming more enlightened about wildlife. Though when you consider the plight of the Staffordshire and English bull terriers at the hands of their often "bruising owners" it makes you wonder which form of life is the more wild. Anyway, I read with interest, and not a little excitement, that DNA may be able to help restock planet with lost species. The more original material that .vives to this day, the greater the chances of success. Apparently .nat rules out dinosaurs as they lived over 100,000 years ago, which appears to be a bit of a cut-off point. Mammoths, sabre toothed tigers, elk, woolly rhinos would all have a second chance of life. So perhaps there is life after death. The poor old dodo is another contender, due to the fact that skin and feathers are in store at Oxford University. If ever a bird was in the wrong place at the wrong time, it was the odod (I'm writing for dyslexics!) Just imagine. You only exist on one island in the world – Mauritius – you provide meat for hungry sailors et al, and just to cap it, you literally can't fly to save your life. What a bummer!

Hot on the heels of animal reincarnation, it's just been revealed that Morris dancers are in danger of extinction within twenty years. How can it take so long! Morris men are on a par with cricket. These are aspects of English life, which I feel I should applaud and support, but really, there seems very little mileage in painting your face bright colours, wearing sashes and bells and stating that it is all in the name of fertility. Seems an awful lot of effort when you can get a tart pregnant in Aldershot at the end of just one evening! Mind you, you have to buy her a few drinks first. Probably best just to pay £50 and forget the drinks. At least you have the rest of the evening to yourself watching "Match of the Day" and checking your nether regions for crabs – well, it's just a thought!

What a false economy it is, and such a waste of money, for the NHS to pay for agency staff. There is no substitute for loyalty, continuity and experience, plus all the other benefits that come from permanent employees. I remember when my dad was in Frimley Park Hospital. Having been brought in by ambulance after collapsing through low blood pressure – the result of emphysema – my wife, mother and I waited in the seated area surrounding a "work station" or some such fancy name. An agency nurse passed with a urine tray – you know, one of those scalloped shaped bed-bogs. She spilled the contents en route to a room, then returned to stand for at least twenty minutes, before wandering aimlessly off down a corridor. The floor was still peppered with the trail of urine. I went to the counter and commented that I thought the nurse would have come back with a cloth and wiped it up. "Not her job", was the humourless reply. "We have a cleaning team for that". The enthusiasm was akin to a cabinet minister being asked to explain his expenses. A slovenly cleaner meandered in some 15 minutes after, and proceeded to wipe the offending area. Slowly, with little interest, he completed the task before retreating from whence he came –Soweto, I assumed. Can you imagine that happening during the good old days of Matron?

Another area of waste the NHS never had to contend with was the £50 million a year on translators. Over 300 English hospital trusts were surveyed, and their bill has more than doubled in one year. Manchester Trust spends more than £1.3 million – mainly for the "local" Urdu population. Birmingham shelled out £1.2 million – again, mainly on Urdu. Peterborough and Stamford Hospital paid £460,000, mainly for the Poles. I wasn't aware that 10,000 Polish women have had abortions in this country last year, which is costing up to £10 million, although look on the bright side, at least the abortee won't be claiming benefit, although you can't be really sure. I still mention that when in Rome.....

It was interesting, and not a little refreshing, to read a quote from Mr. Kevin Rudd, the prime minister of Australia. Muslims who want to live under Islamic Sharia law were told to get out of Australia, as the government targeted radicals in a bid to head off potential attacks. Separately, Mr. Rudd angered some Australian Muslims by saying he supported spy agencies monitoring the nation's mosques. "Immigrants, not Australians, must adapt. Take it or leave it. I am tired of this nation worrying about whether we are offending some individual or their culture. Since the terrorist attacks on Bali, we have experienced a surge in patriotism by the majority of Australians. This culture has been developed over two centuries of struggles, trials, and victories by millions of men and women who have sought freedom. We speak mainly English, not Spanish, Lebanese, Arabic, Chinese, Japanese, Russian, or any other language. Therefore, if you wish to become part of our society – Learn The Language! Most Australians believe in God. This is not some Christian, right wing, political push, but a fact, because Christian men and women, on Christian principles, founded this nation, and this is clearly documented. It is certainly appropriate to display it on the walls of our schools. If God offends you, then I suggest you consider another part of the world as your new home, because God is part of our culture. We will accept your beliefs and will not question why. All we ask is that you accept ours, and live in harmony and peaceful enjoyment with us. This is OUR COUNTRY, OUR LAND and OUR LIFESTYLE. And we will allow you every opportunity to enjoy this, but once you are done complaining, whining and griping about OUR FLAG, OUR PLEDGE, OUR CHRISTIAN BELIEFS or OUR WAY OF LIFE I highly encourage you to take advantage of one another great Australian freedom, THE RIGHT TO LEAVE. If you aren't happy here, then LEAVE. We didn't force you to come here, you asked to be here. So accept the country YOU accepted".

The e-mail that was sent to me with the aforementioned upon it was headed "The whole world needs a leader like this". Well, I'd be happy with just Britain having one. I don't know Mr. Rudd, but I like him.

While I think of it, when my dad died my mother requested donations to Frimley Park Hospital, as she wanted family flowers only. Cheques and cash were received by me and banked on my mother's behalf. One cheque was then sent to cover all. She received not a word in response, either by receipt or acknowledgement. We only knew they had received the cheque after a bank statement arrived. I rang the Chief Executive's office; the CE not surprisingly was unavailable. I surmised he was either playing golf or at a meeting to discuss ways of funding yet more agency staff. Cynical, I know, but old habits die hard. His secretary was, in his stead, extremely helpful and very nicely spoken, which, as you know, goes down well with me. She could have almost had a GU1 postcode – and it don't get much better than that! She seemed genuinely surprised and not a little disappointed that my mother had not received a reply. Within the week, mum had received a receipt for the cheque and a very apologetic letter from the Chief Executive, letting her know how sorry he was that the hospital had failed to acknowledge the donation and how all donations were very much appreciated. So, all in all, a reasonable ending. What I did enjoy, however, was when, during my discussion with the secretary, I stated that the cheque would have been for a much larger sum had I not deducted the cost of car parking charges incurred during the months I spent visiting my dad prior to his demise. You could have heard a pin drop! The silence was deafening. (I didn't deduct any money, of course, but it left her wondering)

My dad was a very formal man. Born in Aberdare, South Wales, he came to London armed with a visiting card bearing the name "David Thomas". DT was an outfitters in Falcon Road, Battersea. Dad being Welsh and the store being founded and run by a Welsh family, his employment was probably a foregone conclusion. He worked there until the war, when he became a military policeman before joining the 15th Scottish Reconnaissance Regiment. He spent the war in one of those four-man ferret cars of which I remember having a toy model made by Dinky. Having survived the Hun and army rations he returned to David Thomas's before becoming a rep, selling hosiery for a Leicester based company called Anthony Martin. His last job before semi-retirement was repping for a confectionery firm based almost opposite us in Falcon Road. His final occupation was working for the Church Commissioners in Victoria. He wasn't particularly religious, but they had a snooker table, so you could understand the draw. It was a bit like an old pals' club. Occasionally, he and his chums had to down their cues and operate the Roneo and Gestetner machines. You may remember these old copiers. You got more ink on you than the paper did on it! I mentioned my father was formal. I had to shake hands every time we met – even if I had only seen him four hours previously.

I realised a couple of years after his death that we'd never really had a conversation. We'd always had an interview. He was always very impressed with wealth, material gain and status. Luckily, that never permeated down to me.....

I remember him saying to me once, "Do you remember So and So?" I did, but I could never bring myself to admit it. After seeing him shake his head at my false inability to remember any of his friends, he then went on to tell me that this particular chap's son had just become Area Manager for HSBC. "Every branch from Aberystwyth to Cardiff. He has a large company car and a good expense account to go with his salary – now there's success!" As you can imagine, it left me totally underwhelmed.

I replied, "But what's he like as a bloke?"

"What?" my father retorted coldly.

"What's he like as a bloke? Is he nice?"

"What the bloody hell has that got to do with it?" my father retorted.

"Well, if he's nice, I'd like to meet him. If he's not, then I wouldn't".

"I don't understand you", finished my father, shaking his head in disbelief.

"No", I thought, "and you never will".

And that really sums it up. My father was born in an era when the police and authority were above all comment or criticism. He once said to my eldest son, who is a printer and happy in his job, "Have you ever thought of becoming a policeman?" My son felt slightly worthless at the comment.

My father knew I hated fox-hunting and experimentation on animals, so he would always cut out articles from the newspaper, as if to drum up support for his point of view, and every Boxing Day when the Hunt took place, he would exclaim loudly, "fifty thousand people following the hunt today. Fifty thousand. Are they all wrong?" My answer that 61 million people weren't following the hunt seemed to fall on deaf ears – mainly because he had already turned his back on me, and he was actually deaf – well, selectively deaf!

I am amazed my dad drove for as long as he did. With

emphysema, macular degeneration, which rendered his sight almost at a total loss, and with hearing that was badly affected he drove until he was 89 (he was 91 and eleven twelfths when he died). In the latter days my mum did the "driving". Well, I say did the driving, she actually sat in the passenger seat, handbag poised on lap and told my dad when it was safe to go, safe to overtake, park, exit from a junction and accelerate away from lights, which my dad could never see turn from red to green. My mum, of course, had never actually driven in her life and had no idea of speed. When she told my dad to pull out at a T-junction, there was always a squealing of brakes as cars stopped abruptly to let out a car whose occupants had no idea they were there in the first place! I suspect that when he gave up driving the accident rate in Ash Vale was reduced by 74%. I imagine Guildford Borough Council to this day is still trying to work out why. But we know.

I said my dad was impressed with material wealth. He was also impressed with the Honours List and status. There was an article in the local paper a few years ago about his exploits during the war, with a photograph of him and mum. This was seen by a serving officer whose war interest included reconnaissance divisions. Through the paper he contacted my dad and they became firm friends until he was transferred abroad. What used to amuse my wife and I was that we always knew when the Brigadier and his wife were coming for tea as the china fairly fell off the table – there was so much of it. We get offered mugs of tea; they got offered bone china that had belonged to my grandmother and was the best set in the house. A cake stand with an array of fancies and delicacies was offered to the guests, which had never been offered to other guests – mainly because the other guests never had titles! Their worst fear was that I arrived on a visit at the same time as the Brigadier and his wife. My wife met them on a couple of occasions and said what a pleasant and polite couple they were. I realised long ago that it was never the people to whom my parents introduced me. It was my parents' sycophantic behaviour that pushed me away from their social circle. You try living with a family that is perfect – with perfect friends and perfect neighbours.

Just recently one of my father's heroes died. If my father were here now, he would be extolling the virtues of Sir Dai Llewellyn, who died from bone cancer at 62. Not a great age at all, but I can still remember his name being mentioned with pride because he was "a socialite" and Welsh, to boot. Now I am sure he never sponged off people. I didn't know him, I knew nothing about him, but whereas his claim to have drunk eight bottles of wine, a bottle of rum, a bottle of port and a bottle of vodka in one night would have my father positively creaming himself in a manner that Basil Fawlty would be to Lord Melbury, I failed to be as impressed. Sir Dai (why was he a Sir?) was the brother of Roddy Llewellyn who bedded Princess Margaret over a six-year period some thirty years ago, or basically when she was still alive. Which also impressed my father!

My dad had opinions for both himself and my mother. She has never once held an opinion of her own. She stored my father's. So now he's gone, there is very little conversation, other than a walk down memory lane to her childhood, a childhood that seemed idyllic. She was one of five, two brothers either side of her and is now the last surviving sibling. None could do any wrong. They all ate together, they all slept together, they all had measles together. When one sneezed, they all caught a cold. They all looked out for each other. Is it any wonder, therefore, that they all wore size 7 shoes, except my mother! Her father, who died when she was 26, and was a grandfather I never knew as he died 4 years before I was born, is always described as a "wonderful" man who "never put a foot wrong". As I said, trying to grow up in a family where everyone else is perfect is never easy. My mother did admit to being spoilt by her father and my father carried on this tradition by cosseting her. They both provided financially throughout their lives. My mother cooked, my father never, although he always carved the Sunday joint. He wasn't a particularly practical man, though he dealt with the practical things. He decorated, painted, filed bills, receipts and warranties scrupulously in tidy folders, which helped me after his death. I feel I should have missed him more – but I haven't.

James, a very good friend of mine and wise sage, who lives near

Wokingham said, "You only have one set of parents, you'll miss them when they're gone". I keep waiting. Strange, though, but several weeks ago I dreamt that I was attending a family get-together (we had many in my youth). Cousins and friends stood chatting in this dream. I walked through from a kitchen with a tray of drinks. Everybody seemed in good form. I stood, tray in hand, and looked towards an armchair. There was my dad, holding court. Three friends or relatives were sitting close by, hanging on to his every word as he regaled them with one of his stories. I remember this dream most vividly. As I stood there, tray in hand there was a strange, warm and close feeling. There was respect, an admiration – no more, no less – someone, I remember not who, passed by and said to me, "I thought your father had died". "Yes", I replied, "but he's back for one night only".

I long ago came to the conclusion that my parents heard me talking but never listened to a word I said. I really wasn't the son they wanted. What they wanted was my cousin Simon. You see, Simon, worked for one company in the City for 40-odd years. He took something like the 7.35 am from Epsom and then changed at Waterloo for the Waterloo & City Line, otherwise known as the Drain. The only time he saw daylight was when they were on strike! Unlike me, Simon passed all of his GCE's. He'd even passed all of his Common Entrance exams before he was an embryo! Clever bugger wasn't he! The strange thing is, I still have arguments with my parents in the car every day. Every trip I take to give a talk to a ladies' group or working as an after dinner speaker somewhere in deepest Bedfordshire or the Sussex coast, I argue with them. They are not there, of course, but I still argue. And do you know, the really sad aspect of all this is that I still lose the argument.....

Enough! Anyone reading this will be under the impression I am getting sentimental, but as you know, I am stoic and my inner feelings are reserved for the truly emotional moments in life, like those contestants being thrown off "Strictly", "Dancing On Ice", "The Restaurant" and watching "Sleepless in Seattle!" What do you mean no heart!

CHAPTER TWO

Alfie – What's It All About?

As I write this it is snowing. Oh, and Sainsbury's are still out of ham and egg pie. As you read, cast your mind back to these two days when England was brought to a grinding halt. The news programmes are full of reporters standing in fields alongside noiseless motorways. London is closed. Boris states that whilst it is the "right" kind of snow, the sheer volume isn't! Classic comment. The financial pundits are putting the cost to the economy at £1.64 billion pounds. Well, they've got that wrong. It's actually £1.64 billion and £50, because a talk I was going to give in Swanley has just been cancelled due to the weather. I know how I arrived at my £50, but how on earth do they arrive at their figures. No-one asked me for my contribution before going public on the Beeb. I don't know why they feel it's that important. We waste more than that every day in overseas aid. There are complaints that we do not invest enough to take account of situations like these two days of snow, but surely that's the point, we don't have the severity often enough to make it financially worthwhile. Why can't we just accept it, enjoy it, and take the children sledding or snowballing, subject of course, to a visit by the Health and Safety Officer, who will doubtless invoke a by-law that precludes fun and enjoyment.

I read that dogs are genetically 98% wolf. Ben appears to be 98% woose. He doesn't like the dark and he doesn't like the rain. He puts one paw out of the back door, tests the weather, and then with wetted paw, gives you the look that says "Nah". He doesn't like the Hoover, electric carving knife, and electric food mixer, in fact, anything that has the name Moulinex on it. He doesn't like church bells. We have a church about 200 yards from the house and at 8 am each Sunday morning the ringing of the bells coincides with Ben becoming apoplectic. He doesn't like Midsomer Murders. You try watching an episode without a wedding or a funeral.

Now, Ben loves the snow. Earlier today Maureen took him for a walk up the road. There were some children making snowmen and Ben sensed an audience and immediately rolled over to be tickled by anyone so inclined. Children stroked him and he lapped it up. The trouble is, when he rolls over, his willy pokes out in an effort to show his excitement and I know our luck, we will be the first dog owners in the country to be fined for encouraging canine paedophilia. So much for the old joke about sheepdog trials! Which reminds me, I'll always remember the gag concerning a man who was seen with a cabbage on the end of a lead. A passer-by queried the man's choice of companion. "Oh", replied the man holding the lead, "I thought it was a collie!" Well, blame Ray Martine, if you can remember him. His show, I believe was called Stars and Garters, and introduced you to the beautiful Kathy Kirby – a pin-up and no mistake!

Anyway, talking of paedophiles, I note that the number of registered sex offenders said to be "missing" has risen considerably. Three hundred and seventeen of the buggers – and they probably are – remain unaccounted for. That information is taken from thirty eight police farces, as opposed to the previous list the year before last, when three hundred and twenty two were absent, but spread over forty nine police areas. The "Met" have lost one hundred and twelve, the West Midlands, thirty-four, Manchester, eighteen, Kent, thirteen, Northumbria, twelve and Sussex, ten. Thirty-four sex offenders, eh, with a West Midlands accent. Crime doesn't get worse than that. I mean, if you were being abused in Sussex, the chances are that the perpetrator may well have spoken nicely, which should help your therapy. There – always think positively! It didn't go unnoticed by the way that none appear to be missing in Surrey. I don't suppose we have any in Farnham! More likely to be in Croydon, now a London borough – which is, of course, Surrey's gain.

The Home Office gave their usual bullish response, stating "We have one of the most robust systems in the world for the management of sex offenders which enable the police to manage their risk and protect the public". A confident and vigorous riposte, but slightly less convincing when you are made aware that registered offenders are able to exploit loopholes in the system, enabling them to register vague addresses before vanishing into the social ether. Still, I am sure these mandarins will be able to justify an above inflation rise in their pay packets when the public sector pay reviews recommence.

Sometimes it's the little irritations in life that create the greatest stirrings in our quest for common sense to be displayed. A vicar, conducting a funeral service, was issued with a parking ticket, even though he was displaying a disabled badge. His sin was to display the badge incorrectly – it was upside down on the dashboard. When confronted by mourners who were sympathetic to the vicar, the traffic warden replied, "Tough". If ever there was a "Jobsworth" it's this chap. The sad thing, of course, is that the council concerned, Torbay, have contracted out parking issues to a profit making company, so targets and box-ticking take precedence over compassion and common sense. And here's another "Jobsworth" traffic warden. This one has issued a £70 fine to a mother who had stopped her car close to a bus stop because her daughter was having breathing difficulties. Her doctors had advised that should this happen, the nine-month-old child should immediately be given an inhaler. "That's not my problem", responded the automaton when told the reason for stopping. Hull City Council, the employers of this complete arse, commented, "If a member of the public feels they have wrongly been issued with a parking ticket, they should make a formal appeal". Yes, I thought their reply was friendly, as well.

Sad to read that Birmingham City Council have decided to drop the apostrophe from all name boards and signage within its domain. This is another example of our standards being reduced in order to appease those who maintain only the lowest common denominator as their bench mark - or those on benefit, whichever is the lowest! Still, if it helps the pass marks for English A Levels, then so be it. As I read this article, I became aware of a group called the "Apostrophe Protection Society". I bet we're the only country to

26

have one. Quickie: What's the difference between a Boeing 747 and a Brummie? The Boeing stops whining when it gets to Malaga!

I never understand the lack of punishment for serious road crimes. We now have the news that a 21-year-old woman has been jailed for 21 months (presumably one month for every year of her life) for taking same from a 24-year-old female. This woman was texting moments before she ploughed into the back of the victim's car as she was waiting for the RAC to arrive, having suffered a burst tyre. The unfortunate girl's car was pushed into a concrete barrier on the A40, where she died from brain injuries.

Here's another one, Lynne-Marie Howden, aged 43, and old enough to know better, killed a 55-year-old radiographer named Patricia Frostrick, having veered across the road and into the path of Mrs. Frostrick's car. She stood no chance at all, as once again the perpetrator was distracted, due to talking on the currently legal, hands-free with headphones jobbies, that I would ban tomorrow. You cannot concentrate on both a phone conversation and driving. This woman had been talking for a combined duration of over thirty-one minutes, of which twenty-seven minutes were to her boyfriend, the rest being business calls. She describes her Mercedes CLK 220 as being "effectively my office". If she's on the phone for that long, she should stay in the office more. The article describes her as a director and head of sales at a consultancy firm. Consultant/radiographer? Radiographer/consultant? Errhh, yup. I think I know which would be the most important, given the option of survival.

A sentence of several years without appeal may make these people think. I remember the case of a Sussex policeman who killed a lady when speeding through a red light near Gatwick Airport. He was convicted of careless driving, fined £2000, given 9 points on his licence and a four-year disqualification, plus having to re-sit his test. Reasonable sentence, some might say, but no, he wasn't prepared to accept his punishment. The Appeals Court reduced his ban by one year. Why? They also set aside the order for him to re-take his test and the 9 points. So he will now have a clean licence. I ask again. Why? I was caught speeding on the A1 in Lincolnshire – 80 in a 70. It was a clear, sunny evening with little traffic. At the bottom of the hill was the camera. Result, 3 points and a £60 fine. That's 3 points and I wasn't even involved in any skirmish. He kills someone and receives nil points. (Please pronounce this the French way, my wife informs me we spell it the same, I wanted to spell it pwar). Bloody strange world! But then I don't belong to any of these strange societies that I understand have acted as insurance agents for certain professions. Now I am not, of course, saying that he did (or does) but you are always wary. I remember my father, who was a mason, returning from a Wales-England rugby match in Cardiff and being very impressed that at an after-game get together where drinks flowed, a local south Wales police bigwig reminded "club" members that if they got into trouble through drink/drive, he could only protect them to the Bridge. Please forgive my misgivings about secret societies, but.....

Now here we have the sort of stories that I love. Ones to warm the cockles of your heart and no mistake. Benefit claimants breed benefit claimants, well, they certainly do in the Peters household. There's a photo taken of the parents, Alan and Lorraine, whilst on holiday in Spain. And what a picture of health and happiness they both look, but then looks can be deceptive – about as deceptive as this pair! Our 56-year-old patriarch has apparently been so poorly that he was unable to leave the family home without an oxygen cylinder. Heavy to lug about, I would have thought, but no matter. Matriarch Lorraine has needed a stick since becoming breathless at the slightest exertion. Big Al has claimed over £32,000 in benefits while the missus has acquired over £40,000. During these years of taxpayers' plenty, both were working under false names cleaning windows – greedy bastards. Or should that be bastard and bastardess. No matter, their eldest son, Gary, was not to be outdone. He has netted over £38,000 himself in incapacity benefits, due to rheumatoid arthritis, whilst younger son, Martin, aged 28, has received £10,000 due to being an alcoholic. Well, I think they could all afford to be, don't you? Not a family to be exclusive, this family free-for-all now includes the mother's brother, one Compton Mackenzie, 51, who walked away with a not to be sniffed at £10,600, due to his fear of open spaces. Now that is someone who should get out more! The younger son has received a 12-month community order – whatever that is – and told to carry out 160 hours unpaid work. What a pity it wasn't in addition to the money he had received. He is paying some back, but the judge stated, "To put it bluntly, the money will never all be paid back". Well, it won't all the time we make it easy to claim without the appropriate punishments being enforced when caught. The others are to be sentenced later, but I won't be holding my breath or the taxpayer's wallet.

The next story is in similar vein. The accompanying photo is of an elderly gent, sporting regimental beret and looking somewhat like a kindly uncle. But once again, it belies the fact that whilst the cove in question, one Bernard McCartin, aged 66, is the former mayor of Horwich and a Lib-Dem councillor; he still received over £18,000 in benefits. Again, he claimed he needed constant care and could only walk with a stick (these sticks come in handy, don't they? They could almost be described as a claimant's crutch!) He slightly over-egged his case by stating that it took him half an hour to cover 25 yards. It must have been another trip to Lourdes, because he was caught on camera bending, kneeling, standing without aid, while he stained his garden fence and cleaned his porch whilst on stepladders. Five months' surveillance by the Department of Work and Pensions, at great cost to us, followed a tip-off by an anonymous caller to the fraud hotline. This ex-special constable is now repaying his country the paltry sum of £12 per week. In one way you hope he lives long enough to pay it off and in another, you just know that in some way we will still be supporting this greedy exploiter of our benefits system.

Just to round off this list of miscreants, here's another couple. Shashi Bacheta, 52, and Jeffrey Cole, 58. The female of the species claimed she was so ill she needed 24 hour care. Fifty thousand pounds was lavished from the tax payers in the form of housing benefit, disability living allowance, council tax relief and income support. The Cole man helped her to claim an additional £12,000 by stating he was her landlord, when they were actually living together, he being the postmaster and she being the newsagent at the other end of the shop. They were caught when council investigators tracked the pair sailing their way around the world in the postmaster's £100,000 yacht. What a bloody cheek! This pair is also to be sentenced next month. What you do know, as I said before, is that the punishment will never replace the taxpayers' contribution.

Right! Time for a joke. During a visit to a mental asylum the visitor asked the director, "How do you determine whether or not a patient should be institutionalised?" "Well", said the director, "we fill up a bath tub, then we offer a teaspoon, a teacup and a bucket to the patient and ask him or her to empty the bath tub". "Oh, I understand", said the visitor, "a normal person would use the bucket because it's bigger than the spoon or the teacup". "No", questioned the director, "a normal person would pull the plug. How do you fancy a bed near the window?"

Oh, go on then. After the success of the above, I'll tell you one more!

So there was this chap. He was very sad and lonely so he decided that life would be more fun if he had a pet. Off he went to the pet shop and told the owner that he wanted to buy an unusual pet, something that would make him stand out from the crowd. After some discussion, he finally bought a centipede, which came in a little white box for use as a house. He took the box home and found a good location for it. He then decided he would take his new found pet to the pub for a drink, so he asked the centipede, "Would you like to go to the pub with me and have a beer", but there was no answer from the box. This bothered him a bit so he waited a few moments, then asked him again. "How about going to the pub and having a drink with me?" But again, there was no answer from his new friend. He waited a little longer thinking about the situation. He decided to ask him one more time. He put his face up against the centipede's house and shouted, "Hey, you in there. Would you like to go to the Coach and Horses and have a drink with me?" He listened and a little voice came out of the box. "I heard you the first time, but I'm still putting my bloody shoes on!"

I find the intrusion of CCTV cameras very hard to take. If I thought they genuinely led to a much greater conviction rate for criminals, then fine, but I'm never convinced that it isn't surveillance for surveillance's sake, in other words – control. George Orwell had nothing on this government. Everything comes under the heading of anti-terrorism. It's sold to you as being for your own good. Now, records are to be kept of all telephone calls and e-mails for a period of one year. This little exercise is to be funded by the taxpayer to the tune of £47 million. This not untidy sum will go to the Internet providers for storing the information. Sounds like another nice little earner to me. It comes as no surprise that this idea started life as an EU initiative, to which our government doubtless complied enthusiastically. As a Home Office minister commented, "It brings us into line with our European counterparts". Even Stella Rimmington, the ex-chief of MI5 has publicly stated that anti-terrorist measures are creating a police state.

The terrorism law is being used to spy on parents by councils who feel they are being given false addresses in an effort by parents to send their offspring to a perceived better school. That is surely not what the law is for? And that's the problem; we never know when to stop. There's no substitute for police officers on the beat. You know, last week, my wife and I were going to bed at about 12.30 am. The windows were open and arguing could be heard. The female seemed to be quite distressed from the tone of her voice, the male aggressive. The argument came from the side road, not our lane – we could see nothing. With the argument showing no sign of abating and becoming more heated, my wife decided to call the police. Having been put through, my wife was asked by the male civilian operator if she felt the woman was being assaulted. My wife replied that she had not gone out to see what was physically happening. The operator then told her that the incident would be logged, but priority would be given to more urgent cases. However, if my wife felt that someone was being assaulted, or even murdered, then she should feel free to ring back! I rang Surrey Police HQ the following Monday to question their policies on 999 calls, but it was snowing and no one was available. I lost the will to live after that.

Those of you who know me, or have read previous tomes, will know my dislike for financial gain from compensation. I remember commenting, gleefully, about a chap who lost his case for easy money after he slid on a grape in an M&S store in London. We now find a "happy shopper" in the form of Jeanette Plummer, a 62-year-old who has just been "gifted" £27,500 after slipping on two grapes – not one, but two – in another M&S store. She broke her shoulder – Christ knows what the fee is for a broken neck! Not surprisingly, "the fall has affected my life, I am now restricted in what I can do". Well, she is £27,500 less restricted now.

You have to laugh; the management at Warrington Bank Quay Station in Cheshire (why did I think it was Lancs?) have put up "No Kissing" signs by the taxi rank. This is in an attempt, apparently, to dissuade couples from a long and passionate embrace (as opposed to full blown sex, presumably) in the back of a cab. If lovers insist on kissing goodbye, they will have to make their way to a specially designated area. The sign consists of a red outer circle, with red line running from 11 to 5, with a couple whose pronounced lips are almost touching. The chap, on the left, wears a hat, presumably to denote that he is, in fact, a chap, while the chapesse appears to have an Afro hair do. As the couple are silhouetted in black, presumably the ban does not extend to the ethnic white minority, (well that's how you feel – unless you are shopping in Waitrose, which is generally very white!) Just a point, but aren't they going to get some flak from same-sex couples whose silhouettes are not displayed? Mmmm, what's that I can smell? Is that litigation in the air?

Sainsbury's, who by the way still have no ham and egg pie available, has stopped selling battery hen eggs. Better late than never. They follow M&S and Waitrose. The villains of the piece are Tesco and Asda, who quote as follows: - Tesco advised, "We will continue stocking caged eggs to cater for families on tight budgets", while Asda noted that many customers could not afford to "trade up" to free range eggs. Strange how the benefit brigade still manages to consume vast quantities of lager, fags and lottery tickets, yet can't afford a wholesome free-range egg – or more importantly, give a fig about animal welfare – which they wouldn't give anyway, as a fig is nutritious and therefore not part of their diet!

I've always admired someone with guts, someone who stands up, or sits down, for what they believe in. Esme Jenkins is just one of those people. Esme recently celebrated her 100th birthday. The picture of her in the Daily Express is one of a feisty, grey haired lady whose face oozes determination and independence. Wrapped in a red dressing gown, she is holding a cigarette in her right hand. She says that smoking has never caused her any harm, adding that she has smoked since the age of 15 or 16. She enjoys a whisky and dry ginger at "elevenses". I love the dismissive way she talks of smoking, and as you know, I cannot abide smoking, but you have to smile. She says, "I am sure it is smoking that has kept me going. I don't inhale, of course, I just puff them. Everyone is always telling me to stop smoking, but I tell them to sod off". Now that's class!

I'm bloody glad to see that the BBC stood up to all parties, plus some little nonentity who goes under the title of the Archbishop of York, who wanted the Beeb to plug disaster appeals regarding Gaza. It's nothing to do with us. When will the do-gooders, the liberal spenders of our tax, and the ideologists get it into their thick heads that you will never change Israel's policies on Palestine any more than their hero really changed water into wine. Anyway, what makes this appeal so appealing? Every hour of every day another appeal is set up for some cause. The BBC should remain independent of them all. Report the news truthfully, informatively and equally, but not be a party to what sounds more like political pressure. There's an actress called Samantha Morton. I've heard of her, but can't recall the face, who states that she'll "never work for the BBC again until they have changed their minds. It's very wrong, it's not a political message". (Not 'arf.) She then says that it is all about raising money for children who are dying. So? Christ Almighty, they're dying all across the world. Imagine the housing pressure if they all survived. Hopefully the BBC will forget to invite Ms. Morton to audition next time they are casting a period romp.

A lot of my working time involves giving talks to various social clubs, and amongst them are ladies' clubs who not only socialise but do good. I say good, but then good is very subjective. Whilst recently at a well-known ladies' club, the chairlady (as opposed to the char-lady) came to an item on their meeting agenda which made mention of the collection of "shoe boxes" that were being filled to be sent abroad to deprived children. At the end of my talk, when the highlight of the evening approached – tea with bickies – I asked one of those ladies present where the boxes actually went to, and what was inside them. "Oh", she enthused, "small toys, trinkets, pens, pencils, notebooks, you know, things which will come in handy and aren't readily available in Swaziland". I appeared pensive but she seemed eager. "What would you put in one?" she enquired. And she really should have known better than to have asked! "Oh, let's think", I replied, savouring the moment. "Anti-rape alarms, sterilisation kits, abortion kits for the 10 years old and over, and for those who survive long enough to make it to adulthood, how about a doll, white naturally, clothed in evening wear, to show how one dresses for dinner in Farnham!" I have to tell you, she didn't appear overly impressed. Now, I know these ladies are sincere in helping Africa but how much longer do we have to keep funding these countries, either by overseas aid through our unbidden tax, or by the gestures of good-hearted people whom I consider misguided and naïve. Me, I feel my shoebox of tricks would be far more effective.

While I think of it, I want to die while asleep, like my grandfather, not screaming in terror like the passengers in his car!

There was a lovely piece I read regarding a dating agency that rejected a prospective male applicant. Their letter of refusal read thus: "Sorry, your application to join our match-making service has been declined. You failed question 14. 'What do you like most in a woman?' 'My dick' is not an acceptable answer".

Here we are, a little quip for those of you old enough to have received a rounded education, though pointless for those of you who have recently attained a degree in geography or anthropology – standards just aren't quite what they used to be.

"I thought I saw an eye doctor on an Alaskan island, but it turned out to be an optical Aleutian".

Last thought – no matter how much you push an envelope, it will still be stationery. (Or stationary, if you feel that fits better!)

Our Ben seems to be settling in nicely. Still not overly fussed on other dogs, but loves humans. I take him for a walk along the canal every morning. We go as far as Heath Vale Bridge Road, cross the bridge with "The Swan" Public House on our right, then venture through the woods and onto the army firing ranges. Although the red flags are flying, the authorities appear to tolerate dog walkers, etc. until about 7.30 am. By this time we have turned at Ash Vale Station to go back along the canal. I count the number of lager tins strewn on the ground each day. Proper people take tins home, lager drinkers, or yobs - I never generalise as you know - discard on completion.

The weather is turning milder as spring sets in. And much to the chagrin of my wife, no-one is better placed to tell us about it in the morning than the BBC's Carol Kirkwood, the weather girl – or as my wife says, woman – who always starts my day off with a smile. She always looks freshly scrubbed, and doesn't that raincoat fit her so well? What a pity that when I'm waxing in lyrical fashion about her smile, her complexion, her poise, her bubbly personality, and the possibility that she just might not be wearing anything under that raincoat, my wife declares that it's about time she did something with her roots..... But hey ho, back to spring. A pair of swans, ducks, drakes, moorhens and coots congregate close to or on the lawn of a house that backs onto the canal. If you are there at a certain time in the morning you can watch from the towpath opposite as the lady of the house feeds all and sundry. There's usually a sprinkling of blackbirds, robins and a squirrel eager to pick up the pieces. It's quite delightful. I've got to know one or two of my fellow dog walkers, and Ben is now quite amiable towards a dog called Alfie, who is also a rescue dog. Alfie appears a very independent dog, usually walking about five yards in front of his owner. The other day we were chatting and I noticed Alfie looking out over the canal. Ben was looking at Alfie and I think the caption would have been, "Alfie, what's it all about?"

Ben currently attends dog training classes in Brookwood, in an effort to relax him and to help dispel his fear of other dogs – well, that's what his teacher thinks is wrong with him. We think of it more as an ASBO. Letting him off the lead is a two-edged sword. We love giving him his freedom; the problem is that he buggers off. Oh, he comes back, but in his time and not ours. Teacher says that chocolate drop treats are the answer. Well, they are until something better comes along, like a rabbit, squirrel (forty feet up a tree), pigeon on a clothes line. You try telling him they are all a lost cause. Still, he never disturbs us at night, though should he hear a noise, then he growls like a guard dog. He's a great impersonator.

The first time we let Ben off the lead was early one Sunday morning. We went to Carrington Lane Recreation Ground, which is a couple of minutes drive away. Bordered on one side by an industrial estate, or business park as I think they prefer in an effort to increase the rateable value, the park dovetails into a V where estate meets back gardens. Separating the industrial from the residential is a very small gap, well, it's a dried up stream really. Ben disappeared down the gap, running like a demented dervish. Despite all the name-calling, "Ben", "Ben", "Ben" (he only has the one name), did he reappear? Did he buggery! Having eventually got to the point where we last saw him,

I shouted once more. There was movement, brush and bush parted company and there running out at a fair rate of knots was a deer, followed by another deer, followed by Ben. The deer looked as surprised as we were as they ran towards the end of the park and the roundabout on the main road - and no, he never caught them.

Okay, time for a quintet of blonde jokes, so if you are blonde with a sense of humour – read on. If you're not, well, you probably wouldn't have read this far anyway!

A man needed a few days off work but knew his boss would say no. He thought that if he acted in a very mad way then his boss would be more sympathetic and allow him the time he required. So, he hung upside down from the ceiling and made strange noises. His blonde assistant asked him what he was doing. He told her he was pretending to be a light bulb. A few minutes later his boss appeared. "Good Lord", he exclaimed, "what are you doing?" The man explained that he was a light bulb. "You're clearly suffering from stress", sympathised his boss. "Take a few days off". The man jumped down and left the office, only to find his blonde assistant alongside him. "Where are you going?" he asked. "Home", she replied, "I can't work in the dark".

Or, if you prefer:

An old, blind cowboy wanders into an all-girl biker bar by mistake. He makes his way to a bar stool and orders some coffee. After sitting there for a while he yells to the barman, "Say, d'ya wanna hear a blonde joke?" The bar immediately falls silent. In a deep, husky voice, the woman sitting next to him says, "Before you tell that joke, cowboy, I think it's only fair, given that you're blind, that you should know five things –

(1)   The bartender is a blonde girl wielding a baseball bat
(2)   The bar bouncer is a huge, blonde woman and
        champion mud wrestler

(3)   I am a six feet tall, one hundred and seventy five pound blonde gal who has a black belt in karate

(4)   The woman sitting next to me is also blonde and a professional weightlifter

(5)   The lady on your right is blonde and a professional knife thrower

Now think about it seriously, mister, d'ya still wanna tell that joke?"

The blind cowboy thinks for a second, shakes his head and mutters, "Hell, no..... not if I'm going to have to explain it five times!"

Of course, this may be more – or less – to your liking.

Three girls all work in the same office with their female boss. They notice that the boss is beginning to leave work early. One day, the girls decide that when the boss leaves they will leave right behind her, as she never called or came back to work. Therefore, how would she know they were also leaving early? The brunette was thrilled to be home early, as she spent the extra time gardening and playing with her son. The redhead was elated as she was able to go for a quick workout at the gym before meeting her boyfriend for dinner. The blonde was happy to get home early as she could surprise her husband. However, when she got to her bedroom she heard a muffled sound from inside. Slowly and quietly she opened the door and was mortified to see her husband in bed with her boss. Slowly and gently she closed the door and crept out of the house. The next day, during their tea break the brunette and the redhead once again planned to leave early. They asked the blonde if she was going to join them once more. "No way", the blonde exclaimed, "I almost got caught yesterday".

Just two more:

A lorry driver stops at a red light. A blonde catches up in her Peugeot 106. She jumps out of her car, runs up to his door and knocks. The lorry driver lowers his window. "Hi", she says, "my name is Sharon and you are losing some of your load". The lorry driver ignores her and proceeds down the street. He stops at another red light. Again, the Peugeot catches up. The girl jumps out of her car once more and knocks on the door. Again, he lowers his window. As if they have never previously spoken the blonde says, "Hi, my name is Sharon and I have to tell you that you are losing some of your load". Shaking his head the lorry driver ignores her again and continues down the street. At the third red light the same thing happens. Now out of breath the blonde alights from her car, runs up and knocks on the door. She again says, "Hi, my name is Sharon and you really are losing a lot of your load". The light turns green and the lorry driver revs up and races to the next light. This time he hurriedly alights from his lorry and runs back to the blonde. He knocks on the window of her Peugeot 106. She lowers it to speak, but before she can say anything, he shouts at her, "Hi, my name is Mark, it's winter, it's freezing, and I am gritting the bloody roads!"

Right – the quin of the tet:

Two Irishmen are standing at the base of a flagpole looking up. A blonde walks by and asks what they are doing. Paddy says, "We're supposed to be finding the height of this flagpole but we don't have a ladder". The blonde takes a spanner from her purse, loosens a few bolts and lays the flagpole down. From her pocket she pulls a tape measure and announces, "It's eighteen feet, six inches", before walking off. Mick looks at Paddy. "Ain't that just like a blonde. We need the height and she gives us the length".

I think that last one evens things up a little.

We are looking forward to going away for a few days in the middle of June to Dumfries and Galloway – yes, both of them. We are driving up with our good friends, Jacquie and Peter (who are first mentioned on the CD, "A Mann For All Reasons" when the four of us went to the Isle of Man for a long weekend – we don't have many friends!) Anyway, we are booked into a hotel in Castle Douglas for four nights and are really looking forward to it. Maureen and I went away for two nights last December to celebrate her coming of age as she called it, or 65th birthday as I called it. We came home after night one. Now, the Peak District isn't somewhere I know that well, and after a perusal of the Good Beer Guide, we decided to book in to an 18th century pub, with low ceilings, beams and brasses and more especially, real ale. It rained on the way up and for most of the next day. Of all the views our room could have afforded us in the way of hills, escarpments, valleys – just grass – but no, we looked out from what I took to be the smallest room in the outbuildings (within which one couldn't swing a rat) onto the car park containing nothing more varied than a range of Ford, Vauxhall and Toyota vehicles, plus our Kia. The television was placed on top of the wardrobe, which had to be viewed from a supine position on the bed. We didn't watch much TV!

After breakfast, which was more than adequate, we drove to Hayfield, Arthur Lowe's hometown, which looked nice in the rain but would probably have looked much better in the sun. We travelled on to Bakewell, which was very nice and full of tarts. And Buxton, which wasn't nice, but still seemed to be full of tarts. In short, it was full of people you'd find in Asda. Actually, for a moment I thought we must be back in Farnborough. Disappointed, we headed for the Crich Tramway Museum for a ride or two in a tram, and the company of proper people. It was closed for repairs. What about the Midland Railway Centre, we thought. Sadly that appeared to be closed as well. Off we trundled to Chatsworth House and joined the throng of cars, presumably with occupants like us, at a loss as to where else to go.

The rain was, by now, absolutely torrential. We made our way through the gates and followed robot style along the conveyor belt of tarmac until we arrived at the queue for the entrance and were then asked to pay £2 to park the car in a very muddy car park. We went to the toilet, which even by today's standard is still quite steep at £1 a pee. I remember the days when it was a penny a pee. However, we walked to the House entrance where signs exalted the magic of a "Chatsworth Christmas", where, and I quote, "Spectacular, unique decorations transform the beautiful rooms on the two lower floors. Trees decorated by the Duke and Duchess and their grandchildren" (where were their parents, then?) etc. etc. There then follows a footnote, advising that the top floor of the House, including the five staterooms is not open during the winter season. This is two weeks before Christmas. It was no good trying to see the gardens, even if they were available, as it was still bucketing down. To cap it all, they wanted £16.50 per adult or if you required a family ticket (two adults, plus up to four children) it would set you back the tidy sum of £49 – not to be sniffed at. We declined on the basis that the titled two would not go short without our contribution, and the £33 would be better spent on fuel in an effort to get us home. We arrived back just in time for "Match of the Day".

I have just read that Surrey Police will cost each taxpayer £181.57 for the next financial year. I do hope that not a penny is being spent on erecting a striped "Rainbow Flag" over Guildford Police Station, in the manner that has recently bedecked Limehouse Police Station in East London. Apparently, someone replaced the Union flag with one that has become the Gay Rights Banner. All this bowing down to minorities does not impress Middle England. Even more worrying is the news that Kent police are to hold a gay essay writing contest, open to all children under 14, which I did find slightly amusing, not to mention disturbing – which I will mention. What the hell do they think they are doing? Children of that age should not be subjected to this sort of narrow view promotion. The winners will apparently receive a £25 book token, presumably to be spent in a gay bookshop. Oh, and they also receive a Kent police shield, (tacky pink with a fluffy emblem, and a helpline number as well?) I can just see it. This essay competition is part of a series of events including quizzes and a dinner/dance. This is not confined to the under 14's (though doubtless there are those who would prefer it). Oh, no, there's a 15-17 category and an 18+ section. There's also a category for police staff. Can you believe it? Apparently, and once again you have to laugh, Kent police are considered one of Britain's most gay-friendly employers. So speaketh the Stonewall Workplace Equality Index. They are ranked fourth in the country, which is up eighteen places from last year. I can almost hear Alan Freeman, pop pickers! Who compiles this rubbish? And more importantly, who cares? You see, not content with getting their members (so to speak) into the police, they then have to force it down your throats (so to speak, again). I have no problem with anyone doing anything to anyone, providing two principles are adhered to. One, is that both parties are over the age of consent, and two, that both parties are consensual. They really should not be allowed to push their pet cause at the expense of "normal relationships" comprising a mummy bear and a daddy bear. And why are the police involved in this? They should be doing what they are best at doing. Basically, booking you for doing 32 mph in a 30 mph area. Now – that's policing!

Human rights supporters have a lot to answer for. European HR legislation is responsible for two homosexual sex offenders being able to live together and abuse even more children. Stephen Carruthers and John Bates (wonder if, as a child, he was ever known as Master Bates?) were listed on the Sex Offenders Register after their release from jail for attacking children. They were allowed to live together at a seaside address on the basis that they were now partners. The police and probation service knew these two were living together but were unable to do anything about it or inform local parents due to breaching laws relating to co-habiting same sex couples. They've now been jailed once more for abusing young boys aged 13 and 14.

There's another paedophile here called David Williams, 44, who has spent most of his adult life abusing children, some as young as four. He is currently serving time in Exeter Prison and isn't overly fussed on some of the conditions. He isn't best pleased about his cell lacking a toilet, hot water and drinking water, so he is seeking damages under the Human Rights Act. He claims to be suffering from a sub-standard lifestyle. There are many similar cases now in the pipeline since the case of Robert Napier, who was awarded £2,450 after claiming that slopping out his chamber pot aggravated his eczema. A judge then upheld his compensation, which has paved the way for many similar cases. The cost to the taxpayer is doubtless enormous. Why are these criminals and paedophiles listened to? Their actions alone led them to a prison sentence. You really do get the feeling that the do-gooder originators of the Human Rights Act really didn't think through their responsibilities to the law-abiding public, or more importantly, to the victims of the crimes concerned. I mean, call me slightly to-the-right-of-centre, but in my world they would all have been put down.

CHAPTER THREE

It's Di-Ja-Vu All Over Again

Just come back from taking Mutley along the canal for his early morning constitutional. Ah, Spring. Heavy rain has raised the water level; everything smells and looks fresh, including the discarded lager tin, which wasn't there yesterday. As ducks and drakes swim up canal, a Foster's tin flows down. The one lying in the bushes was a Carlsberg variety. The two swans have now had their young – seven cygnets are gamely to be seen swimming between dad and mum, or maybe mum and dad. I'm not sure of swan etiquette or tradition but I'm fairly sure that they're not a homosexual or lesbian couple. They look..... well..... put it this way, they don't look ducky!

You can tell it's Monday, the dustmen have been. No, not the dustmen who collect the black sacks (thank someone, though not God, that Guildford Borough Council haven't yet succumbed to wheelie bins), no, it's the second coming, where they take the green and purple plastic containers. We only have a green jobbie, as our ex-neighbours across the road reversed into my purple version, but I never sued or sought counselling, though a replacement or a swap would have been nice. Still, he did smile out of his car window and say sorry, which I also thought was nice. Anyway, you can tell that they've been (or bin!) because not only are they empty and upside down, but they are thrown hither and thither, some landing close to within 30 yards of the property from whence they came. Still, it's the thought that doesn't count.

You remember I mentioned our trip up to Derbyshire before Christmas, well, I forgot to mention that the one gem of a village we visited was Castleton. It was here that we found, in a gift shop, a wicker basket containing golliwogs of differing sizes. We chose one as a present for a friend who collects the Robertson metal golliwog badges and also possesses a few of the stuffed, cloth examples. "We'll have this golliwog, please", I proffered. The assistant seemed hot and bothered as she looked around the shop, presumably in an effort to gauge reaction to my description. "Golly Dollies", she replied, "they are called Golly Dollies". "Nonsense", I rebuffed, "always were golliwogs and always will be". Nice as she was, I still felt it was another human being who had been got at by the PC brigade.

I see that a new musical about the life of singer Al Jolson will have the lead role portrayed only as a white man. Al Jolson's trademark was to "black up", that's what he did. I also note that the television series "Robin Hood" has introduced a black Friar Tuck, totally contrary to what we were brought up with, but it probably helps towards the ethnic acting targets. It's a slippery slope changing history and that's what we are in danger of doing in these sanitized climes. I shall stick to watching my boxed DVD set of "When the Boat Comes In". Very Geordie, and all white with me!

Maureen's just checked the e-mails, which arrive by the horde on a daily basis. Among those attempting to sell me something are examples of characters with implausible names such as Cornelius Winslow, Ecu Pupi, Agamenmon Allison and Pansy Tilley. Aquie Davis informs me that I could "upsize my manhood today", whilst Allah Burns (not sure if that's a name or a statement) enquires if "my wife needs attention". Many others seem to be under the misguided impression that I would be willing either to buy a Swiss watch, an alternative form of Viagra, or enter some sort of betting organisation known as Casino Royale. I suspect for SPAM, read SCAM.

We were in Sainsbury's earlier. They had ham and egg pie in stock., but at the checkout we had to ask for carrier bags. It's interesting because at some of the checkouts, usually those staffed by older employees, they still put them out in good measure. The younger staff appears to have been "got at" by those misguided enough to assume that by continually re-using their orange carriers, we are all saving Planet Earth. Or with the population being what it is, should that not be Planet Birth? I always tell the youngsters that I feel liberated, radical and not a little maverick when asking for a carrier bag as it is akin to the old days when one requested "something for the weekend". The bag is slipped to you from under the counter in a furtive manner. For God's Sake, we're advertising the bloody company, aren't we? I also tell them that they wouldn't want me to bring back their Sainsbury's bags for re-use, as we use them for poop scoops when out with Ben. We'd never sully a bag emblazoned with "Waitrose" or "M&S"!

Maureen and I went for Sunday lunch at a country pub near Petersfield recently. The staff were a mixture of Poles, Lithuanians and French. The landlord, who was in his own words "Persian" and married to an English lady, said that their son felt very English and played rugby for a team on the south coast. He was a very decent chap and like you and I considered that when in Rome, etc. etc. The landlord sat with us and discussed immigration and the inability to obtain a local workforce. It was interesting to note that he has advertised for staff in his local village, which not surprisingly has its fair share of what one could term "council houses", even if they are owned by housing associations, or whatever profit making enterprise they are in reality. He said he couldn't obtain employees from this estate. Many of the occupants are unemployed. Now, he is offering £10 per hour – not bad for bar staff, I would have thought – but apparently during interview, as soon as the great unwashed and benefited are told it's taxable and not cash in hand, they don't want to know as it will affect their entitlement. They would be entitled to bugger-all if it were down to me – bastards. And, once again, this estate has the best views of the surrounding countryside. I'd give them a blank wall to look at – something for the yobs to graffiti.

The downturn in the economy is affecting many aspects of business. A lot of shops are closing and one can be sympathetic in many cases, but you can imagine just how gutted I was when an estate agent closed in the village. It brought a smile and no mistake!

It was interesting to note in a recent article that low-income families live less – well, that's good news. It means less benefit is being paid out over a shorter period, surely. Well, every little helps! You know, I reckon a supermarket would pay a fortune for that little banner.

The names given by parents to their offspring never fail to amaze and amuse me, namely, because I haven't got them. I was giving a talk at a ladies' club the other day when one of the ladies (there, told you it was a ladies' club) came up to me and mentioned that neighbours of hers in Lancashire (I think Oldham) had three children. The family surname was Button and they were called Leather, Brass and Pearl. I know of another family whose surname is Sparkes and they have called their children Axle and Diesel. My wife knew a family friend whose name was Ann Mann. How's that for originality. My eldest son knows of a Stan Still and I know of a Wayne Kerr! If my surname was File I would have to call my son Peter, or if my surname was Soul, I would have to call my son Titus R, or if my surname was White, I would have to call my daughter Isla. Whilst on the subject, I do remember meeting a lady at a club whose name was Jenny Taylor. Close enough, eh?

Maureen works in Woking, or for the dyslexic, wokes in Working and every week visits Robert Dyas in an effort to buy up as many 100W light bulbs as we can store for future use. I have been taxed to the hilt by this incompetent and profligate government and I refuse to give in to their latest dictat that we should not be able to sustain the level of lighting we have been used to since the Romans left – well, certainly the last fifty to sixty years anyway. We recycle bottles, both plastic and glass, though only in the green box. We recycle cardboard and paper, but I'm buggered if I am going over to these expensive, long life Euro bulbs that nobody wants. Robert Dyas seem to be the only shop still stocking proper light bulbs. The traditional retailers like Homebase, B & Q and Focus have long since discontinued their sale. Interesting, then, that when requested by me, shop assistants state that they are discontinued although everyone still asks for them. Were they told to discontinue their sales by government agencies? Were they given a financial sop to do so, like planning permission? It makes you wonder. It's not like the aforementioned stores or the likes of the major supermarkets to miss out on a sale.

I know I am in the minority (no, nothing to do with being white). The number of people who ask, "Did you see 'Top Gear' last night", in gleeful expectation that the next twenty minutes is going to be a re-run of the show's highlights. I have seen it, otherwise I wouldn't be able to say I can't stand it. In fact, it's thirty minutes of lowlights for me. I always feel as though I am intruding at a private party – the same feeling I get when I have inadvertently tuned in to a "Question of Sport", where Sue Barker gets girlie and the team captains think they are seasoned comedians. However, the Clarkson Three hold no interest for me in their "boys will be boys" escapades. The only stunt I'd pay to watch is where the three of them are seen at speed in a lorry as it careers along an incomplete bridge, only to disappear over the edge in a long silence before plunging two hundred feet into a fast flowing river. The lorry would, of course, be fitted with welded doors and fixed windows. Oh, how I could relive that moment over and over again.

There has recently been a programme with James May and Ozzie Clark (is Ozzie an anagram of Twat?) where they've toured around the country in search of a good pint of beer. This is another example of what could have been a very informative programme. Sadly, as is often the case these days, even on the BBC, they have turned it into a boys' little jolly, driving a Rolls Royce and towing a caravan. At the point where they were relaxing under an awning, discussing the merits of various examples and belching for the audience at home, I felt it was time to depart.

Just a thought, but have you ever considered that dyslexics might well think of Nyree Dawn Porter as Nyree Porn Daughter?

It looks as if the government have squeezed every ounce they could from a deal with the ousted boss of the "Royal Bank of Scotland". We tax payers are probably lucky they forced him to only take just under £700,000 a year pension. What amused me was that George Osbourne, the Shadow Chancellor, commented that his pension deal was "obscene". I wonder how many of those city fat cats, and getting fatter by the takeover, are Labour supporters? Very few, I doubt. Still, at least we have a few new phrases to add to our portfolio of rip-offs. "Toxic debts", "sub-prime mortgages", "real estate auction marketing" and "quantitative easing".

Barack Obama seems to be a very decent man. I just hope he will not be subject to the politics of the mandarins and those faceless ones who have such influence on party leaders. In interviews he seems very humble, relaxed and with good humour. I do, however, wish that the press would stop referring to him as being the first black American president. It's surely not that much of a surprise. He appeared to be the best man for the job and it should be the best man or woman who gets the job, irrespective. Wouldn't it be nice, though, if the press were announcing that the new president was the first "native" American from, say, the Cherokee, Cree or Arapahoe Indians. Now that would be something magical.

I read with dismay that a lesbian couple have won the right to have a test tube baby on the NHS. Greater Glasgow & Clyde NHS Service refused permission for IVF treatment on the basis that they were not considered to be an infertile couple. Naturally, they took their case to Scotland's highest civil court, and won. Just prior to a judicial review taking place the health board changed its mind. You just watch, as homosexual and lesbian couples vie for their place in the conception queue. They all have rights, remember.

It gets worse! I see that single women seeking IVF treatment will be able to name anyone they choose as the father of the child. And that could be another woman or a best friend. It could also be a platonic male who had no input (so to speak). The only exceptions are close blood relatives, such as brothers or uncles, though they will have to make an exception for Norfolk! But seriously, doesn't this type of action dilute even further the idea of what we used to think of as a natural family? Did you hear about the 12-year-old Norfolk girl who wrote to an agony aunt? No? Well, she did and she asked, "I'm a 12 year old girl from Norfolk and I haven't had sex yet. Does this mean my brother is queer?" It's only a joke! - probably.

There's a story today, one of racism, but unusually where the victim is Indian and the offender if black. Nice to know that no whites were vilified in the making of this story. Actually, it's not so much the fact that a black Lib-Dem councillor referred to an Indian Conservative councillor as a coconut, the reference means you are black or brown on the outside, but a wannabe white on the inside, it's more to do with what they were arguing about. The Inner City Equality Group of Bristol City Council want to spend £750,000 – yup, not £7.50 that could have bought two coffees and a shared cake at Starbucks – oh, no, wait for it, this is three quarters of a million pounds teaching slave trade history. What a disgusting waste of tax payers' money. Has anyone on Bristol City Council thought of asking the poor sod that will be funding this little venture in self-fulfilment what he or she thinks of it? Blacks were using black slaves long before the white man arrived in Africa. They still do in certain African countries to this day. But that's not important, as the white man isn't the aggressor and it doesn't help the ethnic plight against white colonialism. What does bring a smile, once again of a very wry nature, is when the black woman declares, "How can I be a racist when I am black?" Oh, think about it, dearie. It's just that you are the wrong colour to be punishable. In all matters ethnic you are, so to speak, whiter than white.

I never could take to skivers and con artists. What we have next is a case involving one Andrew Hamlyn, aged 54, who worked for a Devon council as an IT officer. Now he's given sick leave for viral chest infection and – wait for it – stress related

50

illness. He fails to arrange a meeting with his bosses on the spurious grounds that he is too ill. Mr. H has been off sick for 92 days. I don't think it's unreasonable to assume that his employers are entitled to know what's happening. It then emerges that he was fit enough to take part in a major cycling event up Devon hill and down Devon vale. Having dismissed him, he appeals on the grounds of unfair dismissal. Thankfully, after a two-day hearing the judges ruled in favour of the council. I just hope he had to pay costs.

It's stories like the following that continue to damage our confidence in the police as protectors of the public. This case centres on a young girl aged 16 who was killed by an armed police officer driving his marked Volvo estate at 94 mph whilst pursuing a car. It might sound like the Keystone Cops or more recently, a terrorist who, if left unchecked, could cause havoc. But no, this policeman's quarry was a Czech family in a car on a shopping run – and driving within the 30 mph speed limit. Apparently, the police car onboard computer told the policeman, one John Dougal, aged 41, to investigate the passing vehicle. He proceeded to rev up in a housing estate, from 30 mph to 94 mph within 600 yards. The young girl, Hayley Adamson, was hit at 70 mph. He took another 90 yards to stop. Do these policemen change personalities when behind a wheel? Do they think they are immune from accident – or are they, as I suspect, extremely arrogant and care even less? He has received three years, which apparently works out at 18 months in real time. The former police officer still denied causing death by dangerous driving, insisting he considered his actions "to be safe". Clearly they weren't safe enough for Miss Adamson. What did we say about arrogance? Judge Hodson stated that he could have given him up to four years, but what with his "exemplary" record with the police.....
You can imagine how the girl's parents must feel.

On the canal the cygnets are getting bigger. I thought two had been lost when I walked along with Ben. Mum was swimming with her wings in the arc position, as she passed me, along with dad and the other five. I then espied the missing two, nestling within her cradle. I know you are going to ask if you can see the photo I obviously took, but sadly, I do not possess a camera – not even one on a mobile phone. My mobile is now at least eight years old and cost me £10, when our youngest upgraded some 25 phones ago. In fact, it's so old I now receive a grant from the Heritage Lottery Fund!

Whilst on the subject of water, the canal will soon be alive to the sport of angling being played out relentlessly over the coming months. I have mixed feelings about this so-called sport. I can understand someone salmon or trout fishing, providing it's in a flowing stream where the specie is native and it is going to be taken home and eaten. What I fail to understand is the distress caused to fish being taken out of their natural environment before being weighed, shown to all and sundry, and then placed in a keep net before finally regaining freedom. Now Robson Green, the actor, was recently shown holding aloft an exceptionally large fish that he had caught off Vancouver for some programme called "Extreme Fishing", which while I think of it is another irritation. It can't just be called "Fishing" can it? It has to be "Extreme", as in "Extreme Living", "Extreme Survival". There's even the Ben Fogle programme, "Extreme Dreams". I suppose the producers fear a ratings drop if they just give a mild title, so they presumably work on the basis that every programme has to be the new ultimate. When will they realise that people are not impressed and that they do have a mind of their own. Anyway, back to this "Extreme Fishing", which I understand is on one of those commercial stations, Channel 5 I believe they call it. We couldn't watch it if we wished to, unless of course we didn't mind viewing ghostly figures through a snowstorm!

Right! The gist of this story is that Robson Green, the actor, has upset his fellow anglers by stating that in his opinion, nine out of ten fish will die once redelivered back into the water. The angling fraternity is not unsurprisingly outraged by such a suggestion. The Angling Trust spokesman commented that, "It has been repeatedly demonstrated that fish can be caught and returned alive to the water without them suffering any significant stress or damage". Do I detect a slight chink in the armour with the use of the word "significant"? It's one of those words which can be stretched or shrivelled according to the argument. And anyway, no-one has been able to ask the fish how he or she feels. My answer is to save any complications, just leave the poor blighters where they were in the beginning. Forget the angler's ego and the story of the one that got away.

While I think of it, you might enjoy this little story. A woman visits Harrods to buy a rod and reel for her grandson's Christmas present. She has no idea as to what she should buy so she grabs one of each and walks over to the counter. The Harrods salesman is standing there, wearing dark glasses. She says, "Excuse me, can you tell me anything about this rod and reel?" He replies, "Madam, I am completely blind but if you place them on the counter I will be able to tell you everything you need to know by using my senses of feel, sound and smell. These senses are always heightened when you lose your sight". Though doubtful she places the rod and reel on the counter. He picks them up and says, "Madam, what you have here is a six-foot Shakespeare graphite rod with a Zebco 404 reel and a 101b test line. This is a good, all round combination and is on sale this week for just £44". She is full of admiration and says, "It is amazing that you can tell all that by merely feeling and weighing the rod and reel. I'll take it". As she opens her purse a credit card falls to the floor. "Ah", says the assistant, "that sounds like a Visa card". The lady is impressed. As she bends down to pick up the card she accidentally farts. At first she is very embarrassed, but quickly realises that there is no way the salesman could tell that it was she who farted. The salesman rings up the sale and states, "That will be £58.50 please". The woman is totally confused and asks, "Sorry, but didn't you tell me the rod and reel were on sale for £44? How can it now be £58.50?" "Ah, yes, madam", he replied, "the rod and reel are £44 but the duck caller is £11 and the fish bait is £3.50".

I note with not a little exasperation that our ability to shell out money like confetti in compensation shows no sign of abating.

Some cove by the name of Alexander Darg, aged 39, who is a civilian car mechanic working for the police, cut two fingers whilst checking an airbag fault. His fingers have long since healed but then they would have, as this little accident happened over seven years ago, but, wait for it, he was left terrified that he might have contracted Aids. The test results were, and I think this comes as no surprise, negative. If it were me, I think I might just have felt pleased with the result and left it at that. Guess what? Mr.Darg was never going to be content with a negative result. Oh, no, why not turn this negative into a positive. Luckily for him this trauma triggered other medical conditions, including chronic regional pain syndrome, and yes, you're right, it left him unable to work. How inconvenient. Four hundred thousand pounds – he's got four hundred thousand pounds. Not bad for a cut, is it? I know where I would like to stick his two fingers.

This compensation is plus one hundred thousand that the Met police, courtesy of you and I, will have to pay in costs. As long as we are prepared to pay compensation, the next claimant will still be knocking on the door.

The "Daily Express" put the compensation culture into perspective when they published the following: -

£284,000 being paid out to an oil-rig worker, who tripped over a piece of scaffolding and sprained his ankle – he suffered from depression - bless, eh?

An RAF policewoman who gained £80,000 after claiming sex discrimination.

£300,000 paid out to a female detective because her male colleagues taunted her about the size of her breasts. They certainly weren't the size of her payout!

£465,000 paid to a London doctor after she pricked her finger on a needle and feared catching Aids. Seems to be a nice little money earner, Aids!

And to cap it all, did you know that over £4 million has winged its way to homosexuals in the armed forces – well, it's kept them in the pink!

It is interesting to note that the tens of thousands of Polish workers who came over to this country to earn a good living when times were good, and then returned to Poland when they were not so good, are now on their way back here because of the recession in their own country. Not to work, you understand, but to pick up British benefits. It will cost the UK taxpayer £200 million a year in handouts, because we pay a rate which is four times higher than any other EU country. So these weren't people coming here to settle for good or bad, they are just journeymen here for their good and at our expense. What a joke this country is.

Jade Goody has passed away. So much for the news space taken up with so little substance. Of course, it's tragic when anyone so young dies of cancer. However, I became weary of the hype and over-abundance of flowers instigated by the cortege of grievers who had never known her personally, but had merely made her acquaintance by watching "Big Brother". The hypocrisy of the newspapers beggars belief. There was the vitriolic abuse that permeated through the gutter press from the day she first appeared on the show, and it then went into overdrive when accusations of racism were thrown into the melting pot. Shortly before her death, photos covered the front pages, pushing all real news to the background. Phrases like "Jade on a precipice" and "Jade wins precious days of life" replaced the previous "anti" tones. Now, we are subjected to "my beautiful Jade is at peace", "How the Essex princess touched all of our hearts". That's in the form of floral tributes. It's Di-ja vu all over again. According to one newspaper, politicians, reality TV stars and royalty all paid tribute. Why? What had she done that deserved so much news space? If I were editor of any newspaper, my article would have been confined to two words – "Oh, Goody"!

I'm off to the Post Office to send a parcel. I now have to use either the one in Ash Vale centre, where it is difficult to park, or drive to Frimley Green, which is two and a half miles distant, but is easier to park. In the good old days, when the Post Office was at the hub of village and suburban life, we also had one opposite Ash Vale Station, very convenient to all and sundry. That, of course, had to close, as did those in Mytchett and Guildford Road in Ash. There was also one in Normandy, a nearby village. Sadly, Normandy is now bereft of all retailers, save one pub and a sound-hire shop. This took the place of the previous general store on the main road. In my thirty years in this neck of the woods, I can remember when Normandy had a butcher's, a newsagent-cum-grocer-cum -video store at the top end of the village, and another general store, which closed a couple of years ago. There was also another pub, which is now - surprise, surprise – housing.

Asians run most of the current Post Offices. Some are friendly enough, the now-closed station post office was a veritable mine of gossip and chat. Mr. And Mrs. Taylor and their son, all Asian, were of the old school, very polite, courteous and had time for all their customers. Mr. Taylor donned a trilby hat and took on a very colonial air, whereas Mrs. T wore a sari, and was very petite. I can recall years ago her English was limited, but she would always smile and attempt to discuss that very British subject – the weather. Looking up from behind the glass screen in the Post Office she would state, in a very strong accent, "It's raining cats and dogs". Their son, who took over the day to day running, was deeply upset when the branch closed. I haven't seen him from that day to this, although I did meet Mr. And Mrs. T in Aldershot some time ago and they both looked and sounded well, he still wearing his trademark hat. And that's the trouble. Many of the current ethnic incumbents seem so divorced from conversation. I often find that I am the first to say "good morning". I only do that in an attempt to make eye contact and it hasn't gone unnoticed how many times I am also the first to say "goodbye". Otherwise, it seems, no conversation would have taken place, other than my request for stamps or whatever service I require. I still have a PO Box in Aldershot, staffed by salt-of-the-earth, dyed-in-the-wool employees, who have worked for the Post Office for yonks. Of course, it's merely a sorting office now, the Post Office counter side being moved within the nearby branch of WH Smith.

I tend to visit the sorting office as soon as it opens on a Saturday morning. The bad news is that you have to traipse through all of Friday night's discarded take-aways. I have to explain here that the sorting office is alongside the taxi rank, which is opposite Aldershot's main (only?) nightclub. I assume that when a taxi appears the polystyrene box containing the take-aways is instantly thrown away. Chips, noodles, you name it, it lies there. The good news about going in to collect my post at 7 am, when the doors open, is that Aldershot is fairly quiet. You can park free of charge and the place is bereft of benefit claimants at that time of day. They are still sleeping off the effects of the previous day's contributions by you and me in the form of tax, for all their alcohol, ciggies and, in many cases, drugs. Still, nice to know we are such an inclusive and non-vindictive society.

It does make you laugh. On entering Aldershit (as it is non-affectionately known locally) signs announce that it is twinned with towns in France, Germany and Poland. They've had relations with the frogs and the krauts over many years, but the "plucky Poles" are a recent and obvious development – there are just so many of the buggers here. If we are going to twin on racial trends I think they'd be better off dropping the original continental ties, and replacing them with Nepal and Somalia.

Talking of Nepal, I suspect I am in a minority of two – the other chap being a Ceefax contributor – in not welcoming every Ghurkha to be allowed to stay in this country. Yes, they fought for this us, but as far as I am aware, they were not promised residency upon termination of their active service. Much as I am fond of Joanna Lovely, who now takes pride of place as the Forces Sweetheart, I do feel that this is a platitude too far. Why should we have all and sundry, plus their aunts, their aunt's aunt and a brother-in-law once over and twice removed, being allowed in, just because a distant relative served his time. Letters, petitions,

TV interviews and JL holding talks with top brass in Downing Street have naturally been too heavy a political burden, so the government has caved in. Goodbye more Green Belt, hello cheap housing and another Nepalese takeaway.

There was much firing last night on the Ash Ranges. Pretty normal stuff, but there then followed three very loud bangs. I took it to be cannon fire. Is it our chaps, I wondered, in my half sleep, or have the Taliban bombed Aldershot. Sadly, neither Bill Turnbull nor Kate Silverton mentioned anything on Breakfast TV concerning any improvements being made overnight to the Hampshire town. Oh, well.....

Years ago, discussions surrounding education in this country centred on the rights and wrongs of public and private schooling versus the secondary modern. I've long been of the opinion that all private education should stop forthwith and everyone be educated in non-fee paying schools. There is always a "but", and the "but" in this matter would be that all secondaries, comprehensives, academies, whatever their title, would be raised in standard to that of the private and public school. Ill discipline would not be tolerated; parents would back teachers, headmasters and headmistresses, who would, by the way, be wearing mortarboards and gowns. Male teachers would be suited and booted with ties at all times, and female teachers would dress appropriate to their calling. It is no good expecting pupils to develop social graces if those in authority do not set standards. And that includes good diction and grammar. Sadly, any discussion on the above is now overshadowed due to the worrying increase in rights. Everyone has rights as we know, and pity the teaching staff that now has to be all things to all men and women ethnic!

As I am writing this, and sifting through the myriad of research I have to hand, I realise that the subjects truly are in two parts. Firstly, we have the lack of discipline and the inherent pupils' rights. Can you imagine years ago reading of teachers being regularly punched, kicked, intimidated or spat upon by their charges? It would never have been tolerated in the fifties or sixties. We never had the exclusions and expulsions that now seem almost common place within the education industry. Swearing and sexual abuse is also prevalent and this is in primary school! The social structure within our society is in serious disarray. We have many cases of false accusations by pupils in an effort to get teaching staff sacked. It seems very one-way when teachers are instantly suspended, but the enquiry takes months to begin, and even longer to complete. In many cases the teacher is innocent, but his or her working life is shattered and the accuser is never answerable for their actions due to their age.

That, however, is where my sympathies for teachers end. I took a group of teachers for a brewery tour not long ago. You have never seen such scruffy individuals. I did, to be fair, ask if they had been home to change, just to give them an excuse, but no, they had come straight from work. I did make the comment, in passing, that I assumed no member present taught sartorial elegance! I think both words went over their heads – well, they were multi-syllable.

I read recently that teachers at the St. Laurence School in Bradford upon Avon, Wilts., encouraged 11 and 12 year olds to shout out swear words and other obscenities during a – wait for it – sex and relationship lesson. The words were then written with chalk on the blackboard, with the teacher explaining their meaning before doubtless asking the class to "discuss".

At Pingle Secondary School in Swadlincote, Derbyshire, two drama teachers have been suspended having apparently asked pupils to act out a rape scene. Schindler's List was the basis for this little play act. Naturally, it's part of their GCSE syllabus. The teachers wanted the children to "get into the minds" of characters from the film – all very art nouveau.

English language as a subject is about as non-PC as English nationality. English has now been replaced by Literacy. So, instead of being conversant in their mother tongue, many youngsters are totally lacking in the basic knowledge of word formation or speech. How many times do you hear, "like", and "stuff", and "you know"? Traditional English lessons are being replaced with sound bites that achieve the GCSE results, tick the boxes and hit the target. Sadly, this leaves the successful pupil on a high, with 34 passes (and all with A*) though they fail to address an envelope correctly.

We've recently been told that the NUT is demanding that teachers reduce their classroom time by one fifth to a four-day week. This would mean only 22 _ hours teaching, with the rest used for preparation and marking. They really do know how to garner public support.

I'm on a roll now! There's a school in Manchester, a school you will not be surprised to learn that has one of the worst truancy records in the country, where the pupils have been fitted and kitted with designer uniforms. Prince Charles's tailor, one Thomas Mahon, has specially designed at a reduced rate – very charitable – a uniform for the 750 youngsters. This little exercise in haute couture has been part funded by Manchester Airport as sponsors, the parents to the tune of £22 each, and oh, yes – the taxpayer. Manchester City Council was rather coy about how much the good taxpayer of their city contributed without their knowledge, but hey ho! Included in this makeover are spare shirts, satchels and PE kit. Naturally, the school has been renamed, as that always improves the image, hopes and aspirations of all. You wipe the metaphorical slate clean. The school is based in Wythenshawe, so not too much hope then, eh! Previously "Parklands High School", the new name is "Manchester Enterprise Academy" – there's posh!

As you know, I am all in favour of uniforms but it all smacks of a sop, a con. All show, no substance and a lot of wasted taxpayers' money. Actually, I'm so bloody annoyed I will come back to the subject of ethnic school rights later – what, I hear you say, you're glad? You're so right; I think we're both in need of some light refreshment. Time for a soothing piece of poetry. It's called, "The Pube, The Cube and the Tube". You have to read this with a Lancashire accent. You know, Rochdale, Bacup, somewhere around there. Just roll your R's. What? No dear, your R's. Some people!

Whilst standing in front of urinal,
Pointing Percy in time-honoured way
I were transfixed by disinfecting crystals
'Bout twenty of buggers, I'd say

Now normally I'd not take much notice,
But when pees taking time, what's to do?
So I counted each one as I sprayed them.
There were eighteen, all lemon in hue

I started to shake our willy,
Quite vigorous, as you do.
Only one thing's worse than wet patch in pants
And that's trousers when pee has soaked through

Last drops were by now few and far,
Though I thought twice 'bout doing up zip,
When on crystal I spied a lone public hair
Clinging like sandals to shit

Though there were n'owt I could do about it,
It's colour were familiar – silver grey
So I undid me flies in me trousers
To check if one of mine had gone astray

It's not easy to tell if one's missing,
But I considered it could have been mine
So I drew a deep breath and extracted
A single strand, hardy yet fine

There both of them clung to crystals,
Chatting 'bout places they'd been
I could tell they were getting on champion
Though a part of me felt a tad mean

The cistern then hissed as it opened its valve,
A torrent clean flushed them down waste

61

Where they'd end up is anyone's guess
I just hope two more will grow in their place!

But then, as you know, a backward poet writes inverse.

You can tell the fishing season is underway. The litter left on the canal towpath has shot up tenfold. Crisp packets, high energy drinks bottles, low energy drink bottles, Mars bar wrappers, baked bean tins..... Ben is coming to the end of his £60 plus worth of ASBO lessons in doggy harmony. It really hasn't worked. He still slows and begins to stalk as another dog approaches. Apart from Alfie, he really isn't happy in the company of other dogs, which is embarrassing. We didn't realise that he had problems with his nasal passages until we found the Vick Sinex stick chewed up on his bed. It was lying between his paws as I went to pat him and call him a good boy. Still, it saved a trip to the vet's. Mind you, I had to go and get an interim prescription renewal for the diabetic tablets I take. They usually last a month, but yesterday, two weeks in, the health centre had to issue replenishments. We had discovered evidence in the garden in the form of an empty foil packet, from which 14 days' worth of medication had been eaten! I had no idea Ben was diabetic. He never said! I asked Ben if he was able to inject, but he replied that he was all dewclaw and paws! Okay, realms of fantasy, but he did eat over 20 tablets.

Interesting to read that in these harsh economic times a poll of Brits found that one in four women would pose naked for £6,500. Typical! I've only got savings of £6000! One in five would apparently sleep with their boss, and there's me who can't afford to employ anyone. Bugger! And another one in four said they would happily bed a sugar daddy if it meant they'd be better off in life – what, with my diabetes! Did I tell you I was a loser? No? I can still remember taking a girl to the Empire, Leicester Square. In the sixties the commissionaires were burly ex-military types with peaked caps, epaulettes and braid. Their word was god. They'd count the couples as they entered, 220, 224, 232,

246, 250! Me? I just missed the cut every time. I was always number 251 and 252! You give me any level crossing in this country and the barrier swings down just as I approach. Traffic lights always change just as I arrive – I see red for England. I was at the Dartford Tunnel the other day - fourteen tollbooths were open and I was stuck behind the only person in Kent without the means to pay the £1.50. Twenty-two minutes I was there. If I had known what the problem was, I'd have paid her fee. But it all seemed cloak and dagger as the security man took photographs of the number plate, of the car, of the girl and apparently he couldn't move it to one side so that everyone else could get through, as everything has to be filmed on CCTV.

The Christmas before last my wife bought me one of the remaining Woolworth's advent calendars – all the windows were boarded up. You see, no luck. When the doctor told me I had diabetes, she said, "There's Type 1 and Type 2". I have Type 2. I can't even get a first in diabetes!

It's such a pity that housing targets are still the mantra for those in authority. Do they never listen, or is the power of the building industry such that common sense and long-term sustainability pale into insignificance? Despite flooding being widespread, along with the cost of rebuilding and rehousing those affected, we still continue to build on flood plains. Last year major developments took place on areas "subjected to flooding". The Royal Institution of Chartered Surveyors state that 1.7 million homes are at risk from river or coastal flooding, but that won't stop councils from their lemming-like desire to appease central government on their quotas or their greed re the income from council tax. Once again, it's all about the price of everything and the value of nothing.

Talking of value, I read with not a little amusement that Leicestershire County Council has spent £6,000 on fitting their ride-on lawn mowers with sat-nav systems, so that the drivers know which area of grass is to be cut. It's funny how different people view these ideas. Brian Rayner of the National Society of Allotment and Leisure Gardens commented that it was "bonkers", while council leader, David Parsons, enthused that he was "pleased we are embracing innovative technology". You almost feel as if you would have got more for your money if it had just been left in an Icelandic deposit account.

Still, the £6,000 paid out by Leicester CC is nothing compared to the £400,000 that has been paid by Ashford (Kent) Borough Council, Kent County Council, English Partnerships and something called the EU Interreg Fund (whatever that is, when it's at home!) This not insignificant amount is for lampposts within a so-called regeneration area surrounding Ashford Station. This works out at £7,000 per lamppost and is seven times the average cost. Interesting to note that these posts were designed (I've seen the pictures so I use the term loosely) by an art graduate who comes with a very non-English name. I mean, call me cynical, but did he win because of his ethnic origin? Once again, it's interesting to note the opposing views on these works of art – or a complete waste of tax payers' money. The Taxpayers' Alliance describe them as "ridiculous", whilst the designer, one Nayan Kulkasiu, tells us that they are intended to create a "multi-faceted night-time experience that adds an element of drama and delight". So, there we have it. Obviously well worth the money just for the quote!

I had a funny dream last night. I have to tell you, I dream every night. Some are slightly skewed, others downright odd and some, like a holiday to distant climes, with fantastic scenery and weather to match. In fact, by the time I wake up I am so exhausted I'm suffering from jet lag. Last night's, however, was a bit off the wall. I was starting work at a car showroom in Farnham (where I worked in the late seventies). It was called "Heath & Wiltshire", or "Thief & Pilfer" as it was affectionately known within the trade. I always know when I am feeling particularly insecure – that's more insecure than usual – when I dream of past jobs, including that where I am a milkman once more and telling customers I'm only back for a few weeks. Anyway, this dream centred on the re-opening of the garage and all the people I worked with all those years ago being re-employed, including the two Peters, Ken and Bernie (they know who they are). The odd thing was that Susan Tsvangirai, Morgan's wife who died in a car crash earlier this year, was enacting the re-launching and cutting of the ribbon. Isn't it strange the things you dream of. I have to say, she performed the ceremony impeccably before joining us for drinks at the "William Cobbett" Public House – which was nice for her – and would no doubt have been something to tell her grandchildren, if only she'd have lived!

I saw the young lady who has re-opened Woolworth's, Dorchester, as Wellworths, being interviewed earlier. What a pleasant and down-to-earth lady she seemed to be. I wish her all the best. It's a great play on names, Wellworths. Woolies was part of our life. We grew up with every town of importance having one. They lost their way over the years, sadly. Their branch in Aldershot supplied us with loganberry, raspberry and blackcurrant bushes that came in sealed packs at £1.99 each. They bear fruit and prosper every year. On a visit to that same branch some six months before closure, the only plants within the "gardening section" had not seen water for weeks. It epitomised the lack of care and enthusiasm and general demeanour of staff and management. If only someone in authority had bothered to take a trip in the lift from their ivory tower down to street level, walked to the nearest Wilkinson's and saw the difference, they may have woken up before it all went pear-shaped.

WH Smith's are, for me, in the same straits – dire. Another household name that has lost its way. They may now be offering sweets and drinks, but the range of stationary, books and CDs is at best awful. Many shelves are empty, little choice where there is stock and not what you want when you reach the relevant section. Other than at checkouts, staff appears to be as rare as hens' teeth. The only area where queues are to be found is in the Post Office section, which is a complete nightmare. I am sure it is profitable and convenient for WH Smith and the Post Office, but it's bloody inconvenient for the poor sod who has to wait and wait and..... I now by-pass Smith's altogether and buy all my stationery in Rymans.

I wanted to visit the Post Office in Bramley, Surrey a couple of days ago. Having scoured the High Street unsuccessfully I eventually asked in a newsagent's. A very pleasant lady told me it was tucked away to the side of the library, across a car park. The postmaster was polite, but the litter strewn across the floor was very noticeable. A lady I took to be his wife, or whomever, was sitting behind a sweet counter devoid of customers. No "good afternoon" as I entered and obviously no intention of keeping the shop floor clean. Do they not want business? It does make you wonder.

While I think of it, I was giving a talk the other day, and having arrived after an hour and a half's journey, it's always nice to freshen up. The sign above the sinks in the Gents read, "Would all food handlers please wash their hands before leaving the toilets". Does that mean that anyone not handling food is exempt? I remember visiting a village hall in deepest East Sussex where the notice in the Gents read, "Would you kindly wash your hands in the sink"! I mean, when given the options..... For those of you reading this book somewhere to the north of Rickmansworth, if you ever visit Surrey you will find our signs read, "Would you mind awfully washing your hands – thanking you in anticipation".

What? You're just about to have your tea. Okay, I'll be quick then you will be able to tell this little joke to your other half over duck a l'orange, if you are in Farnham, or duck a la Peking from the takeaway, if you are in Aldershot. Right'o. Now, there's this chap walking along a beach. What? Which beach? It doesn't matter; it's just a beach. Now, he espies another chap throwing this large ball towards the sea. He notices that the ball is being thrown with some force, but as soon as it slows down and stops, it starts to gain speed back towards the chap who threw it. This happens several times. "Good afternoon", he says, for he is a polite sort of chap. The other chap returns the acknowledgement.

"That's an interesting ball", he comments. "It is", replies the other chap, as he throws the ball once more towards the sea. "It's a ball that always comes back, no matter where you throw it, it always comes back". "That's amazing", says the other chap as he fingers his chin. "Though the wind is coming in from the sea", he adds. "Oh, that doesn't matter", replies the man, as he turns inland and throws the ball with the wind. The ball scoots off, before finally slowing, bobbing and making its journey back against the wind and into the man's arms. "That really is incredible". He asks, "Can I have a go?" "Of course", offers the man cheerfully (isn't it nice to have a story so lacking in aggression?). So he throws the ball with as much strength as he can muster. Once again, off the ball flies before stopping, bobbing and then returning to the thrower's arms. "There", said the man preening. "Told you, it's the ball that always comes back, never lets you down, it always comes back". "Where did you get it from?" enquired his companion. "Oh", said the man, "I found it!"

Go on, go and have your tea!

I know the BBC are under pressure, like the police, fire service and every other industry subject to the race-aholics, but why do we need some Aussie (or if not, antipodean any rate) presenting the financial services bulletin in the morning. Is there nobody in this country worthy of this position? He always emphasises the words in the manner I feel I am being sold an insurance policy. The southern news on the Beeb is sometimes presented by ethnics only. Dani Sinha gives you the news and Reham Khan gives the weather. Nothing wrong with either girl, they both seem very pleasant, but it's a bit like watching Asian TV, where, I understand, one doesn't find white presenters. Strange that. But at least you know Carol will always be along in a minute. So mesmerised am I that I have no idea what the weather will be like. Not that it matters.

And on the subject of news and weather, can they please find someone to replace Robert Peston by, let's say, tomorrow? His intonation, his delivery in general is frankly nauseating.

Do they make these decisions to employ people like him, knowing that they are not "easy on the ears" on purpose? Is it some great in-joke, or do I just feel persecuted. Yes, the latter probably.

An interesting indication of the change to Britain's society is when you see the list of surnames in the 2008 rankings. Top, not surprisingly, is still Smith, followed by Jones, Williams, Brown, then comes Taylor, Davies, Wilson, Evans, Thomas and Johnson. So far, so English, Scottish and Welsh. But coming up on the rails are the newcomers in the form of Shah, Patel, Ahmed, Singh and Ali. Apparently the fastest growing surname in this country is Zhang. At the last count there were 95,000 Shahs and 53,000 Patels in our somewhat overcrowded little island. As minorities go, they're not quite so minor.

The faceless PC brigade would have a lot to answer for if they weren't so unaccountable. No one these days is allowed to have a sense of humour, it seems. Take the case of Jonathan Yardley. He is a Tory councillor representing a West Midlands ward. During a council meeting where members of the public were given handsets in order to answer questions, the presenter said, "Let's start with an easy question to get us going. Press A if you are male, and B if you are female". Someone in the audience piped up, "What if you are trans-gendered"? Councillor Yardley, who obviously has a quick sense of wit replied, "Press A and B together". Everyone found his retort amusing – well, nearly everyone. The chap who asked the question was the boyfriend of a man dressed as a woman – still with me? Well, it wasn't them who complained. Oh, no, it was someone else (nameless of course) who reported the councillor for homophobic comments. This unnamed person should not even be allowed to get a life, they should be put down!

Now, as we know, the police have much better things to do like posing for cardboard cut-outs to be made of their likeness, and then there are always children to run over, but no, Councillor Yardley was informed by none other than Chief Superintendent Richard Green (wasn't he Robin Hood in a previous life?) of the complaint. Common sense should have told the Chief to laugh it off, not to mention telling the complainant to sod off, but we have sexual orientation to deal with, which is on a par with race – a far more heinous crime than rape or murder. Councillor Yardley was questioned for two hours at his local police station. The police stated that as a complaint of homophobia had been made, they were going to take him through the early part of the complaints procedure in case a formal complaint was received. Didn't know you could have an informal complaint. Still, you live and learn. He was then informed he could be prosecuted for his "crime". I really do think the public and the police should grow up and get a grip on reality.

I remember the case of a care home worker who was suspended from his job because he had the temerity to express – in a private conversation – that he didn't agree with same sex marriages, or that practising homosexuals should be vicars. Once again, I ask – are you no longer entitled to your views or more worryingly, to discuss them? The Society of St. James's Charity in Southampton stated in their letter to the blamed one, David Booker, that he would be investigated over claims of "gross misconduct". He apparently had "broken the code of conduct by promoting religious views which contained discriminatory comments regarding a person's sexual orientation." Trevor Pickup, the Charity's Chief Executive, said, "We are housing vulnerable adults and we need to demonstrate our respect to them and the integrity of our staff". Pompous arse!

On a lighter note, but still expanding the point on the lack of humour, David Starkey (who I actually have little time for) is in trouble for calling Scotland a "feeble little country", with "awful" bagpipes and a "deeply boring" poet in Robert Burns. Scottish MPs in the Houses of Parliament and in the Scottish parliament all went off at a tangent, tossing their cabers, waving their skean dhus and raising their kilts in anguish. Get a life, chaps – people are entitled to their views – it's what freedom of speech is all about.

BT is no better. They recently suspended thirty staff whilst an investigation is under way concerning the sending of an e-mail, which contained an Irish joke. Well, here's another one. Just cut me off?

Mick met Paddy in the street and said, "Paddy, will you not be making sure you draw your bedroom curtains before making love to your wife in future". "Bejaysus, why?" Paddy asked. "Because", said Mick, "the whole street was laughing when they saw you making love yesterday". Paddy smiled. "Stupid bastards, the laugh's on them..... I wasn't home yesterday".

Maybe the e-mail concerned this joke:

After having their eleventh child an Irish couple decided that enough was enough, as they couldn't afford a larger bed. So, the husband went to his doctor and told him that he and his wife didn't want to have any more children. The doctor told him there was a procedure called "vasectomy" that would fix the problem but it was expensive. However, a less costly alternative was to go home, get a large fire cracker, light it, put it in a beer can then hold the can up to his ear and count to ten. The husband said to the doctor, "Bejaysus, I may not be the smartest guy in Killarney but I don't see how putting a firework in a beer can next to my ear is going to help me with my problem". "Trust me, it'll do the job just fine", said the doctor. So the man went home, lit a cracker and placed it in a beer can. He held the can up to his ear and began to count, "One, two, three, four, five", at which point he paused, placed the beer can between his legs so that he could continue counting on his other hand.....
This procedure also works in Somerset and Norfolk!

Or maybe it was this:

Paddy was recently asked if he'd like to run a three-mile race. "No", he replied, "It's not for me". "Oh, go on", they said. "Go on, go on, go on". (Think Father Ted). "It's for handicapped and blind children". Then Paddy thought, "Jesus..... I could win this"!

Of course, any criticism by homosexuals of heterosexuals is an entirely different form of abuse. Basically, it's one that isn't. I watched an episode of "Have I Got News From You", when that

70

smug, smarmy Tory, "wannabe comedian", Mr. Alan Duncan was on the panel. Doubtless because he is a homosexual one of the questions centred upon an American beauty queen who stated that she did not believe in same-sex marriages. She was apparently stripped of her title because of these views. So? That was her belief. Again, I ask, is she not entitled to an opinion? Apparently not, it goes against all things homo. Instead of showing any statesmanship by saying that he obviously didn't agree with her, "Duncan the Twat" as he has been known in this house for some time stated that, "If you read Miss California is murdered, you will know it is me". Duncan is a 51-year-old politician who aspires to be in government, should the Tories reach that not unattainable status. We all like a laugh, but it was the venom with which he delivered his lines that afterwards were described by him as "just in jest" and "in the spirit of the show". As worrying is the fact that the lady concerned was so vilified by those with opposing views. Their right of opinion never seems to be queried whereas any non-PC opinion is something to be bullied into submission instead.

There was a recent case of a homosexual postman who is not unnaturally suing the Royal Mail (GPO as was) for the not inconsiderable sum of £25,000 after his boss called him effeminate, girly and bitchy. The poor love describes the first two as derogatory terms which should not be used in the work place. Such a sensitive soul! He is now hoping to become an air steward, the logical and natural step for any aspiring homosexual, I would have thought.

The following is a perfect example of what most people see as the single-mindedness of those groups with a cause – as opposed to the Corrs, which is or was a group. Anyway, I read that Canterbury is coming under fire from a group called "Pride in Canterbury", (naïve me thought of litter free streets and flower tubs). But no, it's the Gay Pride lot with nothing better to do than bore the arse off people – which is, of course, something they have an A-level in.....

Anyway, PIC are not happy about the lack of a drop-in centre – drop-out would be more appropriate – for lesbian, gay, bi-sexual and trans-gender people. Why should they have their own little closet, funded by the good citizens of Canterbury? I really do think there would be better causes – most causes in fact. So disheartened are PIC that they have lodged an official complaint with the local government ombudsman, stating the local council see them as a problem, not an opportunity. I'm saying nothing! Interesting then, that the Tory run council countered "It regularly promotes gay events". Why? "Provides funding". Why? And "offers support services to the city's gay community". You see, there was me thinking that funding for any group or scheme was on the basis that the social work was inclusive. By having their own bars, centres, et al, it just shows how exclusive these people are. Mind you, how inclusive is the black police federation? But that's another page, or two.

Oh, no. I have just read on. Last year Canterbury Council held a Gay Open Day at the council offices. Another sop to those with pink rights.

CHAPTER FOUR

Macclesfield – A High Security Risk Area?

Freedom of speech is a precious asset, to quash is to destroy the very civilisation men and women have fought for. When I was a young lad we all went train spotting. Admittedly, it was a different generation, a more gentle, naïve generation, but we came through it and ended up owning our own model railways! These days modern trainspotters are being barred from this extremely harmless and competition-free hobby on the grounds of security. A retired accountant, aged 54, was told by Virgin Trains to turn off his camera as he took photos of trains passing through Macclesfield Station, due to the risk of terrorism. Please don't tell me that the world hasn't gone mad.

Interesting to note, of course, is that whilst National Express, who operate the east coast main line and are cracking down on all trainspotting activities, Google are allowed to swan unchallenged around the length and breadth of this country mapping everyone's road, lane, home or barn without you or I having any say in the matter. Many privacy campaigners and homeowners have reacted with alarm to Google's Street View, which gives 360° views. I have no doubt that the present mapping is the thin end of a very potentially and profitable wedge. The "Information Commissioner's Office" – presumably another expensive government quango with no clout and all expenses – rejected claims that Google's Street View breached the Data Protection Act. Cars are driving around this country with cameras fixed to their roofs, taking photographs which then have to have faces and car registration numbers deleted before being made available to all and sundry. And if that's not an invasion of your privacy.....

Apparently, the risk of security to householders in the form of burglars sussing out the area are not considered to be worth bothering about, although a man on a platform with a camera pointing at a train is! The onus is on the person who does not want his or her home on public view to do something about it. Google – how good of them – have created easy-to-use removal tools. Should Google not have asked us if we wanted our house on screen in the beginning? The Queen isn't overly enamoured about Google snooping around Balmoral, for fear of aiding terrorism, though I suspect she will have a tad more luck stopping anything going on-line without having the hassle of having to apply for it first to be removed. But then, all pigs are equal, though some are.....

It's the same as junk mail and unwanted telephone calls. It's always down to us to try to stop these intrusions into our privacy. Google's little scheme smacks of something more sinister, however. Is there going to be, or is there already, a deal with local councils in an effort to increase their knowledge of home improvements in their endeavours to raise taxes? I won't hold my breath!

I am surprised that more of a furore hasn't been made but sadly perhaps that is what happens now. Our inability to comprehend so many decisions by those in power just causes us to be lethargic and indifferent and consider all acts inevitable.

That indifference is aptly demonstrated by an article tucked away on page 19 of the "Daily Express". This bottom-of-the-page item concerns a 59-year-old man who had the temerity to face up to hoodies and tell them to be quiet. Their drunken response was to bang on his flat window. He and his neighbours dialled 999 six times, but were told that the police were busy and suggested a non-emergency number to ring. James Straiton, the taxi driver, went outside to confront the hoodies. He was beaten and stamped on and died two weeks later. Two 20-year-olds have been given life sentences, whatever that is at the moment – so they should be out in a year or so with a full benefits package and a paid holiday to help them readjust to society – bastards!

It is not without a tad of truth that I make the above comments. The Works and Pensions Department Secretary has allocated £10 million over the next two years to a fund, to be administered by Job Centre staff. This fund would see the jobless, or work shy to you and me, taken on shopping trips to..... wait for it....."give them a glimpse of a salaried life!" Have you ever heard such bull? Backers of the scheme have referred to it as "taste of affluence" days out. A single mother could, apparently, be taken to a hair salon, followed by lunch. Me? I'd take her to a sterilisation centre. Once again, privatisation raises its ugly head as this idea is one of a number put forward by companies hoping to take a profitable slice of the £10 million by acting as an agent for the government department.

I've just been flicking through the Surrey County Council magazine that finds its way through our letterbox every so often. There are an interesting couple of pages on Woking, which is a surprise, as I never realised Woking could fill more than a sentence in interest. To be fair, the article centres on the older aspects of the town – Woking Palace, St. Peter's Church, the Basingstoke Canal – and the Shah Jahan Mosque. All locals know there is a mosque – well, most of them attend! It's situated in Oriental Road. Appropriate – huh! What I wasn't aware of was the fact that the mosque was built in 1889 and is the oldest in Britain. It is also a Grade II listed building – bet there's always enough money available for this monolith's upkeep!

Has it ever occurred to you that "kinky" is using a feather – "perverted" is using the whole chicken! No? Oh, well!

Which reminds me – were you aware that a chicken crossing the road is poultry in motion.....

The following was sent by e-mail from my friend Peter in Cornwall (yes, I do have more than one friend).

A man and a woman were sitting beside each other in the first class section of a plane. The woman sneezed, took out a tissue, gently wiped her nose, and then visibly shuddered for nearly fifteen seconds. The man noticed, but continued to read his book.

A few minutes later the woman sneezed again, took out a tissue, wiped her nose then shuddered quite violently once more. The man assumed the woman might have a cold, although he was still curious about the shuddering. A few more minutes passed before the woman sneezed yet again. Once more she took a tissue, wiped her nose, her body shaking even more than before. The man, now unable to restrain his curiosity, turned to the woman and said, "I couldn't help but notice that you sneezed three times, wiped your nose then shuddered violently. Are you okay?" "Oh, I'm sorry if I've disturbed you", replied the woman, "I have a very rare medical condition; whenever I sneeze I have an orgasm". The man felt slightly embarrassed, but still curious. "I've never heard of that condition before", he said, "are you taking anything for it?" "Oh, yes", the woman replied, "black pepper!"

Right! Now to another minorities group who seem to be doing awfully well under this government – what have they got against Middle England? The wheels on the gypsy caravan of fortune really started turning under John Prescott, forcing councils to make provisions for sites. Government inspectors have overturned twice as many council rejections of site applications than before the Prescott order made in 2006, at which point in his lack of career he was the Deputy Prime Minister. The Shadow Communities and Local Government Secretary, Eric Pickles, said earlier this year that there seems to be "one law for the gypsies and another for ordinary citizens". I am surprised he wasn't hung at Newgate for that little gem of truth. However, when you consider that South Cambridgeshire Council is to spend half a million pounds of erecting a sound barrier along the A14 because site occupants complained of noise, you do get the feeling that Mr. Pickles might just have been rubbing shoulders with the ordinary man in the street. This is on top of the £15,000 earmarked for road improvements to the site that is home to fifty – yes, fifty – gypsies. And the problem is that these people are never satisfied. Some chap called Basil Burton of the National Romany Rights Association commented that, "It's disgusting that local authorities have placed a gypsy site next to a motorway (dual carriageway, actually, Baz) in the first place". I bet there were far less problems with planning consent than an imaginary, though very real, Mrs. Travis of Acacia Avenue who merely wants an eight foot extension to her bungalow, but is refused permission on the grounds that it's out of keeping with the area!

We now have the case of one Malcolm Godden, aged 62, who owns a 19th century home in Hampshire. His view has been blighted by a gypsy who has bought the fields next door. Mr. Shea is claiming "gypsy status" which, as you know, entitles you to fast track any planning applications and ride roughshod over rules that apply to proper people – people like Mr. Godden. Without waiting for planning permission, Mr. Shea brought in two mobile homes, two touring caravans and then built a utility block. A gate used by local people for country walks is now padlocked shut with barbed wire wound around the top – there's friendly! Mr. Shea currently owns three homes in Bordon, not far from where he has set up camp. He won't comment on his activities, apparently, but leaves it all to a female by the name of Alison Heine, who – wait for it – specialises in gypsy planning applications. Imagine being a specialist in white middle-class planning applications. If there were, I hope it would be somebody with the name of Henrietta Featherstonehaugh-Smythe. Just a dream!

Seriously, what is worrying, is Ms. Heine's comments that, "Although the family own property, Mr. Shea and his son continue to follow a travelling way of life, preferring to live in caravans. The applicants have a genuine need for a site, as they have strong local connections". She goes on, "The applicants' gypsy-traveller status adds a very special dimension to this case. It permits exceptions to be considered on account of the need to facilitate this way of life". What rot! The fields he purchased do not seem to be overly level. I really do hope that East Hampshire Council reject his application and tell him to tinker elsewhere. You wouldn't mind if newcomers join in with village life, but these people are generally very antagonistic. They have such a chip on their shoulders, they could almost be Welsh!

Only last week I read of a farmer, Mr. Lee, in Devon, who wrote a letter to the council objecting to a planning application for a travellers' site a half a mile away from his farm. Having lived with a travellers' camp next door to him for thirty years, you might think the council would take into consideration the views of such folk, but no, when our man sent in his letter, he commented that horses had been turned out into his fields, that the police were regular visitors trying to trace stolen goods and breaking up fights. Were his comments heeded? Strangely, no. He received a letter back from the gutless ones at Mid Devon Council stating that they "Take no account of representations of a racist nature". Mr. Lee was even warned that he could face legal action from the police and the equality watchdog. The good news is that fifty other complainants persuaded the council to refuse permission. But who are these faceless and nameless unelected wonders that make it so easy for the minorities and so difficult for taxpaying working people?

Now you know what I think of arse holes! But occasionally, an arse hole comes along that you can't help liking, though maybe not so much liking as admiring – although you still wouldn't invite him round for dinner – or even afternoon tiffin, as one does in Surrey. No, Michael O'Leary, head of Ryanair, is just one of those arse holes. I saw him interviewed at breakfast time on the Beeb, having made the headlines once more with further outrageous schemes for increased revenue. Among his more outlandish ideas are charging for the use of the plane's toilet, only being able to check in on-line, penalties for taking luggage, fines for being forgetful passengers and even the staff now having to pay for their own training. He called the company who run Stansted Airport "a bunch of overcharging rapists".

It takes a certain type of personality to get away with that. Most people couldn't. And that's why I admire his balls – not literally, obviously, as he would probably charge you extra! I would willingly place Mr. O'Leary within the ranks of government ministers, with a brief to "sort it out". Any department, any subject. I think we could safely say a few feathers would be ruffled. His first brief would be to sort out the PC brigade, that dangerous bunch of self-satisfied, humourless prolls that wield such power. His first assignment within that role would be to tell a certain Scottish BA pilot to "get a life". Douglas Maughan, aged 54, going on 9, claims that he suffered racism in the work place – wait for it – I can see you champing the bit – due to the fact that he has been called a "Jock". Even when he was marked down on his flying assessment, he claimed that this had nothing to do with breaching operating procedures but "victimisation on racial grounds". And they wonder why we have so little time for those in the provinces and colonies.

Which reminds me, as we are talking of airlines you may have read that Ireland's worst air disaster occurred earlier this morning, when a small two-seater Cessna plane crashed into a cemetery in Limerick. Irish search and rescue workers have so far recovered 1,826 bodies and expect the number to climb as digging continues into the night!

I also read that passengers watched nervously as two men in pilot uniform and dark glasses using white canes to feel their way, made it into the cockpit of a 747. The plane belted its way down the runway as the frightened passengers screamed as the plane headed towards the end of the tarmac. Just in time, it soared into the sky and the relieved passengers cheered and laughed at having been conned by the pilots' practical joke. In the cockpit one of the pilots said to the other, "You know, one day they are going to scream too late and we are all going to cop it"!

The role of carnival queen in Weymouth is no more because it is too sexist. The local Round Table used to organise the carnival for charity each year. But this year, some group called the Weymouth Community Volunteers have taken over. As soon as you read the word "community" you know that everything will be brought down to the lowest common denominator and sanitised to kingdom come. The carnival organiser, Sue Follan – bet she's a Ms – said, "The carnival queen contest is a closed shop as it only applies to glamorous women and we think it is time for a change". So bugger what the good folk of Weymouth think – and I bet they will be ultimately funding it.

The European Parliament mandarins, or "jobsworths", have decreed that the words "Miss" and "Mrs." are to be avoided by Euro politicians. At great expense, the EU has published guidelines which aim to stop these words and others such as "sportsmen" and "sportswomen". They don't like the idea of "manmade" either. They would like it to be "synthetic". This little exercise is all part of their "gender neutral language" initiative, which is there so as not to offend women. Once again, they are faceless, non-elected arse holes who should be stacking shelves in Asda. You would never let them near a Waitrose.

If you live in Sheringham, Norfolk, then you will no doubt be aware of one particular Pay and Display machine in one of the town's short-term car parks. The machine is only three feet high. This is to help the disabled, and presumably dwarfs, midgets and elves, to obtain their tickets. The fact that the majority of motorists are of "normal" height – oh, how I loved using that word – is neither here nor there. We are, don't forget, an inclusive society, even if a three-foot high machine is appropriate for less than 1% of the paying population. Everyone else has to bend down or get on his or her knees. It's ludicrous, though typical.

My mother barks at Banclays and the other day I had to deposit a cheque she had received for her birthday. Queuing, as one does, I noticed only two of the four tills open. There were three at normal height (there, I've written it again!) and one dwarf-height till. Yes, you've got it. One of the open tills was at "normal" height, the other open till being at "dwarf" height. I did enquire, and, yes, they have to have the till open at all times in case a wheelchair-bound customer appears. I have no problem with a window being there for the disabled. It's a very good idea, but I see little logic in opening it all day in the hope that you achieve your target of disabled or dwarf-size customers, which no doubt will be caught on the bank's CCTV cameras. Everyone else has to stoop, but then that's okay. When enough of us have strained our backs to the point that we're crippled, that window will really come into its own for us!

Now, here's another example. The DVLA spend £120,000 per annum translating documents, including licence applications. Some of this is spent on Braille! Now doesn't that sound slightly worrying?

Before we move on to the blossoming industry that is health and safety, I thought you'd like to know that Carol Kirkwood looked wonderful again this morning. As you know I never remember anything she says about the weather, there's just something about our Carol..... (My wife has just stopped typing this tome and said, "I bet she can't type as quickly as me!")

Anyway, swimmers at the London Field's outdoor lido in Hackney have been notified that if there's a burst of heavy rain they could be told to leave the water on the grounds of health and safety. Officials state that rain makes the water cloudy and hinders lifeguards from spotting swimmers in trouble. Meanwhile, not far away in Kent a 64-year-old was ordered to leave Erith Sports Centre swimming baths as he committed the heinous crime of diving into the pool. New health and safety regulations require you to "lower yourself into the water".

And just to complete the trio of swimming stories, just north of the Dartford Tunnel in Dagenham the leisure centre there has banned visitors from swimming lengths in the pool. They say it's easier for lifeguards to keep an eye on people if they are swimming widths instead of lengths. I know, I know.....

The council in Bourne, Lincolnshire, have banned the union flag from being flown from the town hall mast on Armed Forces Day, deeming it too dangerous for a man on a ladder to attach to said pole. It's an eight-foot ladder, for God's sake! Who are these people?

Talking of ladders, a clown who performs with the Moscow State Circus has been told to remove his size 18 shoes when he performs tricks on a wire, because they are in breach of health and safety regulations. Soldiers returning from Iraq and Afghanistan have been banned from putting up regimental pictures once back home in Blighty, because – are you ready for it – they may hurt themselves knocking a nail into a wall. What an insult to those concerned, though of more concern is the fact that under government guidelines jobs like these now have to be performed by private companies under their "private finance initiative". One regiment has been charged £500 to put in an electric socket! While we, the taxpayers, are helpless to act, a lot of people at the top are making a lot of money out of this expensive farce. The health and safety industry starts with the young these days. Children are now banned from playing conkers on the spurious grounds that they may injure not only themselves, but also others. They are also banned from using empty egg boxes on the unlikely grounds that there will be an outbreak of salmonella. They now have to wear goggles when using BluTac and there is a 5-page instruction leaflet on the use of Pritt Stick glue. Still, I'm sure they know best.

Then there are those in life who just ask for trouble. A chap in Shamley Green, Surrey, where cricket has been played for 168 years, bought a house next to the green – well, forty yards from the batsman's crease to be precise. He is now complaining about balls hitting his property. Is it me? Us? Why buy a house near a cricket pitch? This chap apparently likes cricket so you would have thought he might have been aware of what happens when willow strikes leather (I'm sounding awfully poetic!). Shame is, bats are probably no longer made of wood, nor balls from skin. I've never liked the game – too long and too boring. Any sport where you can play for five days and end up in a draw due to rain is somewhat pointless in my book. However, as you know, I am nothing if not fair. The case made against the cricket club on the grounds of health and safety has been thrown out at Guildford County Court. Isn't it nice to see common sense take precedence for once? I'm sure it won't last.

It's been a relatively good month. Neither Andy Murray nor his mother won Wimbledon – which was good. A more miserable looking cove, on and off the turf, I have yet to encounter. Even when he wins there's no smile or warmth. Mr. Federer won, which was good, as he has all the appearance of a rakish gent.

He dresses well on court and afterwards in his whites (or creams – it could be our tele). No rants, no outrages, just a professional. Andy Roddick is okay, except that he wears a cap even when the sun is not an issue. He has been seen on many occasions wearing it backwards as well, for which he loses even more marks. It also makes him look more American, which is the last thing any self-respecting American would want to look like!

Which reminds me; picture yourself if you can on a train travelling at speed through the French countryside. It is crowded. A US marine has walked the entire length looking for a seat, but the only seat left has been taken by a well-dressed, middle-aged French woman's poodle. The war-weary marine asks, "M'am, may I have that seat?" The French woman just sniffs and says to no one in particular, "Americans, they are so rude. That seat is for the use of my little Fifi". The marine shrugs his shoulders and walks the entire length of the train again, but returns to find the dog is still taking the only seat left. "Please, m'am, may I sit down, I am so very tired". She snorts. "Not only are you Americans rude, you are also very arrogant". This time the marine says not a word. He just picks up the dog, opens the window and tosses it out before sitting down. The woman stands and shrieks. "Someone must defend my honour. This American has to be put in his place". An English gentleman sitting nearby calmly folds his paper and says, "Sir, you Americans appear to have a penchant for doing the wrong thing. You hold your fork in the wrong hand, you drive your cars on the wrong side of the road and now, sir, you seem to have thrown the wrong bitch out of the window". Oh, how I would have loved to have been on that train!

Greedy MPs have been wringing their hands, claiming that they acted within the rules of the House of Commons over their excessive expenses. Some have resigned, some have hung on, the local council and Euro elections came and went. The Press were up in arms about the BNP taking seats – oh, what a surprise. I would have voted BNP but I felt their policies were just too left wing.....

I did actually vote UKIP on both counts, though I never held out much hope of massive inroads into the Tory or Labour votes, and this at a time when you think, if they don't make it count now, they never will. I think the problem with UKIP is that there is no-one of prominence in the party. There's no-one with political balls. They should be making more of the Euro waste that we pay for in the form of subsidies, grants, MEP expenses, etc. But, of course, they themselves are now part of the gravy train, so perhaps one becomes like the rest – you know, it's all within the rules. I feel their main problem is actually their leader, Nigel Farrage. He always appears austere, distant and with little humour. He never smiles. Perhaps he has been taking lessons from Andy Murray as, to be fair, they are similar in other aspects as well. Both have the personality of a soggy chip, and neither has won Wimbledon.

The ray of sunshine on the gloomy political horizon is seen in the shape of Peter Davies, who has been elected Mayor of Doncaster with an overwhelming majority. His first move was to cut his own salary from £73,000 pa to £30,000 pa. He wants to reduce the number of councillors from 63 to 21. As he says, "If a hundred senators can run America, why does Doncaster require sixty-three!" He's taken Doncaster out of the Local Government Association and the Local Government Information Unit. This little exercise will save Doncaster's ratepayers £200,000 at a stroke. He is to "untwin" Doncaster – good man! And stop funding all the minority jollies like the Doncaster International Women's Day, Black History Month, Lesbian, Gay, and Bi-Sexual Transgender Month. Even better news! It will be interesting to see how he gets on – or is allowed to by the "Rights Brigade". Interestingly, he was elected as a representative of the English Democratic Party which advocates the flying of the Cross of St. George from all public buildings. Can we clone this man? Wouldn't it be nice if mayors sprung up all over the country in his idiom? But as they say, in democracy it's your vote that counts, whereas in feudalism it's your count that votes!

The government still seems incapable of understanding the indigenous thinking person's love of the BBC and Post Offices.

The idea of using part of our licence fee to fund commercial stations is about as big a liberty as when they transferred funding for worthy causes courtesy of the lottery, to the ill-conceived Olympics or the sating of Sebastian Coe's ego, whichever is the bigger. Still unable to find a buyer for the Post Office, that grotesque and hideous epitomy of all you wouldn't trust even when he's dead, Peter Mandelson, still continues his quest to sell off part of our heritage. He's the sort of person you wouldn't have confidence in to hand out dead batteries free of charge.

This government is no different to the Tories they succeeded. I voted Labour for the first time in my life when Tony Blair ran for presidency – sorry, Prime Minister – back in the nineties. I wanted so much to get rid of the greed culture that Mrs. T had reeked upon this country, along with the rest of the havoc in the form of privatisation of our gas, water, electricity, railway system, etc. etc. It seems plain to me, you obviously, and the rest of Middle England, that once you sell off a public service or utility to private investors, it is no longer a publicly owned service. So why do we still prop up the railways every time Network Rail get into financial trouble. Shareholders still get their dues and the bosses still attract enormous bonuses. Why? We have gutless industry overlords in the guise of regulators, who have very little in the way of teeth and everything in the way of meetings, lunches and expenses. Everything we held dear is owned by foreign companies. When push comes to shove, and scarcity really bites, be it gas, electricity or water, these countries will naturally look after their own. That's what happens. And we, thanks to "Grantham woman" have sold off our silver, as she did with our school playing fields and the NHS. Part privatisation came in with partnerships and public finance initiatives. Whichever way it is put, private investment equals profit. No-one should make money out of our utilities, transport, NHS or schools. I honestly thought that Labour opposed these greedy and short-term developments, but I was wrong. They merely embraced them and continued the bad work .

Right! Fancy a joke or two? Okay, always ready to oblige. What? You're going out this evening and want to be able to amuse those in your company. So, no pressure then. Here goes:

The first joke concerns Sally. Sally was a contestant on "Who Wants To Be A Millionaire?" She had reached the final stage. If she answered the next question correctly she would win £1 million. If her answer were incorrect she would pocket only the guaranteed amount of £32,000. She suspected that the £1 million question would be no pushover. The question was – which of these following species of birds does not build its own nest, but instead lays its eggs in the nest of other birds? Is it (a) the condor, (b) the buzzard, (c) the cuckoo, (d) the vulture? Sally was on the spot. She hadn't a clue. She had used up both her 50/50 and Ask the Audience lifelines. All that remained was her Phone a Friend. She had to use it. Her friend, however, was blonde. She called her friend and gave her the question with the four choices. Her friend's response was unhesitating. "Oh, that's easy. The answer is (c) – the cuckoo". Sally had to make a decision, and make it fast. She considered employing a reverse strategy by giving any answer except the one that her friend had given her. After all, her friend was blonde, and it seemed the logical thing to do. But her friend had responded with such confidence, such certitude that Sally could not help but be convinced. She crossed her fingers and bleated out, "(c) the cuckoo". "Is that your final answer?" asked our Chris. "Yes", said Sally, "that is my final answer". After an inordinately long time the answer came. "You are correct, you are now a millionaire". Three days later Sally hosted a party for friends and family. Naturally included was her blonde friend who had helped her win £1 million. "I just don't know how to thank you", said Sally, "how did you happen to know the right answer?" "Oh, come on", said her friend, "everyone knows that cuckoos don't build nests. They live in clocks".

What's that? You can't tell that one because there will be women at the party who might be offended? Okay, how about this one:

A man and his wife are awoken at 3 am by a loud pounding on the door. The man gets out of bed and goes to the door where a drunken stranger is standing in the pouring rain. He asks for a push. "Not a chance", says the husband, "it's three in the morning". Annoyed, he slams the door and returns to bed. "Who was that", asks his wife sleepily. "Oh, just some drunk asking for a push". "Didn't you help him?" she asks. "No, I did not, its 3 am and it's pouring with rain". "Huh", says the wife, "you have a short memory. It was only three months ago when we broke down and those two men helped us. I think you should go out and help him. You should be ashamed of yourself". The husband tuts, does as he's told, gets dressed and walks out into the pouring rain. He calls out in the dark, "Hello, are you still there?" "Yes", comes back the answer. "I'm sorry I was so short with you earlier, do you still need a push?" "I certainly do", came the reply from the dark. "Where are you?" asks the husband. The drunk replied, "Over here on the swing".

I'm on a roll once more. What – a couple of quickies? Oh, all right:

Did you hear of the thief who stole a calendar and got twelve months, but to be fair the calendar's days were numbered.

Or:

She was only the whisky maker's daughter, but he loved her still.

Oh, you're off are you, well enjoy your evening and I'll see you tomorrow.

Well, it's tomorrow. And the world and Carol Kirkwood are still with us. And it's no good calling me a dirty old man, because I am now over sixty and taking tablets. Us men of a certain age have all had our favourites through the years, from Jane Fonda and Shirley McLaine, to Toyah Willcox (as much for her lithp as for her looks), to Twiggy, who still makes me freeze-frame M&S ads on the rare occasions when I have recorded an ITV programme. Okay, then, let's be honest. I'm not really recording a programme, I'm merely recording an M&S advert. I still have my Kylie Minogue video – "I Should Be So Lucky"..... My wife reminded me as she is typing this that in September we will have been married for forty years. She said it was Ruby, I thought it was Rust! Oh, how she almost laughed!

One of the greatest irritations to the driving public, other than road tax income not being used on road maintenance, is the proliferation of speed cameras. Oh, what joy when you physically see one burnt out or damaged. You know me, I deplore violence, but there is always an exception in life. I had no problem with cameras placed at what were regarded as "accident black spots". There then came the realisation that filthy lucre could be made just by them "being there". That's where the balance between support and greed tends to blur. In 1996 there were 262,000 speeding fines and prosecutions. Ten years on, and there were 1,865,000 – not an insignificant increase. We now have police insidiously hiding behind beach huts in Bournemouth in an effort to catch cyclists exceeding the legal speed limit of 10 mph. During this time a hoodie is holding up a convenience store, raping a female or assaulting a pensioner. But then, speeding fines are income. There is now a new type of speed gun arriving, one that catches you speeding at night. These radar guns work over a distance of one and a half miles and can note the registration number at a hundred yards.

Still, it's not all bad news. I see that the Chief Executive of Serco, the people who make speed cameras, one Tom Riall, was convicted of speeding – 102 mph in a 70 mph area. He already has two motoring convictions, one for speeding. He was fined £300 and ordered to pay £40 towards prosecution costs, plus that other nice little government earner, the £15 victim surcharge. He was also banned for six months and had six points added to his licence. You just can't help but smile, can you.

But that smile can quickly turn to a scowl when you consider the case of the Hull City Football Club chairman, a team I rooted for last year in their quest to survive their first season in the Premier League. Paul Duffen had been banned from driving after being convicted for a fourth time for speeding, but he told the judge that while he could afford to pay for a chauffeur, it didn't give him the privacy he needed when on the telephone buying players. Now admittedly, he was only doing 55 in a 40, but with three previous convictions he doesn't seem to learn that easily. His appeal for the ban to be overturned was granted on the basis that "talking in the presence of a driver would be wholly unsuitable" so the judge decided it was a case of "exceptional hardship". What absolute bollocks! It didn't go unnoticed that in the article it mentioned Mr. Duffen lives in Surrey. I take it he isn't really one of us, merely an incomer, as a proper person would have taken his medicine without the usual whinging one so associates with northerners.

Aren't our policemen wonderful? Sorry, I meant useless. I was thinking of life forty years ago..... Everyone is up in arms this morning as they read their paper and find that a dog handler has left two Alsatians in the back of his car on one of the hottest days of the year. The temperature in that car would have reached 116°F - no wonder the dogs died. He hasn't been suspended but there is a chance he will be prosecuted. The RSPCA in Nottinghamshire is holding an enquiry. Chief Superintendent Khan commented, "We are taking this incident very, very seriously. We will take any lessons from this tragedy, put them into place and make sure it never happens again". Well, if he's ever on "Mastermind", you know his specialist subject will be the bleeding obvious! Didn't he sound like any head of a social work department, when another child is abused and killed? I mean, what have they got to learn? I really do hope that the person concerned suffers as much as his dogs did.

Those of you who know me will be aware that animal welfare and cruelty play a large part in my feelings at either end of the scale. I remember reading earlier in the year of some cove by the name of Roger Venton, who received a suspended jail sentence for illegally using a trap and allowing a colleague to snare birds of prey, but then he is/was a gamekeeper. I suspect his activities come high on the list of "unuttered credentials" at interview. Both men were apparently motivated by the desire to protect 40,000 pheasants and 20,000 partridges on an estate in Shropshire. The word "protect" is an absolute joke. The protection runs as far as the money that can be earned from the shooting of these birds. This estate "boasts" – and it really does boast – top drives, plus a shooting lodge with spectacular views. Please don't bore me and talk of conservation, it's all about profit. This Venton fellow had kept a diary, which showed that in the previous year 102 buzzards, 40 badgers and 37 ravens had been killed on the estate. One can understand the pressure on staff to "deal" with alternative predators, especially when those who get their kicks from shooting are paying up to £10,000 per day. Venton was sentenced to two concurrent three-month jail terms, suspended – naturally, although he does have to spend 250 hours on unpaid work and pay £2,000 costs. He admitted to using a spring trap and permitting his colleague to use a cage that had been baited with a raven, in order to catch birds of prey. What sort of low life could even contemplate killing such beautiful creatures? The spring trap, by the way, was banned in this country over a century ago. Both would be rotting in cells in the newly built Newgate Prison, if I had my way, but then, animals cannot give evidence of torture and pain.

The EU has proposed banning both halal and kosher meats, as the killing process is considered cruel. I can't see either of these proposals getting off the ground. Such will be the resistance on tradition and religious grounds. I have yet to find anyone in a position of power with enough guts to stand up for animal welfare. No-one wants to offend the Jews, let alone the Muslims. If those in power truly cared the EU would have told Spain to ban bull fighting and goat throwing, but then gutless is the EU's middle name. Just tweak the edges and claim the expenses.

The pleasure any human can receive from shooting an animal or bird for fun is totally beyond my comprehension. Over the years there have been many articles, some with photographs, that have truly sickened me by the sheer cowardice shown by the perpetrator against his or her quarry. We now have hunters paying thousands of pounds to travel to the Arctic and shoot polar bears. These morons of high financial standing and extremely low mentality pay £25,000 for a fortnight through an organisation called "Adventure North West". This is a Canadian company (not going there again) whose boss, Boyd Warner, said, "You can track one for days, but a single shot through the heart kills instantly". He added that he gets lots of Mexicans, Americans and Europeans too. His description of this scum as "just genuine, ordinary folk" defies the definition of the words "genuine" and "ordinary". He does, however, add that they have a lot of cash! Can anyone explain to me how shooting a polar bear is "fair game"? The picture accompanying the article shows the hunter – or sick bastard, as I prefer to think of him – lying prone behind a white screen about to shoot. The bear does not stand a chance. How can this complete and utter arse that has been given a gun and sadly for humanity, survived his mother's pregnancy, take any sense of pride from this act of animal murder.

The other photo that got my goat was one showing some female who had killed an elephant She is seen standing proudly in short sleeved top and army fatigue trousers, held up with macho belt, her right hand resting on hip (a sure sign of someone who is very pleased with themselves) and the left hand holding a crossbow. This woman, a description I feel should be challenged under the gender description act, is American, so no real surprise there, of what appears to be German ancestry. It really doesn't get much more unfortunate than that. Her name is Teressa Groenwald-Hagermann. She is 39, so once more, old enough to know better. The smile she gives confirms that she is apparently the first woman to have killed an elephant with a bow and arrow. So proud is she that pictures of her "accomplishment" have been posted on the Internet for all to see and enjoy. She killed the animal at dusk in Africa. What a brave lady she is. She notes that she found the animal in a family of thirty-seven elephants. She crouched twelve yards away, and then fired. She smugly explains that the elephant staggered for five hundred yards before collapsing. How proud she must now feel. She did it for a bet, apparently. Sadly, she adds on the website, "That has to be one of the best examples of setting a goal and working hard to achieve it". Like the aforementioned polar bear hunters I wish them and her nothing but a slow, lingering death from cancer at best, or something worse if that is possible.

So, if you are up there god (you have to earn a capital letter) do your stuff and right a few wrongs. There really should not be a place for these people who extract so much pleasure from killing something that cannot fight back.

Closer to home we have recently seen a fisherman jailed for eighty days - that's eighty days for clubbing twenty-one seal pups to death on a Scottish island. James Stewart admitted mutilating, beating and crushing the pups. How could he do it? This crofter earns £74,000 a year. Not a bad income, is it, for crofting? I always thought they earned less than the minimum wage. Perhaps they just whinge like other northerners. He told the police that the seals were suffering and he had to put them out of their misery. Again, he didn't even have the guts to stand up and be counted for his sins – bastard!

Some good news! And to be fair the "Daily Express" has helped enormously in exposing the shame that is the Greeks' treatment of donkeys. These under-privileged animals are used to transport tourists on the Island of Santorini up 800 feet climbs. Do tourists not notice the poor condition of these beasts? Probably not. But then, that speaks volumes for the mentality of those who visit Greek islands. Tourists should stay away on principle, but these people wouldn't. They are no different from the ones who visit Spain. I am not awash with principles, but I do try. You'll never find me in any country that has traditions of using or abusing animals for financial gain from tourism or spectacle. From now on, these donkey owners will have to be licensed and vets will carry out checks every three months – well, that's the theory. One can only hope.

Oh, and another article with photos to match, but this time one to preen over. Someone has been gored to death as opposed to bored to death, which is what happens when you visit my mother! Anyhow, a 27-year-old male has died of injuries sustained when a bull's horn pierced his neck and left lung. It was during one of these 8-day animal fiestas in Spain, where bulls chase runners through the streets of small towns. Small towns, with even smaller-brained residents and tourists. What annoys me is that written within the newspaper article the beast is described as a "killer bull". Well, they're not known for their docile personalities, and when thrust into the scenario that they are, it's no great surprise that they become a tad tetchy. If ever there was a case for health and safety and animal welfare to work together, it's this obscenity, but then H & S are never there when you really need them.

Just to lighten up the proceedings, I thought you might like to hear a little story concerning teddy bears.

Picture yourself as you will in a crowded bar in a city centre. A man meets a woman. They talk; they get on well and at the end of the evening they leave together. He invites her back to his place. She feels assured and safe. Once back he shows her around his apartment. It is completely filled with soft, sweet, cuddly teddy bears. In the bedroom there are three shelves, with hundreds and hundreds of cute, cuddly teddy bears, carefully placed in order, covering the entire wall. It was obvious to the woman that he had taken quite some time to lovingly arrange them and she was immediately touched by the amount of thought he had put into organising his display. There were small bears along the bottom shelf, medium bears covering the length of the middle shelf, and huge bears running along the top shelf. She found it strange for an obviously masculine man to have such a large collection of bears. She was quite impressed by his sensitive side but didn't mention this to him. They shared a bottle of wine and continued talking long into the night. After a while she found herself thinking, "My God, maybe this could be the one. Maybe I'm looking at the man who could be the future father of my children". She turned to him and kissed him lightly on the lips. His response was warm and caring. They continued to kiss, the passion building before he romantically lifted her into his arms and carried her off in to the bedroom where they ripped off each other's clothing before making hot, steamy love. She was so overwhelmed that she responded with all the passion, creativity and heat that she could muster. After an intensive, explosive night of raw sex with this very sensitive man, they found themselves lying together in the afterglow. At length, she rolled over, stroked his chest, looked deep into his eyes, and asked coyly, "So, how was it for you?" The man smiled gently, stroked his cheek, looked intently at her and with a waving of his right arm said, "Help yourself to any prize from the middle shelf".

Right! I don't know about you, or where you are off to this year, but Maureen and I are leaving early tomorrow morning with Jacquie and Peter for Dumfries and Galloway. What do you mean, you've forgotten? It wasn't that many pages ago I imparted the news of our impending break, so I'll leave you with a jolly jape before we go.

It's the joke about the cabbie and the nun. A cabbie picks up a nun. She gets into the cab and notices that the "very " handsome cab driver won't stop staring at her. "My son", she says, "why are you staring?" He looks in the mirror. "I have a question to ask you but I don't wish to offend". "My son", she replies, "you cannot offend me. When you are as old as I and have been a nun for as long as I have, you get a chance to see and hear just about everything. I am sure there is nothing you can say or ask that I would find offensive". With not a small degree of embarrassment he splutters out, "Well, I've always had a fantasy to have a nun kiss me". She responds in measured terms, "Well, let's see what we can do about that. One, you must be single, and two, you must be Catholic". The cab driver becomes excited. "Yes, yes, I am single and I am Catholic". The nun nods. "Then pull into the next alley". The nun fulfils his fantasy with a kiss that would make a hooker blush. They get back on the road but the cab driver starts to cry. "Dear boy", enquires the nun, "why are you crying?" "Forgive me, for I have sinned. I have lied and I must confess. I am married and I am Jewish". The nun smiles. "That's okay my son, my name is Kevin and I am on my way to a fancy dress party!"

CHAPTER FIVE

Of Galloway and An Arthurian Maiden

Well, we're back, that was fun. What? Where was it we were off to? Dumfries and Galloway, how many more times do I have to tell you! You travel up the M6 until you reach Gretna, then you turn left. We stayed in a hotel in Castle Douglas. We left our house at about 5 am, P & J picked us up in their car, then we drove fault-free to the independently owned Tebay Service Station on the M6, which is the example of what a motorway service station should look and feel like. How many other stations have a delicatessen selling local produce? A lake has been built outside the cafeteria where you can watch ducks and drakes doing whatever ducks and drakes do. It's a far more relaxing way to unwind and has rightly earned accolades for variety, quality and service. Good on them. Breakfast completed we skirted Penrith and by-passed Carlisle before Gretna beckoned. I'd love to say that Gretna was a mere disappointment but sadly it wasn't even that good. But hey ho, ever onwards, or westwards if you are following me on the map. Into Annan, full of low Scottish buildings in red stone. Sombre and severe, but with a town clock. Out of Annan, we headed along the scenic coastal route beside the Solway Firth. We stopped for afternoon tea in a very twee family-run shop next to a ruined abbey. The abbey looked interesting, but they demanded an entrance fee to walk around a pile of stones you could see from the road. We didn't go in.

We visited Kipford, a small harbour village full of pleasure craft, but lacking the atmosphere of a fishing port. There was a gift shop called The Ark that Maureen and Jacquie appeared very interested in rummaging through. Luckily for our Visa cards they were closed on every visit – well, two anyway. Over that 5-day break we visited Dalbeattie, a small town now ruined by unimaginative and bland social housing. Naturally they had the best views of the surrounding countryside, as with all social housing it has been built on the town's outskirts.

Wigtown was a sleepy little place, with a silted-up harbour, which I found atmospheric and Maureen found eerie. At the back of the town centre and on the walk towards the harbour there was a field containing cattle alongside some lovely country houses. Ominously, a sign proclaimed with all its usual pride that social housing was to be built on the field. The place was already surrounded with enough homes better suited to the benefit classes, as it housed incumbents sounding not too dissimilar to Jimmy Knapp.

We all liked Port Patrick, which did have a small fishing port and character. And none of us liked Dumfries. I thought it was going to be a bit like Guildford, but with a Scottish lilt. Sadly, it was run down with drunks and obesity in full flow and view, more like Aldershot but with a Scottish tang. We espied a health food shop. I thought if anyone is having an uphill struggle, it's them. But at least it was open. Many shops were closed, pubs took on the face of the last chance saloon and the town generally felt tired. Stranraer was also visited. It reminded me of Folkestone. We never got out of the car.....

Lockerbie cemetery was a very humbling experience, and not a little emotional when you read the stories of individuals and whole families who had died. Stories of people, all of whom seemed to have been in the wrong place at the wrong time.

Every town seems to have a clock tower. We stayed opposite one at the "Douglas Arms Hotel". I have to say that the quality of food, be it breakfast or evening meal – come to that all we consumed throughout the holiday – was terrific. Even though Castle Douglas has its Tesco, it is still a town full of individual shops, including three butchers. The local produce available everywhere made us very envious when compared with the dearth we have down south. The friendliness of the people was second to none. Opposite the side entrance to the hotel was a Gospel hall and at breakfast every day I faced out onto the street and would read the following, which was painted on the Gospel hall wall:

"Ye must be born again" John Ch3 V7. I thought it strange that someone would take the time to write that, not add his surname but enter his postcode.....

The scenery was very enjoyable, alternating sharply from flat estuary sands to the Galloway Forest, with some lovely rolling hills and spectacular views. We saw a colony of red kites being fed on a farm not far from Castle Douglas. Some fifty of them gather daily at 2 pm, knowing that a lady is going to walk with a bucket of carrion into a field at 2.30 pm. It is then they commence their swooping. Interesting was the fact that seagulls tried and failed to compete for the meal. The crows, however, stood on the ground and collected that which fell off the table. Canny buggers! We continued our ornithological day by visiting a couple of hides alongside a nearby loch. After breakfast at the "Douglas Arms" you needed a long walk before you ate again, and the walk to the hides was perfect. We were the only ones present. We took to our seats and watched over a forty-minute period as a red squirrel busied itself eating nuts and scurrying about, thereby amusing us touring southerners. Crested thingies were spotted, and spotted whatsits abounded. We duly made a note in the log provided. Coloured photographs and diagrams helped you identify the local wildlife. We read what had been seen before and the excited manner in which entries had been made. By the scribble at the end of some of these notes it seemed that several orgasms had been achieved over a not inconsiderable period. Nothing so stimulating for us, however. Well, certainly not for me, not with my diabetes! I can only speak for myself, of course, but I wasn't aware of anyone else in our party, though you never know.....

Anyway, boredom soon set in, as did the giggles. Questions were raised as to how long it would be before anyone spotted a penguin, which seemed almost reasonable until someone suggested a tiger, followed by a buffalo. I'm sure you've got the picture. Maureen had her turn with the binoculars and shouted out very excitedly, "Vauxhall Astra", which she claimed to have seen on the road yonder, bordering the other side of the loch. But as she was the only one with binoculars, we dismissed her observation as fanciful. We left when a party of seasoned twitchers appeared, donning waterproofs, boots, hats, plastic sheeted maps, cameras, four-foot long extendable binoculars, pens and pencils. We realised that we were going to be usurped.

There was one strange happening – that was when we turned off a road in the Galloway Forest, having seen a sign to Bruce's Stone. This apparently had something to do with Robert the Bruce, as opposed to Bruce Forsyth – oh, the power of television, well, Forsyth is a Scottish name. Anyway, we parked in the woods by this loch, followed the very springy trail – I say springy because, although the path was gravel, as you flexed your knees the ground moved beneath you, but it wasn't one of those situations where somebody whispers endearingly, "Did the earth move for you?" It was similar to standing on the belly of a very obese person. Not that I have, but I realise how much you will appreciate the analogy. Having viewed the stone, and been singularly (or in our case quadruple-lally) unimpressed, we returned to our car. As we sat there discussing our lack of find, a woman appeared, walking along a path towards the small car park in which we were, well, parked. She was dressed in Arthurian garb. She wore a grey/black cloak or long coat that looked like chain mail. Her under-garments were medieval in style. She donned a scarf, which she slowly unwound as she approached the car park, revealing centre-parted black, crimped hair, which cascaded down her neck. She was to all intents and purposes, Guinevere. She walked slowly and purposefully behind our car, sticking to the gravel path, bare-footed, which I would have thought must have been fairly sore, although we detected no sign of a grimace. Actually, there was no emotion, no expression. She passed by and headed towards the stone. We all saw her. Strange. All, in all – a good holiday, rounded off with fish and chips, paid for with the remains of our "privy purse", which was partaken at "Jacks" in Bagshot.

We're off to Norfolk next year. What do they say? A county with two million people and only eighty-four surnames! And now a game all the family can play – incest! I remember reading of a letter to an agony aunt once. It read, "I am a girl from Norfolk. I am twelve years of age and haven't yet had sex. Do you think my brother is queer?" Must remember not to say that up there, or I will probably be whacked around the chops with a sugar beet, and I wouldn't want that – not with my diabetes!

Our Ben overhead me describing him as a "Mutt" on the phone the other day and aired his grievances over dinner by informing me that he was going to sue on the grounds that he was not a mongrel, and that the terminology I used was discriminatory, undermining and made him feel under-valued. I understand he had been reading the piece I wrote about the Scottish pilot who objected to being called a "Jock". He added that whilst he was not a pure pedigree, whom he observed never complained about the phrase "pampered pooch", as one of the "unbred" he's been counselled by the Canine Advisory Trust – or CAT. They have told him that he has the same level of legal protection as travellers, which to be fair, I wasn't aware of! Though I am now. You give a dog a home and all of a sudden they've got rights.....

Enough of this Benfoolery! I took him this morning along the canal. The female swan is still with five of her hissing brood. Two appear to have left the family to fend for themselves. I did see them on another section of the canal a couple of days ago, so they are still around. The father has flown the nest once more and is nowhere to be seen. Probably can't find any work in this area, as all local jobs seem to have been taken by the Canada geese. There was a holiday canal boat moored by "The Swan" Public House on Sunday. The curtains were drawn, there was no sign of life, and it was early, 6.45 am-ish. But what struck me was that the boat was flying the skull and crossbones. It did cross my mind that Somali pirates, probably the Basingstoke Canal branch, had hijacked it. Well, stranger things have happened. I mean, Peter Mandelson's been entrusted to run the country for one!

Getting back to diabetes, one of the effects is that it takes so much longer for cuts to heal. I recently visited Frimley Park Hospital where my appointment was for 10 am, only to be told that I should have been at Fleet Hospital instead. Didn't know they had one and no, it wasn't my fault. The form sent by Frimley Park Hospital made no mention that the appointment was anywhere other than Frimley. So off I trotted to Fleet. Oh, what a joy! An old-fashioned, cottage hospital with parking spaces and not a meter in sight. Pleasant staff, clean seating area with good quality up-to-date gardening magazines, and most importantly, proper outpatients. In other words, it didn't take on the persona of a drop-in centre for the homeless. A nurse announced my name at the appointed time and smiling warmly ushered me into an office. Examination took place and within 20 minutes I was being shown by the same nurse to the Reception Desk, and having made another appointment, bade me goodbye, by name, and thanked me for visiting Fleet Hospital. Doesn't it set you up for the day when people are pleasant, especially when you aren't expecting it? Among the many things that irritate me is the over-use of the word "community". It's Fleet Community Hospital. What's wrong with "cottage" or "town"? Mind you, it's the same on television – everything's a community – community centre, no longer a village hall, the community is suffering, the community is sharing its grief. I wonder if it's another political sop in order to make everything and everybody inclusive. Still strikes me of being Orwellian.

Well, I've returned today, five weeks after the initial appointment. I arrived at 8.45 am for a 9 am consultation. I parked in one of the thirteen spaces available, two spaces from the front door, the other being metaphorically unobtainable as it is reserved for the disabled. I did check as I had time, and there was not one mother-and-baby, mother-and-toddler, obese mother with genetically modified child parking spaces anywhere. What a pleasure. Once inside, the same smiling faces greeted me, although the magazine rack was conspicuously empty. I read the sign that hung from the rack. At least the writing was in upper case. It said that due to the contagious aspect of swine flu, no magazines would be available until further notice. Strange to tell, but books were available to take and read from a bookcase some twenty feet away. I sat chatting to another couple that were alongside me. They had come from Aldershot, but were old school. They spoke nicely. Well, put it this way, Farnham wouldn't have rejected them!

I mentioned to the doctor, actually a consultant this time – there's posh – about the magazines not being available in Fleet, although they are at the Ash Vale Health Surgery. We came to the conclusion that swine flu hadn't managed to cross the River Blackwater, which is the border between Hants and Surrey – and neither should it. They don't call them Hampshire hogs for nothing, you know.

The BBC really doesn't understand their viewers; their arrogance is stupefying. What is it about staff that has reached a certain age? They don't perform badly just because they have hit fifty, sixty, or even eighty. Or in dancer Karen Hardy's case, thirty-nine! She is going to be replaced on "Strictly Come Dancing" by a younger dancer. Arlene Phillips is also off the cast list. She is to head a government inspired quango, teaching the country to dance its way to fitness – which will be nice for it. Alesha Dixon is replacing Arlene, aged 66. I have absolutely nothing against Alesha. She seems very pleasant when interviewed, but the only reason the two older women have been replaced as far as I can understand, is due to their age. The same has happened to newsreaders in the past. They don't forget their lines and they don't have trouble reading the autocue. Their crime was reaching a certain age. Someone in authority a couple of years ago felt that Jimmy Young should no longer host a radio show. Why? And when they are replaced, the replacements are generally of an inferior standard. Take Nick Knowles, and I wish someone would. His barrow-boy delivery style always grates. I never watch anything he fronts. You know it will be trite and superficial. The ex-policeman in "Crimewatch", who takes part in the programme, drops so many h's and t's it's not worth watching, even if you like watching it, which I don't.

I've just remembered a lovely joke which Arthur Smith told on Radio Four:
"Doctor, I can't pronounce my t, h and f's". "Well", the doctor replied, "you can't say fairer than that then!"

Just getting back to "Crimewatch", Nick Ross used to host that, didn't he? But now it's Kirsty Young. Very pleasant young lady, but I never found much wrong with Nick Ross.

As a child, I remember reading Archie comics. They were American and centred on the activities of Archie, Reggie, Jughead and two high school girls whose names I remember not. I was reminded of these comics recently, and I'll tell you why. Yes, I will, whatever you're doing, let it wait. Now, there was a character in these comics called Richie Rich who was the spoilt little brat who had everything. His cousin – it could have been Reggie – had very little, so he orchestrated a situation which meant he'd be the centre of attention and he would have a taste of the limelight so frequented by his cousin. When the deed was done and the newspaper article appeared, the headlines read, "Richie Rich's cousin....." with no mention of the cousin's name.

The same happened for real earlier this year. An equestrian called Ian Olding, aged 47, was killed by his horse during trials in Lincolnshire. He was a friend of Zara Phillips. The article heading made no mention of Mr. Olding's name, but ran with the lead, "Horror As Horse Kills Zara's Pal". Some weeks ago two soldiers were killed in Afghanistan, one was a commanding officer, the other being a foot soldier. Whilst the foot soldier's death was noted in all the papers, the background of the officer – friend of Prince Charles and known at No. 10 –was played out in a sycophantic way, day in, day out in the press. It was noted on Ceefax with some letters complaining about the unbalanced coverage. Both deaths were equally sad and unnecessary.

You remember the policeman who left his dogs in a car when it was hot and they died? Well, the RSPCA are prosecuting him. They say there will be no cover up and the officer will be treated like any member of the public. Is this the public where some dogs are treated more fairly than other dogs? It will be interesting to see the outcome of this one.

A lot of well-known personalities and those described as stars have died this year. Wendy Richard, Molly Sugden, Danny La Rue, Karl Malden, Michael Jackson – who took up several front pages for several days. The death of Bobby Robson, the ex-Ipswich, Newcastle and England manager was particularly sad.

He had suffered from cancer over a long period of time and was always considered a gent and certainly came over that way whenever interviewed, despite all his suffering. This view was confirmed when reading the many tributes from colleagues in the football industry.

The most poignant losses, however, were the last British servicemen who saw life in the trenches during World War 1. Both Henry Allingham and Harry Patch died within a very short space of time. Harry was the last to have been through the horrors of the battle at Passchendaele. It was interesting that he always commented that, "it wasn't worth it, no war is worth the loss of a couple of lives, let alone thousands." It really is the end of an era. A more pointless, senseless waste of millions of lives I have yet to understand, but a hundred years ago we believed in king and country. We have, however, learned nothing when you look at Afghanistan. Over two hundred soldiers killed, and for what? Keeping alive a feudal system where a man can starve his wife or refuse her water if she refuses sex. We have our very own Vietnam. If you kill all the present Taliban I do believe that more will follow in the form of the offspring who hate the west and everything it stands for. To be fair, it's difficult not to be sympathetic with anyone who finds foreign powers fighting on your territory ever so slightly annoying. But then you know that at the end of the day it's all about US power and our "special relationship". I am aware that the Canadians have lost many soldiers but other than them, where's the rest of NATO when the threats are global?

Just a quickie. Bet you can imagine just how gutted I was to learn that Gordon Ramsay's restaurant group's profits fell by 90%. I cannot imagine who would bother to eat in an establishment owned by someone who has made his name and a lot of money out of effing and blinding. The BBC seems to thinks it's fun and presumably, so do the Sun readers who tune into his programmes. Me? I think it's gratuitous and pandering to the lowest common denominator – otherwise known as the Sun reader! Perhaps if it all goes pear-shaped, he could get a job aboard a Scottish trawler preparing meals for the crew. I'm sure his language would be acceptable and in common with his common man.

Time for a bit of nonsense!

There was a young ferret called Eric
Who rejoiced in the surname of Meyrick
He thought it sublime that both his names rhymed
But then so did his brother called Derek

We really are a money-grabbing nation, aren't we? Councils will use every means possible to extract the last penny. I wasn't aware that when you book a cremation or funeral you book a time slot. In the case of Milton Keynes council they are 30-minute slots. A lady spent a few minutes over the allotted time, saying goodbye to her five-week-old son and was charged £86 for her trouble. Yes, the council refunded the money, but it does seem somewhat callous to automatically impose the fine. The couple were told by the funeral directors that there was plenty of time before the next funeral would take place – 50 minutes, in fact – so the mother spent an ten extra minutes beside the coffin before it was cremated. Is this "excess time" taped on CCTV or is there a man lurking behind a screen with a stop-watch? Probably not, but you can't help but hear the sound of coins jingling in the council coffers, as opposed to coffins, when they read through the next day's lists. Woe betide any employee who leaves a blank appointment. I suspect they have targets. My mind now wanders to staff being sent to care homes in order to find suitable applicants for the spare slots. These people could then die conveniently in order to be buried or cremated in accordance with the council's timescale. Mmmm, target achieved and all the boxes ticked, filled – buried or burnt!

I took a tour of the brewery the other day. The group were all either funeral directors or crematorium staff. Great sense of humour, they had. One of them mentioned that he worked at Aldershot Crematorium. "You must know my father", I enthused.

"Really? Does he work there?" came the reply. "Oh, no", I said, "but you've probably walked over him a few times, and to be fair he wasn't the type of man to be easily walked over"! We did laugh.

People get very precious, don't they? I remember a couple of years ago, Kirstie Allsopp – she of a loping nature – though very attractive in a big-boned way, and Phil, did a special Location, Location, where they looked at the best and worst towns and cities in Britain. The programme has just been in the news once more due to Middlesbrough Council not being overly delighted by the fact that their town was deemed to be the worst place to live in Britain. The town's mayor complained to Ofcom, but two years after transmission, Ofcom have noted that the programme was fair and used reliable statistics to back up its conclusions. The mayor, by the way, is Ray Mallon, who was the outspoken police chief who spearheaded the zero tolerance to crime initiatives. So that's what's happened to him! No one likes to see his or her town come bottom of the league, but it's also no good whinging (why do the words "whinge" and "northern" come together so often?) The evidence confirming the town's lowly status included the facts that it has "critical health levels", "double the English average of drug abuse", "eight percent more smokers and over a quarter of inhabitants admitted to binge drinking". Ninety percent of residents never exercise and few eat healthily. Robbery, burglary, sexual assaults, violent crimes and car theft are all more than twice the national average. I wonder if it ever thought of twinning itself with Aldershot – just so much in common!

As you can imagine, I've never been a fan of the Duchess of York, but even I have to side with her on what is one of the greatest of uphill struggles she will ever encounter. ITV have made a documentary called "The Duchess on the Estate". And, no, I didn't see it. If I want to watch common people I'll sit on a seat outside Asda in Farnborough. Anyway, Fergie apparently spent ten days in a B & B on the edge of

Northern Moor. It's a housing estate in Wythenshawe, Manchester. Wythenshawe has never had a good name and I take it the residents of Northern Moor are not helping their lack of case. The idea of the programme was to bring mums together in an effort to engender what Fergie referred to as the "Blitz spirit", as opposed to "Blithe Spirit" which none of the incumbents will have heard of! But nevertheless.....

Fergie noted that young people go out with mobile phones and knives, and there was a lot more violence. She also noted a lot of bad language. Part of the remit was to open a community centre (that word again!) A man who disapproved of the centre got a gun and shot out the windows. Well, it's nice to know freedom of speech is alive and well and firing from all barrels. The quote that made her earn my respect was when she said, "The hoodies I spoke to thought I was a toffee-nosed git and were effing and blinding". Sad to see that so many youngsters are influenced by Gordon Ramsay.

Yesterday was not a good day. Maureen was told that her services were no longer required at the place where she has worked for twenty-one years. As you know, she passed 65 last December but was allowed to work on at the reduced rate of three days a week for a further year. At the meeting yesterday she was informed that her birthday this year would also be her last day and she would not be offered another year's contract. It was obviously "nothing to do with her or her performance and she shouldn't take it personally", but..... you know, best practice, best value and the move towards statistics means there is no longer a job for her.

The other news, which nailed the day's coffin, was the realisation that Ronnie Biggs was to be released by that gutless Injustice Minister, Jack Straw. Back in June reports started flying around that due to the fact that he couldn't walk or feed himself, he should be freed on compassionate grounds. The only two people, as far as I could see, who supported this move were his son and his lawyer. Who pays the lawyer, by the way?

The equally gutless parole board had erred on the side of Biggs and were recommending his release. I can understand his son wishing to see his father free, but his emotions must be countered by the fact that his father escaped his punishment, absconded to Brazil where he gloated over the fact that he was untouchable and as far as I am aware, has never really demonstrated any remorse for the needless attack and subsequent death of Mr. Mills, the train driver who never went back to work and died some four years later. Biggs only returned to this country in 2001 when his money ran out and British funding by dint of the NHS seemed an inexpensive alternative. Extremely inexpensive when you think that he had never paid into our system. In fact, I think it was all take. It's no good his son, Michael, arguing that he has served his time. Actually, he hasn't. As we know, at the time he should have been in prison he was poking fun at the British establishment and making himself a personality. For a paper that crusades for justice and sometimes does it very well, the "Personal View" column by David Robson in the "Daily Express" dated Saturday, 27th June, really does make you want to vomit with disgust and have a word in Mr. Robson's shell-like. He starts by telling you how poorly Biggs is, accepts that there is no reason to think that he is a "nice man" and then adds "He has at least supplied the nation with a reasonable amount of amusement over the decades". The rest of his comments are equally flippant. I think he should be made by the editor to visit Mr. Mills' family. A little bit of humility is what Robson requires and a clip round the ear by his mother for being a complete arse.

On 2nd July there appeared an article whose headline read, "Unrepentant Biggs To Die As A Prisoner". This encouraging line came on the back of Jack Straw's refusal to allow his parole. The following day it was announced, "Biggs Is Close To Death". His son explained that the robber was not responding to hospital treatment. He has pneumonia, fractures of the hip, pelvis and spine, not to mention MRSA. He is apparently in a lot of discomfort – aahh. And just to labour the point, his son added, "He cannot read, write, eat or drink and is very disappointed with Jack Straw's decision". Well, he obviously rallied as he was still alive on 29th July. His son announced that he "only has days to live". Well, it suits me. Apparently, according to Michael, "It is the worst he has ever been. The doctors say there is not much hope. They are talking about not resuscitating my father if his heart stops. I've never seen him this weak". A fresh application for parole had just been lodged.

By 7th August the chink in the parole board's armour and Jack Straw's resolve had finally been punctured. An article appeared, which was headed "Great Train Robber Biggs Will Be Set Free Today At Death's Door". And there was me thinking it was a hospital door! All rather dramatic and accompanied by two photographs, one of him sloshing back champagne in Brazil in order to celebrate the 25th anniversary of the robbery – that shows compassion and regret for Mr. Mills – and another of him taken a few weeks earlier in his hospital bed. Ill, but not too ill to lift himself and his spirits in Norwich University Hospital, Biggs managed to sign a copy of the release papers. Under the terms of his parole, he has to agree to be "well behaved and not commit any offence". I'm sure he won't, but that's not the point. He stuck two fingers up at the country that is now paying for his keep. I understand he is to be moved to a nursing home in Barnet, close to where his son lives. It seems we can't do enough for this criminal. Who is paying for his nursing care? – it couldn't be us again, could it? I'd have let him rot in jail – he should be shown the same compassion that was shown to Driver Mills.

Right! Got that out the system! As you know, for you this is a read, for me it is therapy!

Now the next little joke has a bit of a moral to it. So think carefully if you find yourself in the same situation as Bill.

Bill was a single chap living at home with his father and working in the family business. During a tête-à-tête with his dad he discovered he was going to inherit a fortune when his sickly father died, so he decided he would need a wife with whom to share his fortune. One evening at an investment meeting he spotted the most beautiful woman he had ever seen. Her beauty, demeanour and style took his breath away. "I may look just like any other ordinary man", he said to her, "but in a few years when my father dies, I will inherit £65 million". Impressed, the woman obtained his business card and three days later she became his stepmother!

Women are so much better at financial planning than men!

I don't know whether you know this, but more money is spent on breast implants and Viagra today than on Alzeimer's research. This means that by 2040 there will be a large, elderly population with perky breasts and huge erections. But sadly, with no recollection with what to do with either of them!

If the NHS wishes to save money, it could stop the completely wasteful practice of allowing sex-change operations at the taxpayer's expense. Over the last ten years in excess of 1000 people have changed from Arthur to Martha and from Lesley to Wesley. The ops have trebled since it became a "right". This "right" came about in July 1999, when an appeal court ruled that those who believed they were "in the wrong body" were suffering from a legitimate illness, so the ops became free. Again, I have no problem, and not a little sympathy, but I do think it's way down the list of priorities when it comes to spending our hard-earned money. Trans-sexuals can also have psychotherapy and hormone replacement therapy on the NHS. What a pity there's not a test that can be done at birth, when it could be ascertained whether the sprog would later wish to change bodies. Any surgery could be carried out then. What? I'm not callous, I'm just thinking of the taxpayer.

The word "callous" brings us to a two-page article written in the "Sunday Express" surrounding the publication of a new book entitled "Japan's Gestapo: Murder, Mayhem and Torture In War Time Asia". It wasn't details of the book that struck me, nor the article itself, but the horrific photograph taken in 1943 of an Australian sergeant called Leonard Siffleet, who is kneeling, blindfolded with rope around his arms and midriff as a Japanese soldier is poised with sword about to behead him. The sheer awfulness of it and the helplessness felt by those prisoners surrounding this atrocity behind the attendant armed guards is there for all to see. The Gestapo were nasty bastards, but somehow the Japanese took arrogance and torture to a whole new level. They seem to enjoy the humbling, the humility, and the dehumanisation of all who stood in their way. And I think that's it, really. Germany has progressed to being a part of Europe. Their ministers have acknowledged their past, the Japanese still refuse wholeheartedly to apologise to China for their atrocities and I suspect that any acknowledgement is done out of business necessity, rather than genuine remorse. Any comments seem to be grudging. They are a disingenuous lot. I've said it time and time again, Japanese leopards never change their spots, you only have to look at the game shows.

From Biggs to the Lockerbie bomber. It now appears that he will be released on the grounds of compassionate leave due to the fact that he is suffering from terminal cancer. The world has gone mad, hasn't it? I'm of the school of thought that he should rot in the Scottish jail in which he is serving his sentence. The Americans are furious but there seems to be little comment concerning the views of the Scottish people. For once, I am on the side of the Americans – there is a first for everything. The decision, however, by the Scottish minister should not be influenced by the Americans, though one can understand their feelings. I assume that pressure is being brought to bear on the Scots on behalf of some higher cause – Britain's relationship with Libya? Colonel Gaddafi now seems to be "in" with regards to world politics and is no longer persona non grata. Whilst I agree with the Americans on this point, I loathe the British government's lack of guts with regard to the proposed extradition of Gary McKinnon, the computer hacker. So he managed to break into the security of the USA's defence computers. Frankly, I couldn't help but smile. All they want to do is incarcerate him in one of their jails for the rest of his life.

Alan Johnson, the new Home Secretary, has washed his hands, saying he can't get involved.

Right! On to the domestics for a while. A lot of people have asked me what has happened to our offspring since the last book. Well, Glyn, now 37, has finally found the girl of his dreams and they married last November. I didn't just go to the wedding because I wanted to be part of the celebrations, I also wanted to make sure he turned up, but he seems a happy little bunny and is now living in near domestic bliss, just outside Farnham. Debbie, 35, has just finished working at her weekend job in a fashion store, and is set to become a 7-day a week mum, ably assisted by her husband, who is still a graphic designer – designing graphics, I suspect! They now have three children, aged 9, 8 and 2. William is now 26, and after all the angst, the heartache and the quarrels over eighteen years, he's turned out to be a contributing member of society. Having left school and having many jobs in a few years, he and I now run a little gardening business. Funny, but when he was, well, any age up to "grown up", we never thought he'd make it as a human being. He's now the father of an eight-year-old daughter and the most Victorian in outlook you will ever find! But then, what goes round comes round. Mind you, you still have to make contingency plans. We have erected two foot of trellis on top of the six-foot fencing surrounding our home. It's not to keep Ben from straying, but to keep the children from coming back!

I had to visit Frimley Park Hospital after being referred there by my GP. The diabetes is causing all sorts of problems, including shooting pains in the feet and fingers. It's like being stabbed with an electric prod, or prodded with an electric knife – but I'm sure you know what I mean. Anyway, the neurology lady is sending me to St. Peter's Hospital, Chertsey, so I await an appointment. I was asked if I wanted to see the notes on my case. I suspect this comes under the heading of "Patients' Rights". I wasn't overly fussed either way, but I had to make a decision, so I said okay. Anyhow, today I received a copy of the letter sent to my GP with a copy to St. Peter's. I expected to read something along the lines of, "With reference to your patient, Mr. ....." However, the letter started, "Thank you for sending this nice chap....." Obviously a sentiment I agree with, but I wonder how many other doctors start their letters thus. Awfully Surrey, don't you think?

We have a relatively new vicar at St. Mary's Church, Ash Vale. The church is situated at the top of Wood Street. I remember his inauguration in the parish one evening, due to the fact that you couldn't drive down Wood Street to get to your own house. I think some higher being in the ecclesiastical pecking order was present, which I assumed upped the attendance. All the god-botherers and sycophants were out in force, parking wherever the whim took them, which was mainly across everybody else's drive. If there had been a fire the occupants of the properties would have perished because emergency vehicles would not have gained access due to the parking of those involved. It's not the widest of roads – selfish bastards! The new vicar has replaced the previous female vicar, or vicaress. I went to see her once, did the right thing, rang and made an appointment. When we sat down and she asked how she could help, I informed her that I did not want to be one of her flock, having been christened without my knowledge and consent which, to be fair, would have been hard to establish because I was only a few months old. The point is that I have been in their statistics, on their books and you know me, I do not want to be associated with petty cults. She seemed perplexed. There were no forms readily available. Apparently people just don't go in to the vicarage and resign! Strange that. She said she would ask the Bishop for guidance and would call me back. Guess what? That's right, she never did.

In the old days vicars took to the streets in order to meet their parishioners. My mum and dad would have loved a visit from a vicar, my mum still would. Sad to report that all the while there is work to do in Uganda and the sub-continent, our new incumbent appears to have little time other than to tell his parishioners via the parish magazine of his sterling work in some corrupt, forsaken African state that pleads poverty but feeds its masters well. I passed the vicarage this morning with Mutley. It's a pity that more time is not spent on sorting out the vicarage curtains – very untidy! And you know me, not one to criticise for the sake of it, or be petty, but.....

This health and safety malarkey is a recipe for copping out. We have the case of a chap called Carl Malton, aged 32, who was hit by a car whilst walking on an unlit country road late at night. He apparently fell backwards into a dyke. The dyke is fifteen feet below the road. Although a pathologist confirmed that Mr. Malton was dead when the medical team arrived some time after 11 pm, the medics did not know that. Did they help? Did they buggery! A paramedic called Fergus White decided it was too dangerous to go down. He described the bank as "steep and unstable". It's only fifteen feet! Senior Fire Officer Edward Halliday also stopped his firemen from using ropes and ladders. He carried out a "risk assessment" but came to his conclusion on the grounds of that old chestnut, health and safety. Ten policemen also followed suit. It seems like an Ealing comedy at this point. All these men looking into a dyke. When Mr. Malton's relatives arrived they discovered all of the above service personnel drinking tea, which whilst being a very English thing to do, also smacks of being the easy way out. Interesting to note that at the inquest the police accident investigator stated that he would have gone down the bank and "would have expected other officers to have done the same". What a pity he wasn't there that night and in charge. Still, I expect the tea was hot and sweet.

I don't know about you, but I scrutinise every form I am asked to fill in these days. Mostly, it's to find the box you tick to stop yet more junk mail from being delivered. When receiving my appointment for Frimley Park Hospital's Outpatient Department recently I was asked to take with me a form they included, which at the top gave the details they had on me, the lower half being devoted to ethnicity. I, as always, crossed through everything very dismissively, circled "English" and where it said "white", wrote "very". Who wants to know? I did enquire and was given the name of a lady who would know by Frimley Park's switchboard. They also gave me her number. I phoned twice. However, the phone rang and rang until I lost the desire to know.

Which government department is it that takes these statistics, and why? Do hospitals have an ethnic or gender target? Is their funding based on the number of disabled, black, single parent, lesbians? These, of course, being single parent by sperm donation – and probably were homosexual until their operation and they're still not sure of their true sexuality and denial remains an issue. Anyway, I am sure it pleases the Race Relations and equality arses, which should be made to sit through films of the fifties and sixties and take note of how Britain looked when it was a nice place.

Meanwhile, back at the NHS, it's a salutary thought that 45,000 staff are on sick leave every day. What does that say about the job? I suspect it says a lot about the paperwork, targets, and pressures brought about by health and safety and the statistics industry. No doubt there's irritation regarding those in their ivory towers who have never come through the ranks but arrived via the banking sector and command a salary (with commensurate pension) while those who graft on the shop floor face a daily drudge with little incentive. The NHS lost nearly £27 million last year. Contract disputes, theft, legal expenses, that old standby compensation and the thorn in the taxpayers' side, foreign patients who refuse to pay. Why the bloody hell did we treat them? What a soft touch we are.

Not far away from Frimley Park Hospital there is a charity called Camberley Care Trust. The charity is council funded, funded not surprisingly from departments populated by what is euphemistically known as bureaucrats – or arse holes to you and me. There are new rules. Any artisan working in the home of an elderly customer now has to ask if he/she/they have Aids or HIV. This is someone who is going to replace a light bulb, unblock a sink, put up a shelf..... A Surrey County Council spokesman (surprised they are still un-PC enough to use that phrase) said, "It is a contractual requirement". They also have forms asking the customer to declare their ethnicity, although the spokesman added, "There is an option to decline information". But at what price? Perhaps there is such pressure to conform that not towing the line renders you liable to blackballing, or whiteballing as it probably soon will be. See! Another form for another department and everybody is nameless. Where does it go, and for what purpose?

A couple of little medical funnies to tickle your fancy, for which there is a cure, but only available privately:

Right!

One of the top cardiac specialists dies. At his funeral the coffin is placed in front of a large replica of a heart made from red roses. When the vicar finishes his sermon and everyone has bid his or her goodbyes, the large heart opens up, the coffin is rolled inside and the heart closes once more. Everybody thinks that it is a majestic tribute to his or her much-loved cardiologist and friend. Suddenly one of the mourners bursts into a fit of laughter. The man next to him asks, "What's so funny?" "Oh", the man replies, "I was just thinking of my own funeral. I'm a gynaecologist"!

Next!

A male patient is lying in the hospital wearing an oxygen mask over his mouth and nose, still heavily sedated from a very difficult, four-hour operation. A young student nurse arrives to give him a partial sponge bath following the surgical procedure. His eyes flicker and from behind the mask he mumbles, "Nurse, are my testicles black?" The young nurse is embarrassed and replies, "I don't know, sir, I'm only here to wash your upper body and feet." Painfully he repeats the question, "Nurse, are my testicles black?" Concerned that he may elevate his vitals from worry about his testicles she overcomes her embarrassment and sheepishly folds back the covers. She raises his gown, takes his penis in one hand and his testicles in the other, lifts them, then moves and inspects them. Then, taking a close look and holding his genitalia very carefully, says, "There's nothing wrong with them, sir". The man slowly pulls his oxygen mask down, smiles at her and very slowly says, "Thank you very much, nurse. That was truly wonderful, but listen very, very closely....." "Are – my – test – results – back?"

And yes, I am aware that the "Norfolk" gag told on page 99 was previously related on page 50, but sadly it was easier to print this acknowledgement than "bugger up" the typesetting! Though looking on the bright side, it should be helpful to those readers suffering from short-term memory loss or alzheimer's!

CHAPTER SIX

The Three R's – Race, Religion and Rights

I saw a picture in the papers today of one of those Smart cars with the letters CCTV emblazoned on the sides. Clamped above the rear wheel was what looked like a drainpipe with periscope attached. This little money earner will be coming to a council near you, if not your own, soon. The cars replace traffic wardens and they photograph vehicles parked illegally. Those caught on camera only know they are to be fined when a notice appears through their letterbox. I understand some thirty councils are now using this form of legalised racketeering. They really know how to alienate the ratepayer, don't they?

What's that? Mention the bins? I was going to, but sticking with cameras for a mo, it didn't go unnoticed that approval for telephone and e-mail information was requested by councils, the police and intelligent services over half a million times last year. That's 40% up on two years ago. These organisations' ability to legally extract this information comes from the Regulation of Investigatory Powers Act, which no-one would question if referring to terrorism, but councils are using these powers to prosecute dog owners who allow their dogs to foul public areas. Not for one moment do I support dog owners who do, but surely things should be kept in context, and I can't help thinking that there are one or two areas in society which would rank higher up the surveillance pecking order, such as anti-social behaviour, assault, and those good old standbys, rape and murder. But no, we have to use these powers to prosecute taxpayers who put their bins out early. Over 630 state bodies are allowed to use these powers and that includes 470 councils. A Home Office spokesman said it was, "Vital we strike the right balance between individual privacy and collective security and that is why the Home Office is clear these powers should only be used when they are proportionate". Maybe, but the trust has gone.

Right! To the bins. The obsession with surveillance of bins has little to do with morality, a cleaner, greener planet or health, but everything to do with European targets and the government's desire to haul in more money. It wasn't long ago that "waste inspectors" in the Lancashire towns of Blackburn and Darwen were spotted standing on ladders looking over garden walls to check that homes only possessed the one wheelie bin they were allowed. Southampton City Council are now issuing their dustmen (I prefer that nomenclature) with satellite tracking devices that will tell those who need to know just who has put their rubbish out on the wrong day, who has failed to recycle and who has put out too much rubbish – bastards!

North Wiltshire Council has spent £70,000 on "dawn raids" to enable them to analyse the contents of wheelie bins. Despite the comments of Andy Conn (appropriate surname) from North Wilts Council that, "We don't know which homes the rubbish comes from", I certainly wouldn't trust their motives and how on earth do they justify £70,000? Not only has the service been diluted to fortnightly collections in many cases, but also if, heaven forbid, you leave out sacks alongside your bins an £80 fine is in the offing. This is the brainchild of Oxford City Council, who says it is to discourage people producing too much waste. What a pity we are not discouraging people from producing too many children! That's the nub of the problem.

Oxford City Council are likewise to employ "Waste Education Officers" or the bin Gestapo, and at what cost? One chap up north was fined £110 for overfilling his bin – by four inches. As he said, "The fine for fly tipping is only £80, I might as well have done that". I've never been a fan of fly tipping, though Thai flipping is an entirely different matter and something I would watch should it become an Olympic sport! But back to the story. Flintshire Council in Wales refused to take a brown garden waste bin from one of its ratepayers who had the temerity to include windfall apples within the waste. The collectors placed a yellow sticker on the bin, indicating possible contamination. They might as well have walked about ringing a bell and chanting, "Unclean,

unclean". Andy Macbeth, the council's Environmental Service's Manager (there's really posh) said, "Spoiled fruit or vegetable peelings may have been inside a kitchen and come into contact with cooked meats. It is difficult, if not impossible, for our operatives (dustmen) to determine whether spoiled fruit or vegetable peelings found in a brown bin have been in contact with other kitchen waste....." He goes on and on, actually, stating various health and animal regulations, but as the bin owner qualified, "We have an apple tree, we have windfalls, they fall off the tree....." True, but not to the taste of Flint Council – arses.

A joke I heard, which I thought you might enjoy:

Paddy has been drinking in his local Dublin pub all day and most of the night, celebrating St. Patrick's Day. Mick, the bartender, says, "You'll not be drinking any more tonight, Paddy". Paddy looks through glazed eyes, and replies, "Ok, Mick, I'll be on my way then". He spins around on his stool and steps off, falling flat on his face. "Shite", he says, as he pulls himself up by the stool and dusts himself off. He takes a step towards the door and once more falls flat on his face. "Shite, shite", he exclaims as he bangs his fists on the floor. He looks towards the doorway and thinks to himself that if he could only just get to the door and some fresh air, he'll be fine. He belly-crawls to the door and shimmies up the doorframe. He sticks his head outside and takes a deep breath of fresh air, feels much better and so takes a step into the side road before falling flat on his face. "Shite", he says. He can see his house just a few doors down and crawls to the front door. Hauling himself up by the letterbox he opens the door and makes it inside. He looks up at the stairs. "No-way", he thinks, "no way". He crawls up the stairs thinking, "I can make it to bed". Opening the bedroom door he takes a step and falls flat on his face. "Shite", he says as he crawls into bed. The next morning his wife, Bridget, comes into the room carrying a cup of coffee and says, "Time to get up, Paddy, did you not have a bit to drink last night". Paddy looks at her, smiles inanely and says, "I did, Bridget, I did. I was pissed all right, but how d'you know that?"

Bridget replies, "Mick phoned from the pub, he said you'd left your wheelchair".

Well, Charlton have won their first four matches of the season. It's early days, but I have every confidence that we'll be there, or thereabouts, come the end of term. A year or so ago I needed the advice of a solicitor and then for him to act on my behalf. The visit didn't start well. I was on time, sitting in the waiting area. He wasn't. I waited nearly 15 minutes before he appeared. He apologised and beckoned me through to his office. I did wonder what it would have cost me if I had been 15 minutes late. Tall, good-looking, a young buck who could have been an estate agent – and he was northern. He offered me a seat in his Yorkshire tones and asked what I wanted. I told him and as he explained how he could help I espied on a rail behind him an Arsenal scarf. "You're not from round these parts?" I enquired in a silly, swashbuckling accent reminiscent of the Buccaneers television programme from my childhood – though definitely not his. He smiled, "I come from Sheffield. All my family are Blades supporters". (Sheffield United for non-footballing fans). "But I've always supported the Gunners". He continued, now enthusiastically, "We're playing a cup match in Italy next week and I'm off with a few mates for three days. You know, a few beers, support your club". I was warming to him. "How about you?" he said. "Sadly, I'm a Charlton Athletic supporter". "Ah", he said – well it was more of a commiseration really. We got on with the business, before he enquired, "I suppose you would like to know how much this work will cost?" Now I did have an idea as someone I knew who had had this work done was charged £1,200 plus VAT. I waited with breath of a bated nature. "Our charge", he indicated, leaning forward and fiddling with a pen poised over a sheet of paper is £1,100 plus VAT." "Oh, right", I replied. He didn't look up, but started doodling. At least I thought he was doodling. "So if I say £700 inclusive of VAT, how does that sound?" I was slightly taken aback. "Actually, it sounds very good, but I have to ask why you have told me your company's fee and then reduced it by over £400". He looked me straight in the eye, smiled disarmingly and said – and believe me this is true – "You can't help feeling sorry for a Charlton supporter". I left elated. Never has supporting Charlton ever saved me money! Nice chap, huh.

My attention has been drawn to a news item where the police have just been called to a nursery because a 3-year-old is resisting a rest! Ho! Ho!

Well, we're two weeks on from when Biggs junior procrastinated over Biggs senior's imminent demise. He's still here.

I received one of those phone calls that generally gets short shrift but I was in a receptive mood for some reason. "Good afternoon", said a slimy voice. After establishing that it was me who he was talking to, he continued, "And how are you this afternoon, sir?" Now normally I say to the caller, "I was all right until you wasted 20 seconds of my time – now bugger off!" I then replace the receiver, muttering, "Pointless bastard", or something similar. Today, however, I replied, "I can't imagine for one moment why you're interested, so I assume you are reading from a script". The slime continued. "Very good, sir, very good". He then exalted the benefits of his bank's new credit card. In fact, his very words were, "Let me tell you of its benefits". "Please do", I said, with a total lack of enthusiasm. He told me how these so-called benefits of up to 57 days' credit, 0% interest on transfer balances and various insurance deals would change my thinking on credit cards. "I think you'll agree, sir, it's just what you've been looking for". "Not that hard, I haven't", I replied, but I'm not sure he listened. "And the exciting thing, sir, is that the card costs only £50 for a year. However, sir, for the first year the card is free. How does that sound?" "Well", I managed to say without the excitement causing me to wet my pants, "it sounds about £50 too dear". "But it's free for the first year, sir". "So it bloody well should be", I said. "I currently have a BT card which gives me £75 off my telephone bill each year. You can't match that, can you? Actually, if I went with you I'd be

£125 out of pocket". He wasn't to be deterred. "Ah, yes, sir, but I haven't yet mentioned the card's value when you're abroad". Aha – my trump card was about to be played. "I don't go abroad, I don't possess a passport any more". That stumped the slime ball. "May I ask why, sir?" We were probably nearing the end of his script. I was now on a roll. "Because the thought of waiting in an airport terminal building for three miserable hours at best, having paid a fortune to park, being subjected to what purports to be coffee at an inflated price even Starbuck's would be embarrassed to charge, served by some servile youth of indeterminable background, who is unable to speak comprehensible English and then queuing to dispose of one's luggage before being strip-searched and eye tested to make sure your biometrics are to an EU standard is beyond my powers of toleration. "Well, fair enough", he countered and wished me a good day. I replaced the receiver – arsehole!

I ordered two pairs of trousers through a railway magazine. I know, I was surprised as well, as I rarely read any adverts, let alone buy from them. But two pairs for £15 looked too good to miss! They came within three days and fitted. The problem now lies with the post that comes from that one order. Today I got a bin-full. Firstly, there's the exclusive footwear collection brochure, followed by the lifestyle living direct brochure, then came the home textiles sale brochure, the men and women's clothing catalogue (with amazing autumn savings) and the piece de resistance – a 5 star customer leaflet. Apparently, I am now considered a 5 star customer (for which they offer me their congratulations and a leaflet!). They then say that I deserve more – and here it is. "It's official. You are a 5 star customer. In recognition of your loyalty and consistent ordering record (remember – one order for two pairs of trousers at a total of £15) it gives me great pleasure to welcome you to this exclusive status as one of our very best customers. As our way of saying thank you we promise to keep improving choice, value, quality and service for you. You can also expect some great extra awards, for example, order within seven days and you can claim a 5 star gift".

So to be one of their very best customers, having spent £15, I am now entitled to buy a luxurious six-piece towel set for £9.99, thus saving £20. Oh, and they are available in green or pink, which is nice. We then come to the free gift. This happens to be a pen, hideous in the extreme. It is a pen with a plastic wart at the end, containing balls with lottery numbers. It's called their "lottery pen" and is described as "fabulous". I don't do the bloody lottery, so they can stuff their pen where the "sun don't shine", bulbous end in first, naturally! Ideal for those ordering the pink towels. Which reminds me, I see that corduroy pillows are making headlines!

Amongst the other dross, which descended to the ground via the letterbox was Guildford Borough Council's newspaper. All the usual self-indulgent backslapping stuff. A list of councillors' expenses, which came to a not inconsiderable £285,000 for the year, and an article with photo of Street Angels. These do-gooders allegedly help Guildford to become a safer place on Friday and Saturday nights. Since their inauguration in October 2008, they've "helped on over 2,500 occasions with revellers and people who find themselves vulnerable in the town centre, many of whom might otherwise need help from the police". Well, that's what it says! So firstly, they are allowing the police to get on with more important tasks – if only they did. Secondly, I have to ask, why should anyone need help and why are they so vulnerable? They are only in the state they are because they are drunk and often obnoxious, so once again, nobody has any personal responsibility, it's all down to others to calm you down, deal with your angst and get you home. Pointless, absolutely pointless! Where they could help is taking the numbers of vehicles parked on grass verges, and lobbying the council to remove them, especially in Ash Vale. Shawfield Road has always been subjected to arses that would rather destroy the verge than park on their own drive, in front of their house or nearby if the first two were not possible. But nobody wants to walk these days. The Vale Road has been home to one selfish sod for a number of years. I rang the Parish Council offices and was told it was Guildford Borough Council's responsibility. They, in turn, said it was Surrey

County Council's responsibility. The lady there made me laugh because she said that grass is a very grey area! It was tempting to respond, but I resisted.

I buttonholed a local councillor one fine day, as he stood atop a ladder along the Vale Road erecting a sign which tells you how naughty you are if you go over 30 mph. I hope he'd been trained on how to climb and stand upon the ladder. He agreed that it made the grass look awful, as it wore it away to mud and dust, but said he was unable to do anything about it as it was..... yes, one of those grey areas. I think the idea of him or someone suggesting that it should be made illegal to park on a verge was a suggestion too far, as we now have up to four cars parking overnight, instead of on the car owner's land. It actually despoils the whole idea of having a grass verge, but then we are talking about selfish bastards.

Went out with Ben this morning, and I noticed, well we both did – the dog's not stupid – that five cygnets are still with their mum. Also noticed that the fly tipping season, or fishing season, is still with us, as leftover cans, bottles, crisps and Twix wrappers were to be seen a-plenty along the banks by the Flash.

Many years ago I remember writing about my concerns with regard to genetically modified food. I didn't want it then, and I don't want it now. My distaste for the food was matched by my distaste for the big multi-nationals that would benefit from the industry's growth. It doesn't take much vision to see a future world where the global agricultural economy is in the hands of a few seed producers, these producers being a world away in size and ethics from seed merchants of yore. Not content in selling their seeds, these faceless wonder companies would be stitching up every farmer with contracts akin to tied public houses. We currently have a situation in the brewing industry where managers and landlords can only buy from the pub-owning company and usually at a much higher rate than they can obtain their beer from the brewer independently. GM crops are already becoming a problem, even though they are not allowed in this country. The ramifications from those naïve enough to be fooled by the industry are having an impact in the UK. The growth in GM soya production in Brazil and Argentina is such that our meat, milk and egg prices could soar by some 20% within a very short space of time. Sadly, this country is dependent on soya used in UK animal feed coming from abroad – in our case, Brazil and Argentina, who supply us with 90% of our intake. We cannot use GM soya but by squeezing the production of natural soya, the price inevitably rises. Isn't this playing straight into the hands of the GM industry? Mark my words, this will be a major problem. Small farmers will be pushed to the wall and unable to compete. Organic farmers will have such an uphill struggle to survive, and once again consumer choice will be reduced even further.

What makes my desire to see the "miraculous recovery" of Biggs take a turn for the worse as soon as possible is the news that he can now claim £95.25 pension per week, backdated to the day of his release. I wonder if that's taken from him and goes towards his care? I do hope so. After all, we seem to be paying for everything else. You certainly wouldn't be looked after like this if you had worked all your life and paid into the system, but Biggs is a man apart. Apparently the criminal told friends (where the hell does he get friends from?) that he is determined to live until at least Christmas to spite all those people who wish him dead. Well, you know where I stand.

Sickening photographs greeted readers of the "Express" last week. The main photograph showed a trainer with three "performing elephants" at a circus. The other two photos showed a trainer beating one of the elephants with a metal stick. I wasn't aware until recently that circuses were still allowed to use wild animals in their so-called shows. The Great British Circus also owns lions, tigers, reindeer and camels. Who pays to see these animals? One of the elephants was living in the wild until its mother was shot as part of a cull. Words fail me. Luckily, an animal welfare group called "Animal Defenders International" or

ADI captured the abuse on video, which in its entirety showed the elephants being hit on the head with a large metal hook, a broom and a pitchfork. You can also hear them crying out, apparently. All this in the name of profit. ADI claimed the circus staff used a "staggeringly high level of casual violence". Sounds on a par with the average care home for the elderly or vulnerable. I'm not actually interested in statements that animals are cared for by these circuses. They shouldn't be there. It's no less demeaning than if the participant was a human freak or Welsh. What? You think that constitutes a cheap jibe against human freaks? Oh, very well. But seriously, it's about time that the government got its departmental finger out of its orifice. At the moment, the Environment Department state that, "Work is under way and reports are due to be completed later this year". How long has this lot been in power?

Now, I've been watching the athletics over the past week on an on-off basis. What I've seen, I have enjoyed. Of particular interest to me are the 800, 1500 and 5,000 yards-and-a-bit races. It's the tactics I find interesting – whether to lead from the start, hold back or rely on a sprint finish. Oh for the days when we had David Bedford, Brendan Foster, Steve Cram, Steve Ovett and even Coe, before his ego became larger than the stadium. But no matter, watching one of the women's races, both Maureen and I took a second glance as the winner, one Caster Semenya, coasted in yards ahead of the other runners. We both thought it was a male in female clothing – and actually the clothing was not that female. The governing body, the IAAF, has said she now has to face a gender test. I heard her speak - certainly sounds like a chap. Her mother says she has a daughter, not a son. She probably is a daughter, but one's natural thoughts turn to drugs, and it wouldn't be the first time. She is now a hero in South Africa, who is not surprisingly outraged at her treatment and is to lodge a complaint about her public treatment under the Human Rights Act. All very predictable and, of course, there's talk of racism. So, again, no surprise. I did watch an amusing part on the "One Show", where viewers were invited to e-mail with suggestions of how you could test whether she was male or female, and one suggestion was to get her to pass a women's shoe shop. If she managed to pass, she was obviously male!

The BBC is still coming in for criticism re its stance on not employing older newsreaders and panel judges. Sadly, public opinion won't change anything. I've come to the conclusion that the BBC is staffed at the top by an arrogant bunch of bastards who always know best, whatever their tax-paying public think. Still, it makes dumming-down all the easier for them.

So, Mr. Al Megrahi is free. Another sop to the do-gooders. Scotland's minister, to be fair, gave a very eloquent 23-minute speech, which I listened to whilst proceeding at a snail's pace between Orpington and Bexley, and frankly with the traffic and retail parks and their attendant roundabouts and traffic lights, you do need to listen to some light relief – if only there had been! One's suspicions were confirmed. The terrorist was to be freed to go home to what turned out to be a hero's welcome. The wrath of America was wrought upon the Scottish decision and as I said previously, for once it was deserved. It was interesting that interviews on radio and television seemed to be confined to parents and relatives of British victims, who agreed with the judgement. Was that decision to show only those with that view made due to any political pressure? Surely the outcome wasn't purely based on future deals for Shell and BP? I mean, that would be immoral.....

Did any of those who voted to join the EEC as was, honestly think that this corrupt behemoth would stop us using 100W light bulbs within our lifetime? From next Tuesday only those remaining in stock can be sold. As you know, we have been stocking up with bulbs from Robert Dyas, Woking, for the last few months. No one I have spoken to wants these dim, expensive alternatives. But for us, choice is now at an end.

Nice to see our local county council still has delusions of

grandeur and not a little disregard for public opinion. Surrey Council Council has appointed, at the not inconsiderable sum of £140,000 over three years, an Olympics co-ordinator. You're right, there's not one event taking place in our hallowed county, but that's not stopping SCC from attempting to host any Olympic-related contracts that might be in the offing. SCC said the new chap, or chapesse, will be "tasked" (oh, how I hate that word) with ensuring the Surrey 2012 programme has maximum impact. He or she will be "a skilled networker and influencer". Already sounds like inflated waffle, and they haven't started paying them yet.

Well, it's Sunday morning. I've just come back from taking Maureen and her sister to London Airport. I was up at 4 am – plane doesn't take off until 9.30 am for New York, but you know how it is. Everything I find horrendous about the airport "experience" Maureen and her sister find compulsive. Their plan – and opposed to their plane - is once having landed, to get to the hotel in Times Square, check in, shower, change and then get to Macy's Store by 3 pm their time, which allows them two hours of browsing. Maureen's not really a shopaholic – well, not here – but there is something apparently about NY that she really loves. Still, Maureen's one week's holiday abroad is my one week's holiday at home, but don't tell her!

Now you know me, never been a fan of religion, never fussed about anything based on power, fear and money. I do, however, get a tad miffed when one lot, however much you loathe or laugh at their naivety, has to play second fiddle to another lot – a lot that has to be cosseted, but then it's all a question of race, when all's said and done. I remember an instance of this in "Coronation Street" some months ago, and no, I wouldn't have seen the episode. I haven't watched CS since Ena Sharples was in gymslip and the programme introduced us to a whole new phenomenon – northerners! The attraction soon wore off. However, I read that two characters in the soap were getting married and having a "traditional" wedding in a "traditional" church. Someone – it was never made clear whom – asked the real vicar of St. Mary's Church in Cheshire, where the scene was filmed, to remove or cover up the cross as it "could offend some viewers". Who? If they mean Muslims, then they should say so. If they mean white liberals who feel Muslims would be offended, then they should say so. See! No-one ever takes responsibility. As the vicar said, and for once I wholeheartedly agree, "This has a resonance nation-wide. It plays into who we are as a nation and I do not think we have a clear idea as English people. We do not know where we are going. There is constant attrition to our way of life". Well said, that man.

Now, to balance a perfectly reasonable pro-Church of England argument, we also learn of a bus driver who refused to take out his bus because of an atheist advert on his vehicle. The advert read, "There's probably no God. Now stop worrying and enjoy your life". Ron Heather, aged 62, should be the laughing stock of his road. What a complete arse! Naturally, the bus company is accommodating his little problem, or pandering, as I prefer to think of it, by finding him a bus that isn't informing people of a choice they may wish to consider. You have to laugh! This clown's verbal reaction when interviewed was to reply, "When I first saw the bus last Saturday I was shocked. I was just about to board and there it was, staring me in the face. My first reaction (over reaction me-thinks) was horror. I was in a dilemma (no, you weren't, you were by a bus) but I felt strongly, I couldn't drive that bus so I went up to my inspectors and told them there was no way I could drive it". Someone else was called upon to cover, and the clown was sent home. Seriously, the words "shock" and "horror" are just a tad over the top. Christ knows how he would react if he read this book! Me? I'd have sacked him on the spot for (a) buggering up the roster and putting people out, and (b) having the temerity to cause such a fuss over something he will never be able to prove. God is a belief, dear boy, not a fact.

What were we saying about pandering to minorities? A Middlesex county cricket team had to change their name from "The Middlesex Crusaders" to "The Panthers". This change came about because "one or two complaints were received from the

Muslim (them again) community" who drew a tenuous link between the cricketing crusaders and the 11th century crusaders about whom apparently they are not best pleased. Talk about long memories. Nobody has any balls – no puns please – these days. The cricket club has a chief executive (who doesn't). This chap's name is Vinny Codrington. Never did like the name Vinny – reminds me of Vinny Jones - like it even less now. He denied that the change had anything to do with political correctness – but then he would do, wouldn't he – conceding that some people found it "rather upsetting". Well, they would. They see it for what it is. Another sop to the minorities. I could be more sympathetic to the "Cod", as I think of the chief exec (there's status) if he hadn't come out with such codswallop by insisting, "that it was time to make a name change (suspiciously convenient) after securing a new main sponsor for the next few seasons. We felt the time was right for us to take a look at our one-day image and unanimously reached the conclusion that re-branding (it's only a cricket club) to a new look would be the right decision....." And so he went on, and on. He didn't say who the new sponsors are – Asian? Muslim? It makes you wonder, dunnit!

All NHS employees have been told not to discuss their religious beliefs with colleagues or patients. So that's another topic off the list. They apparently could be seen has harassing or intimidating others. This follows on from the case of a Baptist lady who was suspended (why?) for offering to pray for an elderly patient. If that was me, however much of an atheist I am, I would have told the lady very politely that in my book she was wasting her time, but if she wished to pray for me, then fine. I wouldn't be that disingenuous. I would have even been slightly humbled that somebody cared, however misguided I felt them to be. The lady, after all, was showing concern, not venom. Why suspend her? She was accused of "failing to show a commitment to a quality and diversity" before being suspended without pay. I'd have told them to "sod off". Hardly a sin compared to the fraud and inside knowledge dealing that goes on day in, day out in the city, and they end up getting rewarded in a most handsome fashion. It's a funny world.

Getting back to the story concerning the bus driver, I see that the Christian Party have hit back against the bus ads by atheists with their own advertising slogan. "There definitely is a God, so join the Christian Party and enjoy your life". We're back to the same old chestnut, aren't we? The difference is, they can't prove it. I think they should be done under the Trade Descriptions Act for the use of the word "definitely" and the Sex Equality Act for not suggesting that God could be male or female, and for good measure, race equality for not stating if he or she was white, black or half-caste (I've been waiting all this book to use that phrase! What fun one has!)?

The Church of England is so out of touch. At a time when unemployment is rising by the month, the Bishop of London, Richard Chartres, has come out with a statement worthy of a complete loon. He says, "Redundancy can be good for the soul", adding, "Being made redundant allows people the opportunity to get off the treadmill and reconsider what they really want in life". Well, surely a job would help! Unless, of course, you live in the north-west, where collecting benefit has always been a constant struggle. You know, having survived a hard night in the pub, traipsing outside every twenty minutes to have a cigarette and then getting up mid-morning to check that your giro has been received in your account, before making a trip to the newsagent to buy your lottery tickets. Perhaps they don't have giros these days, but then, as one lives in the Home Counties (south) one wouldn't know too much about benefits. But seriously, the Bishop is a complete arse. He could always be promoted to "Arse-Bishop". Just thought of that, but however .....the man receives £57,000 a year. Not bad for not having a proper job. A title, yes, but he is at best a waste of space and at worst, someone who is never likely to be out of work, so therefore unable to understand the world inhabited by people who are.

Free speech took another knock, a somewhat one-sided knock, earlier this year when the Government banned a Dutch MP from entering the UK because of his anti-Islamic views. So much for freedom of speech. Every week, some Muslim leader or cleric is slating our country, our values, our soldiers, but that's okay. Our

Government's ban was on the grounds of "community harmony and therefore public security". Naturally, Labour's Lord Ahmed, a Muslim, agreed. He put in his four rupees' worth, by stating that Mr. Wilders is indicted for inciting racial hatred in his country. Well, quite a large number of Dutch voters put their cross against his name. He is a legitimate member of the Dutch parliament. Mr. Wilders claims that the Koran turns Muslims into terrorists. He is concerned about the number of Islamists "swamping" Holland. Well, they've swamped just about everywhere else. Why should his views be stifled when he has been elected through a democratic vote? An unnamed source at the Home Office stated, "The Government opposes extremism in all its forms. It will stop those who want to spread extremism, hatred and violent messages in our communities from coming to our country" – our country, that's a bloody laugh. I think that's if you are white and oppose the spread of Islamic hatred. It's all down to race and colour. What I'd like to know is the name of this Government source, what his position is and just who the hell does he think he represents. It's certainly not you or me (although it could be the chap looking over your shoulder – he tends to look a bit suspect).

This is where religious problems overlap racial problems, nowhere more so than with the Muslims in this country. Governments, whichever colour or political persuasion, continue to ignore the Muslim problem at their peril. Only a few months ago a head teacher was forced to resign after her plan to go back to the old days of a general assembly was scuppered by four Muslim parents who complained about the proposed scrapping of Muslim-only assemblies. A previous head at the Meersbrook Bank Primary School in Sheffield had agreed (I wonder under what pressure) to separate assemblies for Muslim children. FOUR PARENTS. FOUR! How does a minority make such a vocal fuss and clear the way for the head teacher to resign after consulting parents on the issue and receiving their support? What she failed to receive was the support of Sheffield Council who no doubt feels that race is the baton to be handed over to someone else in the shortest possible time. Gutless! Absolutely gutless!

I'm glad to see that the Chairman of the governing board also resigned in protest at the head teacher's treatment. But what of the other governors? For my money, religion has no part to play in assemblies. It would do away with all the fuss about who is included and who is excluded. I understand Jehovah's Witnesses take their children out of assemblies, and have done for years. Assemblies should embrace all schoolchildren at the start of the day, so why religion is still allowed to poke its cultish fizzog in the proceedings is beyond me.

There's another case of a female head teacher, this time close to home in Woking. She went off sick, never to return, because of the constant criticism of her that started when four Muslim governors were appointed. Is four a sacred or optimum number required in order to upset the status quo? For those of you who do not know Woking, and it's better that you remain that way, Woking is one of those towns where the pro-multiculturalists positively cream themselves. It has a very high Asian population. One of the four Muslim governors, ironically a convert by the name of Paul Martin, started raising questions concerning the school's ethos and policies, its stance towards Islam, its links with the Muslim community and the head teacher's management. Education doesn't appear to have been mentioned.

You have to question these people who stand for governorships. You do wonder if it has very little to do with the education of their offspring and more to do with feathering their own political nests. It's interesting to read that Ms Connor, the head, stated after she left and moved out of the area that, "I felt – I will be honest – that this was racism towards me, because I felt that, had I been a Muslim head things would have been conducted in a different way. I felt they didn't have the courage to stand by me in this", "they" being Surrey County Council. Once again, come the issue of race and they all scrub their collective hands so clean there's not a trace of opinion, fact or support left. This lady eventually received £407,781 in compensation. A High Court judge ruled that education officers had been more concerned about complaints to the Commission for Race Equality than the health of a teacher. We never had teachers so stressed because of racial issues that they had to resign when I was a child. But then we didn't have the numbers and we didn't have the "Muslim mission".

Getting back to Meersbrook Bank Primary School in Sheffield, were you aware that they banned the traditional Easter Bonnet Parade? No explanation was given, but I think we can guess why. Good to see, however, that a Muslim parent, wearing the full monty, including the niqab – yes, that's the headgear when you only get to see the eyes – was banned from a parents' evening. This happened at a Catholic school in Blackburn, which refused to allow her in unless she "showed her face". Quite right! Bloody cheek and all the other forms of indignation that one feels! She apparently left the school in tears – the only bit of her they could see! What a pity she didn't leave the country.....

It was disturbing to read that Aberdare Girls' School in south Wales lost its legal fight and will now have to pay a bill of £200,000. That's a lot of money out of the school budget, and all due to a Sikh pupil who refused to take off a bangle on religious grounds. The school naturally had to defend accusations of racial discrimination, that hoary old chestnut of easy money, by stating that it was not part of the school uniform. You wonder why they didn't just give up at the start – the odds were stacked against them. All the ingredients were there, race, religion, minority, non-white, they didn't stand a chance. The local council backed them initially, but presumably got cold feet – same old story. What I find hard to swallow is that the Liberty Group, one I have never felt an empathy with ever since the days when they supported certain IRA members, brought the case in the first place. The school has already paid £60,000 to this group. Why? Once again, a dubious group on a dubious cause, but the greater good of the school budget is without thought.

Statistics do not make pleasant reading. There are ten schools in this country where no-one speaks English as a first language. How can that be? Interesting that four are in Oldham, one each in Blackburn, Rochdale and Burnley, two in Tower Hamlets and one in Hillingdon. There are 116 primary schools where 95% of children do not speak English as a first language. Do not tell me, or the rest of Middle England, that this is not a recipe for disaster.

The only reasons we did not have the "rivers of blood" in the sixties and seventies were because Britain has been by nature a very accommodating and accepting nation. That acceptance has been tested to the limit and the accommodation to the point of overcrowding. Successive governments are now beginning to see the result with the increasing numbers of BNP councillors and MEP's. We have seen a number of racial clashes in Luton, London and Birmingham, along with the growth of the English Defence League. However, I digress. But is it any wonder that we have lost our identity. We just want it back, please.

Woodside High School in Tottenham has four out of every five children who do not speak English. However, sixty-four other languages are spoken in the school. Where is the social cohesion in this case? Still, underneath the article relating to the above it states in an advert that there are big savings to be made at Morrisons – so it's not all bad news!

Something I hadn't given much thought to, well, any as it happens, is the closing of schools due to religious festivals and high days. We only used to close for Christmas and Easter, but now you have to take everyone else's faith into account. I know, I know! In Tower Hamlets (remember them from the earlier statistic) all schools close for something called Eid. It's a Muslim day, apparently. There are other schools with large numbers of Hindu or Sikh pupils who close when their special day arrives. How diverse is this? And how unfair on those trying to plan an education for all. Rod for your own backs springs to mind!

It was interesting to read that an author by the name of Denis MacEoin spent some time looking at school and Islamic web sites in order to discover if there were any extremist links, etc. He found that a number of Muslim schools are promoting extremism, some even encouraging children to grow up despising our country. They also discourage children from playing cricket, board games or listening to western music. Neither Harry Potter nor Shakespeare is being promoted. One web site of a governing body at a Yorkshire primary school praises a woman who "keeps herself indoors or hidden in a veil". Another little piece likens a person who "plays chess to one who dips his hands in the blood of a swine!" Poetic, though still bollocks! What is wrong with these people? One keeps coming back to the phrase, "If you don't like it here – bugger off!"

I have to say, however, all sympathy with teaching staff goes out of the window when you read that twenty head teachers jetted off to Mauritius on a taxpayer-funded jolly to enable them to "exchange knowledge and experiences". They could have done that in Slough! They stayed at the Hilton resort and spa. This was organised by iNet. No, I've never heard of them either. The specialist schools and accommodation trust charity, which last year received - wait for it - £35 million from the taxpayer, arrange these excursions. I'd love to know how they distributed our money.

These people have a lot in common with those who decide on MP's expenses, totally without the knowledge of the lives of ordinary people and their struggle to stay afloat. Apparently they were "sharing ideas with colleagues from around the world". It would have been more useful if they had attempted to derail the Government on the supposition that the "i" before "e" rule is no longer worth teaching. A document, entitled "Support For Spelling" suggests that children use guidelines such as analysing TV listings for compound words, and learn homophones through jokes, such as "How many socks in a pair?" "None – because you can eat a pear". The guidance also states that text abbreviation such as "fone" and "skool" boost literary levels. Dear, oh dear.....

A-Level history students have been complaining about the difficulty of their exams. Apparently they involve words! Words like "despotic tyrant". This was a description of Hitler, apparently, and there was me thinking they meant Gordon Brown, until I read on! Is this not indicative of just how basic English has become as a subject within another? It is the basis of everything we have, be it geography, history, it is the everyday form of communication, unless you reside in Oldham or Tower Hamlets, obviously, but it certainly is in Farnham. But getting back to the use of the words "despotic" and "tyrant", students were not only foxed by what the words meant, but were unable to think of what to do when that foxing occurred. One student remarked, "I thought it meant chaotic". Another thought it meant weak, and a third commented, "My life is destroyed because of this exam". Perhaps with comments like that she should try acting. I mean, it doesn't take much, does it – that's research, not acting. Has none of them heard of a dictionary? Please, please do not tell me that standards are the same as they were when we were young and received a rounded education.

When you get to the situation where GCSE examiners are told by "desperate" education chiefs to "grade gently" it really does show the standards of teaching. They shouldn't have worried, of course, as all the results confirmed an increase in passes, as we discussed earlier. Papering over the cracks springs to mind.

It made me laugh when I read ('cos I can read) that one in four boys cannot write their own names at the age of five. Almost a third are unable to recite the alphabet (but then I suppose it depends on whose alphabet), whilst one in five cannot count to ten. A chap from the Campaign for Real Education, one Nick Seaton, said the results show there's a massive problem, whilst Dawn Primarolo, the Children's Minister, stated that the Government were "making progress"!! Still, as long as she's satisfied and all the right boxes have, once again, been ticked.....

Here we go again – here's another quango funded by us called the Assessment and Qualification Alliance, who work in partnership with local authority youth schemes. The Alliance hands out qualifications as prolifically as benefits are offered to incomers. This waste of paper, gained by a probable waste of space, is for the most mundane of tasks. It is given out willy-nilly and comes in many different forms. One is "The Using of Public Transport Certificate". Now to qualify for this waste of paper that doubtless will underwhelm many prospective employers, one has to walk to a bus stop near one's home, then stand or sit until the bus arrives. One's next task is to enter the bus in a "calm and safe manner", find a seat and observe through the windows. The final test in this quest is to wait until the bus stops before standing up and alighting. Can you imagine anyone with any nous in a local authority wanting anything to do with these half-wits? How the hell do they manage to convince government departments that they are worthy of funding? This little scheme alone is costing £20,000. The AQA advise that these schemes are designed to give youngsters accreditation for success in short projects or pieces of work. I suspect that the "short" refers to their attention span as well. They add that "they are suitable for all abilities and can be made available for almost every activity. They are easy, quick and nationally recognised". (What as?) I'd re-brand them as being ideal for retards - learning difficulties as is. They say the AQA unit award is a great stepping-stone to get you started.

The article went on to note that 900 youngsters between the age of 11 and 15 (presumably with an IQ of those aged 3) signed up for this scheme in Manchester, Rochdale and Bury last year. Aah. So now we know the qualification is commensurate with the intelligence of those in the north-west! But hang on, some lady called Barbara Lewis, who is Bury's Youth Support Services Manager (long title, little substance, I suspect) said, "It's about teaching young people self-reliance and emotional well-being through fun and challenging activities". I can just imagine her going home after an easy day and her other half asking, "And what have you done today, dear heart?" And her replying, "Oh, talking bollocks, as always". And there's more. Wirral Council is offering "Travel Training". This is a subtle variation on the AQA test. Perhaps you get a gobstopper if you pass both. This instructs 16-year-olds on how to climb aboard a bus and then pay their fare. I'm sorry, but that last part was far too fanciful. Do you know anyone who has ever paid his or her fare in the north-west? Anyway, Councillor Jean Quinn of Merseyside Strategic Transport Partnership stated that, "By increasing people's ability and confidence to use public transport, we contribute to improving the quality of life and allow people a wider range of opportunities". Down south that would be considered ever so slightly patronising, but I suppose in the northern wilderness that sort of statement would be acclaimed on a par with anything written by Martin Luther King or Pam Ayres! Oh, and just for the groan factor, I read that a rubber band pistol was confiscated from a pupil during an algebra lesson on the grounds that it was a weapon of maths destruction! Talking of Merseyside and its environs, here are a couple of gags that wouldn't go down well in that neck of the woods – or pit-bull breeding territory, though they go down quite well in Dorking.

Okay, first joke:

The Liverpool Manager, flies to Baghdad to watch a young Iraqi play football. He is suitably impressed and arranges for him to come over to Anfield. Two weeks later, Liverpool are playing at home to Manchester United and with only twenty minutes left, find themselves 4-0 down. The Manager decides to give the young Iraqi striker a chance. On he goes. The lad is a sensation. In those twenty minutes he scores five goals and thus wins the game for Liverpool. The Manager is delighted, the fans are delighted, the players are delighted and the media loves the new-found star. When the player comes off the pitch he telephones his mother to tell her about his first day in English football. "Hi, mum, you'll never guess what. I played for twenty minutes today, we were 4-0 down but I scored 5 and we won. Everybody loves me, the fans, the media, they all love me". "Wonderful", his mum says, very dismissively, "I'm glad you're so happy. Let me tell you about my day. Your father has been shot in the street and robbed, your sister and I were ambushed, gang-raped and beaten and your younger brother has joined a gang of looters, and all the while you are having such a great time". The young lad is brought down from his dizzy heights and is now very upset. "What can I say, mum? I'm so sorry". "Sorry? Sorry? So you should be", said his mum, "it's your fault we moved to Liverpool in the first place!"

And now for the other:

A primary teacher at the Preston Learning Centre was trying to make a good impression on her first day. She explained to her class that she is a Preston supporter. She asked her students to raise their hands if they, too, were Preston supporters. Everyone raised his or her hands, with the exception of one little girl. The teacher looked at the little girl with surprise and asked, "Why, Mary, you didn't raise your hand". "No", replied the little girl, "that's because I'm not a Preston fan". The teacher was shocked.

"Well, if you're not a Preston fan, which team do you support?" "I'm West Ham and proud of it", replied Mary. The teacher could not believe her ears. "But Mary, you live in Preston, why are you a West Ham supporter?" Mary was indignant. "Because my mum and dad both come from Barking and they're both West Ham fans, so I'm a West Ham fan too". "Well", said the teacher in an obviously annoyed tone, "I see that as no reason for you to be a West Ham fan. You don't have to be like your parents all the time, you know. What if your mother was a prostitute and your father was a drug addict and a car thief? What would you be then?" "In that case", smiled Mary, "I'd be a Liverpool supporter".

CHAPTER SEVEN

A Welsh Weekend – There's Lovely!

Well, I'm off into Aldershot to buy some copy paper for the printer. You've no idea how much I get through in putting this book together, in order that your delectation can be sated. Wish me luck, and with that bit of luck I may be able to drive in, park, get what I require and get back home without exhaling! Well, it's a thought, not to mention a challenge.

I'm back! I bought the paper in Rymans, having passed "WH Smith's The Post Office" en route. There were twenty-two people queuing for counter service. The snake extended to the Crime section of paperbacks. You can't possibly peruse the shelves anymore, for the constant shuffle of Post Office customers. For those of you who don't know, the Wellington Centre in Aldershot was its first development of enclosed shopping. This was followed some years later by "The Galleries". It was never a great success and over the years many shops have closed, one by one, or more likely two by two, until we are now left with just three. Julian Graves, an opticians and a kitchen shop, and only today I note that the kitchen shop is extolling the virtues of its closing down sale. From there until the other end of The Galleries, there is a stream of closed shops, many still sporting the name of their last owner. The escalator has long since been put into mothballs to save money. When you venture down the steps on either side of the escalator, you come into an area that once was home to a Wimpy on the left, and the Post Office on the right. Both are now empty shells.

I understand the centre management also reduced the heating in the area to save money. I think I'd reduce the centre management in order to save money. And while I think of it, when taking Mutley around the block this morning, I passed the vicarage. The curtains looked as if they could do with a wash. Pulled hither and thither, though somewhat more hither, they never seem to hang straight. Still, as long as Uganda is being supported. But at what price of domestic tidiness – and the lean-to looks in need of a tidy-up an'all! In fact, it's not the sort of vicarage garden that you'd see in Midsomer Murders where tea parties are held and Cully is bound to be seen involved in something completely pointless.

Now, I've just finished writing that last piece with only one interruption, which was due to the phone ringing. I answered and a voice announced that he was from the HSBC bank and enquired if I had a few moments to spare. I courteously indicated that I did. "I'll just take you through two very quick pieces of security", he stated. I said nothing. He continued, "Now I'll give you the first part of your post code and I'd like you to finish please, so it's GU12....." He waited. I said, "You've rung me, I don't know that you are from the HSBC. What a bloody cheek, you ring me and then you want me to convince you of whom I am when I am at the end of my own phone." He interjected. "It's only for security. My other question relates to your date of birth". "Sorry", I said, "It still comes under the heading of bloody cheek. I've been a customer of HSBC (Midland Bank as was) for over thirty years. If you wish to attract my attention, kindly send me your bumff in the post. Good day". I won't hold my breath.

I read on teletext that Asda are to introduce a range of Asian clothing in twelve stores throughout the country. As you know, I'd never soil my M&S shoes in an Asda store, but knowing where the twelve stores are will act as a good barometer of towns to be avoided, should one move. And before those with a racial cause, itching to find fault, gallop towards me on their silky, black steed, my feelings would be exactly the same if Asda's new range were for "white shell-suited males". But then, I'm never likely to move to Liverpool.

I see there's a new campaign to derestrict Sunday opening hours, so that every day rolls into one. I've never been against Sunday shopping restrictions on religious grounds, it is the sheer greed of those who own the stores and will benefit financially that I oppose. The problem is the public. They won't boycott these shops. If they did, then they would have to close on that one day, but give the great unthinking their head, and off they trundle. It's on a par with those who watch Sky TV and then complain about the BBC television licence. If they hadn't bought a Sky dish, we'd all still be watching live sport on a proper television channel without adverts. It really makes me laugh when I listen to Sky supporters condemning their £140-odd a year for the television licence when they pay Sky £50 plus per month and then suffer the ads as well. Where are the original programmes of the quality made by the BBC? And all to line the pocket of some colonial who doesn't even pay tax in our country. Beyond belief! Anyway, back to the High Street and Sunday shopping.

The article says church groups and unions are against the proposal. Well, the church groups can decide for themselves if they wish to shop, but please don't speak on behalf of us non-believers. Incidentally, I wonder just how many God botherers officially opposed to Sunday shopping actually go shopping on a Sunday. Still, hypocrisy is the fundamental basis of religion, is it not? It was an interesting statistic I read that while four and a half million people go to church each Sunday (why?); seven million go to Ikea (Why 2 – the Sequel). Those who wish to extend Sunday opening times are called the "My Sunday, My Choice" lobby group. Surprised they're not called the "My Sunday, My Rights" group. As far as I'm concerned, if you can't do your shopping in six hours on a Sunday, you have too much choice – and as I always say, when you've seen one shopping centre, you've seen a mall! Sorry!

Right! Have you heard the joke about the Husband Store? No? Good. Then read on:

A brand-new store has recently opened in London that sells husbands. When women go to choose a husband they have to follow the instructions at the entrance: -

"You may visit this store ONLY ONCE! There are six floors and the value of the products increase as you ascend the flights. You may choose any item from a particular floor, or may choose to go up to the next floor, but you CANNOT go back down except to exit the building!

So, a woman goes into the Husband Store to find a husband. On the first floor the sign on the door reads: "These men have jobs," The second floor sign reads: "These men have jobs and love children". The third floor sign reads: "These men have jobs, love children and are extremely good looking". "Wow", she thinks, but feels compelled to keep going up. She gets to the fourth floor where the sign reads: "These men have jobs, love children, are drop dead gorgeous and help with housework". "My God", she exclaims, "I can hardly stand it", but she desists. On she goes to the fifth floor and the sign reads: "These men have jobs, love children, are drop dead gorgeous, help with housework AND have a strong romantic streak". She is so tempted to stay, but decides on going to the sixth floor, where she reads: "Floor six – you are visitor 31, 456,013 to this floor. There are no men on this floor. This floor exists solely as proof that women are impossible to please. Thank you for shopping at the Husband Store".

To avoid gender bias charges, the store's owner opened a New Wives Store just across the road. The first floor has wives that love sex, the second floor has wives that love sex and have money, floors three to six have never been visited!

However well intentioned, most policies and innovations to reduce the problem of binge and under-age drinking fail because they never address the real problem. The price of a pint of beer is raised at the pub, the ordinary working man who simply wants a couple of pints is therefore penalised, but the yobs who get drunk and abusive on cider and lager continue to buy the drink cheaply in the supermarkets. The latest idea is to ban alcohol advertising. Do they really think that it will have any effect? The idea that using the slogan, "Smoking kills" on the front of every packet of cigarettes is not going to make anyone stop smoking - it's a drug! If you wrote, "You'll die after smoking the third cigarette in this pack" it still wouldn't stop people from smoking. And now we have another sop in the form of pint glasses coming under threat, because they could be used as weapons. Once again, the ordinary man (and woman) is penalised due to the anti-social behaviour of those who should have been put down at birth, if not aborted sooner. They never get to the nub of the problem.

Allowing judges to give sentences that fit the crime would be a start. I really do hope that the plastic glass replacement idea is a non-starter. Just a thought – but you do wonder if there's any leverage from the plastics industry by lobbying MPs or conducting polls on their behalf. You trust no-one these days.

As you know, I've always maintained that whilst the NHS should be free to all at the point of delivery, the patient should also be responsible for their own destiny, and a large part of that destiny is via their lifestyle. In other words, I would not treat freely anyone suffering from cancer through smoking, nor would I treat extreme obesity when it is down to sheer gluttony. The same applies to drink and drugs. What a revelation it was to read that a teenager, given two weeks to live after damaging his liver through excessive drinking, may not be allowed a liver transplant. He suffered acute liver failure after drinking thirty cans of lager in one session. It shows what type of person he is by the fact that he was drinking lager and not real ale.

Last Saturday Maureen and I travelled the 3 plus miles to Frimley, where we ate out at a little Italian restaurant to celebrate (well, that was Maureen's word) our fortieth wedding anniversary. We were placed at a table in the middle, there being two aisles with tables running parallel against either wall. On my left, but behind Maureen, sat a couple that fascinated me. She was in her forties, and looked longingly into the eyes of the man who faced her, he being silver-haired, and in his fifties, I guess. He looked the sort who had been manual, but had succeeded financially to the point where he relied on manual labour to make his money. Probably completely wrong, but that's how I saw him! His arms rested on the table before him (they hadn't yet been served), always a bit awkward when you find your arms wallowing in your minestrone. With his hands faced down, she smoothed hers over his, gently easing her splayed fingers up and down his tanned arms before withdrawing them once more. She then cupped his hands one at a time, her gaze never leaving his. Maureen caught my eye. I nodded in their direction. I said, "Have a look at them". Maureen was hesitant. I added, "They'll never notice you". Maureen turned surreptitiously – well, it's the only way she knows how to turn, took in the scene, before facing me once more and said, and "They obviously met on the Internet!" Women really do have that ability to push the right buttons, unless of course, when they're driving and then the windscreen wiper is turned at full blast when they meant to indicate. Oh – by the way – the meal was very good.

Talking of getting things spot on, over a recent meal at my local, "The Swan", the subject of Carol Kirkwood cropped up. There were five chaps, plus Maureen, present. We guessed Carol's age. The guesses ranged from thirty two to thirty seven, except for Maureen who stated quite forcefully, "She's forty eight if she's a day!" "Never", we replied in unison, well nearly in unison as one still had a mouthful, but you've got the principle. Maureen, we felt, was well off beam, obviously driven by jealousy. A few days later my cousin, Simon, phoned to say that he'd looked up our Carol on a web site and found that she was born in 1960, which makes her forty nine. "Maureen was right", he said. "Did she know?" "No", I replied, "we had looked on the web ourselves but the site we found didn't give her age". When I reluctantly admitted to my wife that she was right, all my wife said was, "Well, just look at her. The dyed hair stares you in the face". "A very pretty face", I countered, but by then the "Weakest Link" was in full swing and my wife's interest in Carol had evaporated.

What a greedy world we inhabit. I see that Bristol City Council are issuing perks to traffic wardens as freely as traffic wardens issue tickets. In fact, the more tickets they issue, the greater the perk! How sad is this. Their "team rewards" include a monthly lunch laid on by caterers with the extra perk of having the rest of the afternoon off. Wardens who bring in the most cash in the month are given what is described as a custom-made pen. They must be easily motivated. A spokesman for the Taxpayers' Alliance described the practice as "amoral".

I describe it as sheer greed. Bristol CC brought in £1,294,447 in parking fines last year. Not a figure to be sniffed at, which is more than you can say for the job and Bristol City councillors. I would rather be unemployed than lower myself to that level, but then some people have no pride.

There's a newly introduced ruse to enable officially authorised queue jumping for children suffering from ADHD or attention deficit hyperactivity disorder, and the similarly named ADD (as above but without the hyper). These children will be allowed into theme parks without having to queue. That's right, you just turn up and ride. Tourism bosses have agreed (I can just imagine the Press and the pressure if they hadn't) to allow those affected to operate a pass system in order to avoid tantrums. Some female cove called Andrea Bilbow who operates under the banner, "Chief Executive of the National Attention Deficit Disorder Information and Support Service" (phew!) said that children suffering with the above initials "are very impulsive and just can't cope in a queue or when there is a delay in gratification!" I wish she could hear herself. She adds, "I know many primary schools let them go ahead at dinner times – and if that stops scenes, what's the problem?" The problem, dear, is that this is nothing more than pandering to little sods who should learn to wait. If you extend this principle to all situations, are they to get preferential treatment in a shop, parking space, and cinema? I suspect the parents of these children require as much pandering to, if not more than their offspring. I say this with not a little knowledge. As you will no doubt recall from my previous books, our youngest, William, was in that bracket. Short term attention span. He was given wheat-free this, goat's milk that, and tartrazine free the other. Nothing to do with it – he was just a git! Does he play up now if he queues at Burger King? No! Does he have a tantrum if he has to wait for petrol at the service station? No! Mind you, in most other ways he's still a git!

I heard via the wireless that Elton John wishes to adopt an AIDS orphan. What would no doubt be touching to some is vomit inducing to me - and you I suspect. We wouldn't have come this far if we didn't have something in common! What? You're reading this for a bet? Oh, you're joking – well, I hoped you were. Anyway, where were we? Oh, yes. This news was followed up by a photograph in the "Daily Express". The accompanying article notes that he and his partner, David Furnish (why does the term "partner" make me squirm when referring to another male?) have had their hearts stolen by some Eastern European sprog. The article reminds us that Mr. John "married" Mr. Furnish in 2005 in a civil partnership. I have to tell you that the whole thing makes me cringe. A 62-year-old male with a wig and a 46-year-old male standing together and betrothing their whatevers, I still think it comes under the section headed "ever so slightly sordid and not overly nice". I really do hope they are not allowed to adopt, but I won't hold my breath. Celebrity and homosexual – it doubtless ticks all the adoption boxes in today's world, whereas white, middle-class and representing both sexes no doubt reduces your place in the ranking.

Talking of things odd, I see that the South African runner, Caster Semenya, is not best pleased with the revelations that the tests carried out in order to check if she is Doris or Maurice have found her to be a hermaphrodite. For those of you reading this in Addlestone, it means she has male organs as well as female. What makes me smile – and I do – is that she apparently possesses internal testes – she had them well hidden. Male organs produce muscle bulk (well, she had that), body hair (certainly did on her head) and a deep voice (never sounded to me like a soprano). She was also found, it is claimed, to possess neither womb nor ovaries. Yet her uncle, Lesiba, bless him, said, "I believe Caster is normal, inside and out, we are a normal family who looked at a child when she was born, saw that she was a girl and raised her as any family would do". Normal? Normal? Seems a bloody funny family to me, though I suppose she could always run for Middlesex!

It's always nice to get the opportunity to use a new word in one's tome. I read yesterday that a female accountant who worked for PricewaterhouseCoopers is suing them. She claims they vindictively pursued a campaign to wreck her future prospects. She has asked for £40 million in compensation. Interesting to note that she has previously sued UBS and Credit Suisse over previous redundancies. PwC describe the lady as a "vexatious litigant" (the new word was "vexatious", not "litigant". There are probably thousands of those, though not all vexatious). By the way, our lady of Romania, the litigant, is citing all the good old stand-bys such as "offensive" and "racist" remarks, references to her being a "Communist spy", and "victimisation". All the ingredients enabling her to remain in a very healthy lifestyle in this country, I'd say.

So, a further alignment with the USA is due to rear its ugly, corporate head shortly. ITV and Channels 4 and 5 will be able to push company products during programmes in an effort to rake in extra income. Thank someone, I know not who, that the BBC is immune from such dictat. Does the viewer really wish to be confronted with products subtly or unsubtly thrust within a drama or quiz? All this does is to push me even further from watching anything on a commercial station.

What a sad case Ed Balls is, or Ed Bollocks as I prefer to think of him. The Schools' Secretary, who I wouldn't have cleaning a classroom on the grounds of incompetence, is hoping to promote music in schools. Nothing wrong with that. It's just that having launched the National Year of Music, he recruits a group called N-Dubz (no, I've never heard of them either, which I suspect is good news for us all). N-Dubz have won a Mobo – Music of Black Origin – yes, try finding a Mowo winner! Their material is apparently sexually explicit. Would you say that rap music is ideal for the national year of music? No, neither would I. But it's hip, if not hop, it's ethnic and it's basic, which is in line with the level Mr. Bollocks will be aiming at. This Government's slogan must be, "Always aim for the lowest common denominator". There was not one mention in the article of any music by Jake Thackray, Peter Skellern or Matt Bianco – philistines! I don't suppose that N-Dubz are any different from other rap groups – unintelligible, tuneless songs, sung by people who should spend any financial gain on elocution lessons. I'd make sure they were in the same class as Dominic Littlewood and Nick Knowles.

You really worry about the health of some people. You remember the policeman who left his two Alsatians in a hot car, where they eventually died, well, PC Mark Johnson is not well enough to attend his own court case. He was due to make his first appearance but copped out due to suffering stress, though I suspect not as much stress as his two dogs suffered. Still, a doctor's certificate was handed to the magistrates at Nottingham Court, so that's all right. His solicitor said that, "The defence will be obtaining a psychiatric report regarding his fitness to plead". So, it's all being made very watertight. The PC's brief also made a successful application banning publication of the handler's address. Obviously, they don't want any dead dog heads being left on his pillow. The article commented that the now ex-dog handler could be fined up to £20,000 (but he won't be, will he) or be jailed for six months (same comment). I just hope his stress is as terminal as the heat endured by his dogs.

Ah, some good, welcome and very satisfying news. That obnoxious cove, Alan Duncan, has been sacked by Dave the Brave from his job as Shadow Commons Leader. He still holds a post, however – that of Shadow Justice Minister – but it might go a little way towards curbing his arrogance. These people never seem to learn. Mr. Duncan didn't heed the warning signs by the electorate of their disdain for the MP's financial antics. After his throwaway comments some months ago on "Have I Got News For You" concerning expenses, he recently complained that, "MP's are treated like shit and forced to live on rations". Rations, I am sure, most of us would be happy to be treated to!

What regress we encounter when a situation arises that trains have to be cancelled due to a lack of drivers consenting to work on Sundays. London Midland, the current franchise that runs trains between London Euston and Birmingham New Street, have had the contract for two years. Was it not a forgone conclusion that if drivers are not contracted to work on a Sunday, and you decide to cut costs by terminating double time for working on that day, you might end up with just a tad of a problem? Well, whether it was foreseen or not, all factions have ignored the warning sign. A bit like passing a double yellow signal and hurtling headlong into a situation where services have been cancelled due to an almost total lack of volunteers. Volunteers? Ex BR crews must be laughing on their footplates in the sky. You never had to rely on volunteers under BR, still I'm sure Margaret Thatcher knew best.

Okay, a rail related story starring an un-named 5-year-old and his rather nice mum. I've never met her, but I would imagine her being very nice! So, are you sitting comfortably? Then I'll begin:

A mother was working in the kitchen, listening to her 5-year-old son playing with his train set in the living room. She heard the train stop and her son announcing, "All you bastards who want to get off, get off now and hurry. And all you bastards who are getting on, get on now, because we're not waiting around for anyone". The horrified mother hurried in and told her son, "We don't use that kind of language in this house. I want you to go to your room and stay there for two hours. When you come out you may play with your train, but I want you to use nice language." Two hours later the 5-year-old came out of his bedroom and resumed playing with his train set. The train stopped at the station and his mother listened at the door, as he said, "All passengers who are disembarking the train, please remember to take all of your luggage with you. We thank you for travelling with us today and hope your trip was a pleasant one". She was so pleased to hear the little boy as he continued, "For those of you boarding, we ask that you stow all of your hand luggage underneath your seat and just to make you aware that there is no smoking on this train. We hope you have a very pleasant and relaxing journey with us today". She fairly beamed, before the child added, "For those of you who are pissed off about the two hour delay, please see that bitch in the kitchen"!

Or, for those of you who wish to know the best way of avoiding paying for your train journey, read on:

Three women and three men are travelling by train to a football match. At the station the three men each buy a ticket, but are bemused by the fact that the three women buy just one ticket. "How are the three of you going to travel when you've only bought one ticket?" asks one of the men. "Watch and learn", replies one of the women. They all board the train, the three men taking their respective seats but the three women disappear and cram themselves into a toilet before closing the door. Shortly after the train has departed the conductor comes around to collect the tickets. He knocks on the door and asks, "Tickets, please". The door opens just a crack and a single arm emerges with a ticket in hand. The conductor takes the ticket and moves on. The three men watch this happen and agree it is a very clever idea. After the game they decide to copy the women on the return journey and save some money. When they get to the station they thus buy a single ticket. To their astonishment, the same three women breeze by the ticket office without purchasing even one. "So how are you going to get back without a ticket between you?" asks one of the three perplexed men. "Watch and learn again", replies one of the women. When they board the train the three men cram themselves into a toilet. The three women cram into another toilet across the corridor. Shortly after the train is on its way one of the three women leaves the toilet and walks to the toilet in which the men are hiding. She then knocks on the door and says, "Tickets, please".

If only we chaps had the guile of the female sex!

The following story concerns a schizophrenic who duped health workers into believing he was not a risk to the public, and then murdered a man before eating his brains, which he apparently buttered! (Novel, and not a combination I've come across on "Masterchef"). However, he gained his freedom to commit this crime, having already murdered someone previously. Having been sent to Broadmoor he then murders a patient only weeks afterwards. East London NHS Foundation

Trust and West London Mental Health NHS Trust have both apologised, which is nice, but no-one appears to have been disciplined. So that's all right! A social worker, unnamed, also failed to report that this killer had allegedly assaulted a teenage girl. I've come to the conclusion that there are too many people in mental health whose interest is skewed towards protecting the assailant, rather than the public but as we all know, those who err have far more rights than those who don't.

I smiled, as I did earlier in the book – you know, one of those understated smiles – and why? Well, the lesson learned was not to be seriously ill during the first week of August. It appears that emergency admissions are more likely to die during this week than at any other time, due to the number of newly qualified doctors taking to the wards for the first time. Deaths are 6% up over the previous week. Still, I expect this statistic will allow a PhD to be taken in an entirely new subject – "How to keep the buggers alive against all the odds". So, just remember, don't go out, don't do anything in the first week of August, it's for your own good!

We all make mistakes, even the titled Baroness Scotland. For me, it's the lack of honesty, humility and arrogance that go with that mistake. She, the lady who took on an illegal worker, contrary to the laws she was closely involved in implementing, was fined £5,000 but retained her job. BS says she failed to photocopy the worker's passport. The worker now says she was never asked for her passport during the extremely in-depth ten-minute interview. BS casually dismisses her not so little oversight as comparable to not paying the London congestion charge. I wonder which pot of taxpayers' funding her £5,000 has come from, 'cos it certainly won't affect the Scotland woman's lifestyle.

Well, we've had the first two weeks of "Strictly....." and it was interesting to note the number of complaints concerning Alesha Dixon on the panel and comments that she contributed the square root of naff all (as the Bard once said). I fully understand that she's new to the job, but she's not one who seems backward at coming forward. I would normally give anyone a few weeks to grow into the job. My problem, however, is one which many shows won't address and that is her appalling diction and dropping of letters. What a sloppy Alesha. Arlene Phillips, who I would have back tomorrow, never dropped her "h"s and "t"s. I don't know about you, but it crossed my mind that the dropping of Arlene may well have been due to the closet desire to introduce an ethnic judge. After all, it does look the picture of middle class white England – well, Len, anyway, as Bruno is institutionally Italian and Craig is antipodean, although at least he has learned to speak properly, and has a double-barrel to boot!

What a bloody cheek! Yes, I know, another one. Here we have yet another ruse by this inept, free-spending government. Every household is to contribute 50p per month, payable with your telephone bill, in order to help finance Broadband. Thousands paying this new tax will never own a computer, let alone use Broadband. Why on earth should they be made to pay? So close to an election, it makes you wonder if they really are aware of just how unpopular they are. Perhaps they think that walking on water is a right for all politicians and not just the chap who starred in that best-selling hard-backed novel.

Which reminds me, "The Parishioner", our parish magazine, has just winged its way through our letterbox. There is going to be a harvest supper. Tinned and dry goods will be given to some charitable association in Aldershot, which no doubt will be swapped for booze and fags. Monetary gifts will be used to buy fruit trees for a church in some place called Saluti in Uganda – that country again! With these African states' record of self-dependence, I've no doubt that the trees will be cut up for firewood just as they are beginning to bear fruit. I mean, call me cynical.....

I've just been checking my e-mails. One prospective booking, three offers of Viagra, in different guises, four offers to gamble my lack of money on Casino Royale and a couple from unlikely characters, one Whittenborn Nicholle is inviting me to "take a shower together" – hope it's a female! – whilst Kortney Bellamy states she "always wanted me in school". Strange,

I went to an all-boys' school on Wandsworth Common – and by Christ, weren't we common. I can assure you no-one was named Kortney in those days, even less so with that common spelling. I wonder who sends this soon-to-be deleted rubbish?

Talking of rubbish, Mutley and I wended our way along the canal once more this morning. Two discarded cigarette packets lay where fishermen fish, a Hovis bread wrapper hung from a tall reed and a Green Giant corn tin (empty) sat on the flattened ground as if to give credence to the angler's rest. I suppose smoking must relieve the boredom of sitting for hours and hours looking at the end of a line, waiting for that moment of ecstasy when the thingy bobs and an unguarded moment of temptation by the fish concerned spells a visit to the bank for visual examination, measuring and gloating, before returning to the murky depths (about six feet actually) with presumably very sore lips. There's a chap on a bicycle that I pass most mornings. Very pleasant, cheery type, who always passes the time of day. Bedecked in yellow high-viz jacket and black helmet, I assumed he pedalled his way towards the station en route to London. Wrong! I met him on Saturday (without a helmet – he'd broken the strap). Passing the time of day, yes he stopped long enough as it was a Saturday, he commented that he was a carpenter working for the army and said he worked seven days a week. I know no more about him than that, but if I do, I'll pass it on. I know you are always interested in the common man.

As you know, Clarissa Dixon-Wright is not a soul I hold dear to my heart, or has a heart I'd hold dear to my soul, due to her love of hunting and frankly, her scruffy demeanour does nothing to help her cause. CD-W manages to plumb depths murkier than the canal in the distaste I have for people who see their wanton killing of an animal as sport. We now discover that this woman was filmed attending a two-day hare-coursing event "up north". What I don't understand is that whilst hare coursing is illegal and she admitted to taking part in the event, she was given an absolute discharge. Why? Also charged was some cove by the name of Mark Prescott, a year younger than CD-W at 61. They were both filmed along with "hundreds" of supporters by undercover inspectors working on behalf of the International Fund for Animal Welfare. How on earth do you get so many people attending such an event? If ever there was a case for a mass execution, it will be one of these events. If they were football supporters, they would get an awful press but here they appear nameless and shameless. A private prosecution was launched against what was described by the prosecutor as a "serious and sophisticated event". The district judge stated, "What the defendants did was wrong and unlawful, but there are complexities within the hunting act which make it difficult to enforce". Having been discharged (absolutely, don't forget) neither will have to pay costs. Both admitted attending an illegal event. The photo accompanying the article shows the lank haired one smirking (she may be smiling, though I prefer smirking). It is not the prettiest of sights!

Whilst up north, if I lived in Lancashire, I wouldn't be best pleased with my county council. They are looking to employ, at the not inconsiderable sum of £30,000 per annum, a person to combat negative thoughts regarding immigrants. Have you ever heard anything so ludicrous since you read the last couple of pages? The council states that the project manager will promote "community cohesion" in the county. Another politically correct jobs-worth. Surely £30,000 could be better spent on training police to climb a three-rung ladder, or purchasing additional radar guns. Papering over the cracks springs to mind once more. You can have all the jobs-worths in the world gushing multi-cultural inclusiveness, but walk out onto any street in Oldham and you will see why people voted BNP.

I'm a firm believer that leopards rarely, if ever, change their spots. Once a thief, nearly always a thief. There's this 32-year-old called Mark Hook, who has been jailed after being found guilty of snatching an 80-year-old's wallet in a street. What a tough and brave little Hook he is. His victim weighs six-stone and walks with difficulty. Hooks criminal record goes back eighteen years to 1991. This ungrateful piece of humanity was given a chance to change his life at the age of sixteen. Not many people get this chance, paid for by taxpayers to go on a "character building" trip to Kenya, Egypt and four other countries. He was. Why? It cost Gloucester Social Services – or Gloucester taxpayers to you and me - £7,000 plus interest back then. What a total waste of money. He has a history of thuggery. Who was it that felt he would change his habits of almost a lifetime? Again, no names are ever forthcoming. I'd make them pay the £7,000 back into the council's coffers, and then decisions like this would not be made so rashly. I've never been convinced about a heaven, but I really do hope there's a hell.

One's perception and respect for the police never gets better with time, sadly. Their arrogance is hitting a new high – or should that be low? PC Malcolm Searles, aged 23, now ex-PC MS, killed a 61-year-old lady who happened to be in the wrong place at the wrong time. Mrs. Sandra Simpson was walking home with her husband from a restaurant when Searles crashed his car into her. This happened just off the High Street in Bromley, Kent, or south-east London, dependent on whether you own or rent your property. He wasn't even involved in a high-speed chase, attempting to bring criminals to justice. Oh, no, this Searles character was driving at speeds of up to 100 mph, though 50 in a 30 when he killed Mrs. Simpson. His quest? Well, that was to deliver a birthday card to his sister. He's only just qualified as a police driver. Methinks he must have been fast-tracked. Perhaps the bit about personal responsibility, recklessness and how not to be a complete arse should be enforced more vigorously during their training. Apparently he wants Mrs. Simpson's family to know that he is truly sorry. I'm sure that will help the family feel a lot better.

There was a recent case of a 49-year-old, fed up with ringing 999 and getting nowhere, as a gang of yobs threw apples at him and his wife from the safe confines of a BMX track. After the third day of this behaviour, the husband managed to apprehend one of the perpetrators and made a citizen's arrest. Not once did the police make a visit whilst the intimidation by these thugs was ensuing. But the second the yob made a complaint, the husband, without any previous convictions to his name, was arrested. I'm glad to say he resisted the easy way out, that of receiving a caution, and pleaded not guilty to common assault. This charge was brought about following evidence supplied to the CPS. It is situations like this that fuel the public's mistrust of the police and the lack of confidence in their own rights to defend their home, family and on a wider platform, the civilised world we all lived and felt comfortable in, before the aggressor had rights and the victim had bugger all.

There's a picture in the "Daily Express" of a young Afghan trying to get into this country by stowing under the chassis of a coach. It says in the caption that his hiding place was near to the engine, which could have proved fatal. If only it had, the outcome would have been far more pleasing.

Went to Wales last weekend with Peter, one half of Peter and Jacquie. Peter is one of the gang of six of us who take the layout to model railway exhibitions. Peter and I tend to share a room when attending as we both tend to snore, he worse than I, obviously! We decided to travel to Bridgnorth in Shropshire for a visit to the Severn Valley Railway on the Friday, before wending our way towards Caernarfon later in the day. Deciding to book an overnight stop rather than "take a chance" Maureen scanned the computer listings for accommodation in and around Caernarfon. One place popped up which looked hopeful. Country house, acres of land, close to the golf course, fishing facilities (neither of which we would partake in, but always nice to know it's there). A browse of the rooms looked good, until we delved deeper into the list of advantages of staying at this particular establishment. Among those boasted was the announcement that the premises were "gay friendly". The last thing I want – or Peter, come to that – is to be subjected to the sideways look, the questioning nod, the overt "did you sleep well....." I mean, Peter's not the type to go down to breakfast displaying a sign around his neck announcing "I am not his pet bitch". We scrolled on. So did P & J on their home computer. They found a B & B some four miles out of Caernarfon but without any mention of it being a Stonewall – Rainbow –

Tatchell Accredited Gay Friendly Establishment. It was, however, close enough for both of us to travel in the following morning and take the 10 am bound for the southern terminus at Hafod-y-Llyn. The following night we would find accommodation on the hoof – or to be precise, in the puma (Ford Puma, that is).

Peter picked me up at 6 am; we travelled to Bridgnorth via the M40 and M42 before bypassing Bromsgrove, which is probably the best way to see it! I don't know why, but whenever you are within smelling distance of the West Midlands the grass becomes less lush, less green. There's a sort of pallor that engulfs the provinces for mile after mile, reeking boredom, sleepiness and an innate desire to get into Shropshire asap. At least the Severn Valley Railway runs from somewhere to somewhere, that is Bridgnorth to Kidderminster via the interesting little town of Bewdley. Not that we alighted, but it looked interesting from the carriage window. We did alight at Highley, which is a beautiful example of a restored country station set in a picturesque hilly setting, giving no hint of its heavy industrial mining background.

There is a new museum close to the station, which is very interesting, sporting lovely views of trains arriving and departing from Highley Station. The down side is that someone who spends his or her life exhibiting at the Tate Modern must have designed the museum. Hideous, absolutely hideous. It wouldn't look out of place on Weymouth seafront as a cheap end of promenade afterthought. But as a museum, well..... The museum shop was full of children. I once again enquired of the staff if I was allowed to be within sight of them as I still haven't been CRB checked! I think the sale of a book was more important than the possibility of a paedophile within their midst. Probably not, in fairness, but it's always best to assume that profit comes first.

Late afternoon we travelled via Oswestry and Llangollen, up the A5 towards Caernarfon, where, having reached the outskirts of the county town, we headed for our overnight accommodation. Imagine our delight when we espied the premises displaying "Bistro" and "Sunday Lunches and Evening Dinners". Sadly we were to learn that the signs should both have been taken down the previous year, as the Bistro had become a bar (more like a last-chance saloon, actually). It all gave a whiff of desperation to the place, but never mind, the twin-bedded room (note, twin-bedded) was ample in size and very clean. Having unpacked, showered (separately, you understand!), changed and feeling refreshed, we made our way, by recommendation, to a hostelry situated on the road back towards Caernarfon. Two meals for £10 sounded very good value, and once partaken, the meals were definitely good value. The language of the day was Welsh, spoken by all, although amusingly and liberally peppered with the only English word they knew – "f-ing this and f-ing that". It did sound funny!

A reasonable night's sleep was had, Peter snored loudly through several of the night hours, during which I had four separate dreams. One concerned us both going to the closed Bistro-cum-breakfast room, only to find that the place had ceased trading whilst we had been asleep. It was not to be. At breakfast we found four rooms to be occupied, and after grunts of greeting were exchanged, all eight occupants settled down to what was a very good three-course breakfast. Luckily, black pudding was on the plate. Peter doesn't like black pudding so I had his.

We made our way to the Caernarfon railway terminus of the Welsh Highland Railway, which I had been to three years ago when Maureen and I spent a week in north Wales. The journey was slightly shorter back then. I looked forward to the extension of the spectacular scenery through which the railway travels. The station comprises what I think started off life as a Portakabin. If not, its similarity is striking. You walk to the platform, a platform that is devoid of all seating, lighting and flower tubs. It is merely a raised area alongside the track with a stone wall separating the railway from the pavement. It has all the friendliness of a Taliban held suburb – or Oldham, whichever is worse, the choice is yours. The only colour to be found in the area comes from the lager tins (note, lager) and wrappers, plus spent carrier bags which litter the track. I did enquire of the young lady behind the shop counter as I collected our pre-booked tickets, if someone could not have been despatched to collect the rubbish before punters arrive. Now bear in mind that the first train of the day does not depart until 10 am. She responded by saying that it had all been deposited overnight and that they didn't have the staff. She also commented that the station platform was devoid of furniture and tubs as "it would be all over the railway by the morning". She didn't seem overly enthused but did take time to express her hope that it "didn't spoil my journey".

Our seats were in the Pullman Observation Coach looking out of the rear window – the best seats on the train. Should be at £35 a throw! And that's with the OAP's discount! The journey was fantastic, the scenery likewise. Literally, just after take-off, a uniformed steward appeared and asked if our fellow passengers and we would like tea or coffee. Most of us did. He also asked if we'd like to buy a souvenir brochure at £3 a throw. Most of us didn't. The whole idea of paying the extra to be, well, first-class, is that you don't wish to sit with common people, or those who have just alighted from a Shearings or Wallace Arnold coach and whose average age is "dead" and smell of incontinence pads. For you know darned well that someone in the party will always leak! Never pleasant, especially for the cleaners. So how come that down the end of the same coach was a single woman and a child. Her clothing, her hair colour and general demeanour and shabbiness indicated council housing. Perhaps she is yet another recipient of the government's attempt to woo the unemployed, the benefit ridden scroungers, no doubt hoping they will vote for them once more by giving them days out at the taxpayers' expense. It could, of course, be that she and said sprog were going undercover for some BBC investigative programme to see how common people are treated when in the company of the upper class who had paid. I think my reactions would have been considered true to form. I tutted and dismissed where appropriate. You know, when the little git put his feet on the seat, and when the mother went into full, flat vowelled, Dudley-accented mode. The cleaning staff must really have had their work cut out with their dustpan and brush, sweeping up all the "h"s and "t"s she dropped throughout the journey. They both alighted at Beddgelert.

On the return journey, and some three hours after we had left Caernarfon, Peter and I plus two other couples behind us, decided that teatime had arrived once more. We had seen hide nor hair of any of the three stewards who appeared to be incumbent in the next coach. We all knew this, because at some stage during those three hours, we had passed them en route to the loo, situated at t'other end of the second coach. You would have thought that one of them might have attempted to sell us something else. But, no. The lady immediately behind us decided on our behalf, to walk through and ask. On her return, she commented that she was greeted by indifference and lethargy. It was with all the muster he could summon that one of the uniformed three came and took orders for tea at £1.30, I think, a cup – plus cakes all round. It does make you wonder if they actually want any business.

We travelled inland towards Bala for a ride on the Bala Lake Railway - £8 each and fairly uninspiring. Looking for accommodation in Bala was an insight into mid-Wales life. There were about five or six pub-cum-hotels and hotels in Bala. We tried three before settling on one that turned out to be fully booked. I say we tried three, we actually set foot inside the door, looking at the clientele and the Sky TV that took up three-quarters of a wall. We also listened to the language before beating a rather hasty retreat into the relative safety of the High Street. Youngsters kicked and headed a football in front of shops about to close for the evening, or closed for good in some cases. The B & B we stayed at was very clean and tidy and a very pleasant widow informed us that it was best not to leave the car in a side street as you "never know". Ah, for the confidence that brings! She very kindly rang the hotel (the one we couldn't book into and who had recommended this landlady) and they kindly agreed to our leaving Peter's car in their car park. We repaid that kindness by partaking of dinner in their hotel, which was okay. Loud and raucous company, but knife crime free! Outside, and before we made our way back to our side street accommodation, we strolled up and down the main road. High-pitched voices waxed unlyrically in the High Street. Young bucks congregated outside those establishments we had dismissed earlier – and weren't we right to! Lager drinkers to the man, they were. Meanwhile, outside the kebab-cum-chip shop, elderly men (the Tafia?) grouped, which is probably more acceptable than groped. I watched "Match of the Day" before attempting to sleep.

Peter's snoring surpassed all previous encounters. He is about to try some nasal spray recommended by his doctor. I hope it works, as the only other cure was a recommendation to have him put down which, to be fair, he wasn't enamoured about. Breakfast was excellent, sadly no black pudding, though two sausages each, which was nice. The day started misty, though warm.

We made our way to Llangollen for a trip on the Llangollen Railway. It is, for me, one of the best. If ever you wish to be transported in time to a world of Great Western chocolate and cream, passing through the solidity and cosiness of manned railway stations, with water cranes, signals and platform furniture, you have it all here. The journey through Berwyn towards the present terminus of Carrog is delightful. The railway plans to extend to the westerly terminus of Corwen, with longer term plans to link in the east with the BR station at Ruabon. Standing in a corridor looking out of the carriage door window, awaiting the lowering of the signal, the smell of steam and the bird song that permeates the air, the anticipation of travelling at a leisurely pace, and the dream of continuing to Morfa Mawddach and the coast brings back wonderful memories. Memories of trips to the Festiniog and Talyllyn Railways in the late fifties and sixties came flooding back.

In the late afternoon we arrived at another favourite of mine, the Welshpool and Llanfair Railway, where we trundled along the seven-odd miles, looking back down the track from the "comfort" of the last coach's veranda. It was a very pleasant weekend. In a couple of weeks' time the gang of five are off to Taunton for the Model Railway Exhibition – a boys' weekend away. Peter from Cornwall can't make the show.

We now have the Conservative Party Conference not to look forward to. I really do hope "Dave" doesn't do a Brown and have his missus on stage referring to her other half as "my hero". This is not America, Mrs. B. We do not have First Ladies. The first chink of respect I had for the Brown Lady went when I saw her camping it up at a Gay Pride rally. Why was she there, having her fizzog in the same photograph as the actor, Michael Cashman, and his very blonde other half, both standing with grins looking not uncannily like two very gay Cheshire cats? All three are dwarfed by two drag queens wearing oversized and outlandish blonde wigs. I don't know what sort of statement they are trying to make, other than just what twats they look. Still, at least Sarah B looked normal, but you have to question her decision-making. Norma Major never got involved in any of this "let's be at one with any minority and rights group" as I recall. She seemed, well, normal. In fact she put the Norma in normal! Still, Sarah B's only got a few months left as a PM's wife, as this time next year she will be demoted to that of an MP's wife – sad for her and hubby, but that's what happens when people forget to listen.

Getting back to the minorities, it makes you spit feathers when you read of a Metropolitan Police advert for "royalty protection at London palaces or Windsor." It informs us "applications are particularly welcomed from women, lesbians, gay, bi-sexual, trans-gender, black and minority ethnic communities/people as these are under-represented within the SO14". This post-code like description refers to Scotland Yard's Royalty Protection Branch. Who are these people who make up these adverts, and who gives them their brief? Do they not understand the bile that is produced when reading an advert like this if you are white, English and straight, and therefore feeling very much like a second-class citizen in your own country – which, of course, it isn't.

Three months have passed since an investigation took place as to whether Canterbury is "gay enough". Do you remember some pages back when the Gay Pride lobbyists were feeling slightly affronted (when aren't they?) by the city's attitude to them? Well, it's finally been established that the city has passed its "audit". The Local Government Ombudsman concluded that the council was not "duty-bound to promote gay culture". Neither should it be. Why do these people feel they have precedence over other, more normal activities enjoyed by the masses but lacking in funding? Christ knows how much this investigation cost but it's run into thousands of pounds – all funded by us, who no doubt could think of hundreds of more worthwhile causes than supporting those with such tunnel vision – and no, no jokes at this point, please!

On a more serious point, I remember reading of a guide produced by the BAAF (British Association for Adoption and Fostering). This quango is taxpayer funded. Some female called Nicola Hill, who used to write for "The Guardian" - say no more - wrote the guide! Entitled "A Pink Guide to Adoption for Lesbians and Gay Men" (says it all) it includes the phrase "Children need good parents much more than retarded homophobes need an excuse to whinge". What puerile, trite, pro-homo claptrap. When will Ms Hill - 'cos she's surely a Ms - understand that children need a mummy bear and a daddy bear. How many times do you have to tell these people?

Oh, no! Shock of shocks! Anton du Beke has committed the ultimate sin – well, the same as Prince Harry, actually. He's only gone and called his dancing partner a "Paki". The phrase seems to be all the rage in celebrity circles these days. Naturally, the nation is up in arms. There are calls for him to be sacked by those humourless scrotes who spend all their venomous lives finding fault. Everyone who is anyone within the media is distancing himself or herself from the poor sod. Vanessa Feltz in her column is pinning her colours to the mast by stating how unacceptable his comment was. I tuned in to Radio 5 on the way to Essex and found Victoria Derbyshire entertaining those with bugger-all better to do and who wanted to sound off in disgust. Nearly five hundred complaints have been made to the Beeb. What about the eight million "Strictly" fans who were ever so slightly more circumspect, worldly-wise and couldn't give a fig? No, there was no mention of them. I don't expect these whingers ever to attain a sense of humour but I really do hope that one day they get a sense of perspective.

Talking of humourless scrotes, it was with incredulity that I read of a 9-year-old lad forced to apologise to his friend (who happens to be Polish) in front of his class for making racist remarks. He apparently pointed a finger at his mate, pretending it was a gun, and said, "We've got to shoot the German army". For this, the lad was hauled before the deputy head and then taken in front of his classmates and forced to apologise. His mother commented that what infuriated her was that the head had carried out an official report on the lad which will stay on his record. Those in authority at Purford Green School in Harlow should also get a sense of perspective. Have they ever thought that their heavy-handed, overbearing tactics could easily backfire, where a quiet word may well have sufficed? Blowing things out of all racial proportion could actually have exactly the opposite effect and make, not just this lad, but anyone put in a similar position, become a genuine anti. And anyway, when it comes to world wars, we're still 2-0 ahead!

I see that the husband who was fed up with oiks throwing apples at him and his wife, and who failed to attract sufficient attention from the police, has had all charges against him dropped. So they should be. They should never have been brought by that skewed organisation, the CPS. He tries to make a citizen's arrest, fails and then ends up in trouble himself, while the police once again remain passively incompetent. Was that a chink of common sense being displayed in the court? If so, take their name and award them a government position.

Guildford Borough Council has delivered the dreaded wheelie bins. Apparently, they've trialled them in a couple of areas and everyone's delighted. Surprising, that, as everyone I have spoken to thinks it is a complete waste of time, money and added complication to what was a reasonable system. We now have two bins of differing sizes for differing rubbish, plus purple plastic sacks for something else. I can feel my temperature rising as I write this. If the council genuinely want to do something to save the planet, get together with other councils and tell government to do something about the country's population.

I have to pay a visit to that land inhabited by obese fag-hags pushing prams containing sprogs of differing hues and fatherhood – or Aldershot, as some people call it. That will now be twice in the same month – life's not fair, is it? If it were, Margaret Thatcher would have been born a fly and swatted at an early age, although not necessarily in Grantham. Have to visit Rymans once more as I'm getting through printer ink like it's going out of, well the cartridge, I suppose. So wish we luck. If I don't return, think only this of me, that there's some corner of a foreign field that is forever England - for further details, see Rupert Brooke and his Soldier poem.

The last time I visited Rymans the lady behind the counter cheerfully welcomed me with a "Good afternoon, may I help you?" "Aha", I replied, "I see English is spoken here". I say that, because the last time I walked back from the so-called shopping centre to my car, I failed to hear English spoken once. It was mainly Nepalese, with just a hint of Somali in the background. Very edifying! There's a café outside Wilkinsons store which never seems to have more than six people in it at one time. It must pay, obviously. I noticed the name earlier – it's called Café Prego. I don't know whether this is a chain or whether it's named in deference to the number of pregnant customers that it undoubtedly serves. After all, it is opposite "Mothercare".

Well, I didn't die. I did return. I did, however, get stuck behind a bus marked "Gold Line". A very smart bus it was too, in dark blue and registered on an O8 plate. It was travelling from the Aldershot area through to "Old Dean". The destination is two-thirds of the Old Dean Estate in Camberley, not somewhere you would go for your holiday. I can imagine being on that bus. I would be the only one not on benefit. No wonder it had smoked glass windows – very similar to a police transit van or Black Maria as we affectionately knew them. It should make the passengers feel at home. Having parked in Aldershot, I passed one of a number of derelict or empty shops. There was one that used to house a nursing agency. Their slogan, still radiating towards the High Street, reads, "Investors in Care". They surely meant "Investors in Profit"!

Right! Let's share a joke. Well, more tell one really:

A man walks into his bedroom with a sheep tucked under his arm. He announces, "This is the pig I sleep with when you have a headache or are too tired". His wife, with a withering glance, disdainfully replies, "I think you will find that that is a sheep!" The man, equally disdainfully comments, "I think you'll find I'm talking to the sheep!"

CHAPTER EIGHT

Liberate Freedom of Speech!

Well, what a to-do over the BBC's invitation to Nick Griffin, leader of the BNP, to a seat on "Question Time". I didn't watch the programme. I never watch the programme, actually. I preferred the original concept where audiences and their questions were chosen in order to stimulate debate. They now seem to be clinically chosen so as not to rock any politically correct view. David Dimbleby I find to be extremely ill mannered, his hand pointing with invitation to "that woman at the back", "that man over there in the green top", it's never "that lady" or "that gent". Once more I digress. It was never a surprise that demonstrations would take place all day outside and for some, inside Broadcasting House. It makes you laugh to think that these protesters liken themselves to guardians of free speech and democracy, though they only appear to be guarding anyone who holds the same views as they do. Why not let the BNP leader either surprise everyone with a well-conceived argument, or merely fall flat on his face with one that is ill-conceived.

I've always worked on the basis that if one is confident of one's own view or argument, one has nothing to fear from an opposite view or opinion. Those protesters made the same mistake as MPs. They take the electorate for fools. We can actually make up our own minds listening to a reasoned debate. What got me so hot under my size 16 collar were the comments from that former colonial yob, Peter Hain. How dare he attempt to coerce the BBC into changing its mind about the BNP leader's invitation. Who the hell does he think he is? He ought to be grateful for British tolerance. Does he forget so easily the time he was digging up our cricket pitches for his own causes (and probably his own publicity)? He is an import. The fact that he has got so far in politics in a foreign country is testimony to that same British tolerance. I would have deported him on the grounds that his excavating activities were not commensurate with cricket (or their grounds) and should therefore be sent packing. Any appeal against this sentence would have resulted in the death penalty. He wouldn't dig another hole would he? Arse!

Does Hain not understand that whatever he thinks of the BNP, people voted for them in a democratically run election process, nationally and in Europe – about the only democratic process in Europe and for how long I wonder..... Good to see that Mark Thompson stood his ground and refused to be bullied by the odious Hain, who, if I remember correctly, forgot to declare some earnings last year – pre the MP's expenses scandal. Hain has just been elevated from arse to bastard!

Interesting was the aftermath in the media to the BNP appearance. The audience was described as very anti – no surprise there, though a poll apparently showed a more mixed reaction. Teletext had one short comment from a member of the audience who was very much against BNP policies, but then the lady concerned did have an Asian name, so no surprise there 2, the sequel!

The "Daily Express" who, along with the "Daily Mail", tends to crusade and air the views of those with the least clout – middle England – really got its collective coloured knickers in a twist. Friday's front page showed a full photograph of Nick Griffin with the headline, "A disgrace to humanity". Alongside his fizzog were the words, "Boos as bigot faces fury on TV". On pages 4 and 5 were photographic scenes of the demos outside the studios. The pages' headlines described him as "disgusting, poisonous..... a thoughtless bigot". And all the time I thought the "Daily Express" was against mass immigration. Ah, well, a story is a story.

It's the Saturday after the Thursday night's "Question Time". Ceefax has letters from viewers who saw the edition. Some robustly felt Mr. Griffin was poor in his performance, but more than one commented that, as usual, David Dimbleby never let him answer a question and that's the other thing about Dimbleby's anchor-man qualities. He doesn't have any!

I see that half the drivers in our cities are not insured. That would be five years in prison if it were down to me. Ooops! I forgot. We don't have the room. The police response, however, is as predictable and lame as always. South Yorkshire Police Farce is threatening to have motorists' insurance policies made invalid if they leave anything on display when their cars are parked. So once again, the onus is on the law-abiding citizen to make our cars like our homes – a clinical fortress. The police will spend their time recording the number plates of offending vehicles and reporting same to the insurers via the DVLA's database. So they're not catching any crooks, only penalising the law-abiding public. This creeping surveillance culture is sickening and it doesn't reduce the number of ne'er-do-wells, opportunists or serial thieves, though it probably hits a target somewhere. So where are all the CCTVs in all this, if they are so helpful in detecting crime? Long gone are the days when you left your front door open. Long gone is the key on a piece of string hanging from within that door. I recently drove through Tilbury in Essex just after 6 pm. It was like driving through Shutter Town. Every shop was locked, bolted and shuttered. Is this not indicative of our society? We're not getting to the root of crime, be it at school, through parenting or the fear of capture. Reoffending is all too prevalent because the penalty never fits the crime.

It was interesting to read that in one episode of that foul-mouthed Gordon Ramsay show, "Kitchen Nightmares USA" he used the F word no less than sixty-three times. I am surprised the Americans put up with that. What an awful export Ramsay is to the Americans. Even I feel like saying that I'm sorry to them, and it's rarely that I give a fig for American opinion. Do these TV companies think it's cool or big? Does that arse Ramsay think himself macho, or possibly more important if he swears continuously? In his case it comes over as the frustrated expletives of a bully. Not the sort of person I'd invite for dinner – even if he cooked it himself!

"The Day Di and Dodi Died" is back in the news. The French are again being accused of withholding vital information. Didn't they do that in the war by not mentioning that Hitler was marching through some region laying waste to acres of grapes? I expect we had to find that out by ourselves, by virtue of a holidaymaker from Tonbridge stopping off for a picnic with his family alongside their Morris 8 close to some French village, when goose-stepping drowned out their happy chat. The first the British authorities realise there's a hitch in international relations is when a telegram arrives at the War Office which commences, "I thought you'd like to know....." and ends with, "Hope the above is of use. Weather is wonderful, wish you were here. Teddy Caldicott, France. PS returning Blighty via Dover Tuesday - Hun willing, byeee".

Meanwhile, back in the present, Mohamed Al Fayed still maintains that his son and Di were killed by the Secret Services. It is intriguing and will continue to be so. I have always considered the strong possibility that she was pregnant by would-be daddy Dodi. It never ceases to bring a smile to my face, thinking of the British monarchy and establishment being told, and then coming to terms with a "royal" carrying a Muslim baby. I can see the headlines now. "Sharia law coming to this country soon, due to a right royal cock-up". Oh, what a hoot! I'll tell you what, though, judging by the photos in today's papers, Di never seems to age.....

I remember the story (and you won't forget it either) of the woman pregnant with triplets who was walking down the road as a masked robber ran out of a bank. He opened fire on all and sundry and shot her three times in the stomach. Fortunately, all three babies survived. The surgeon decided to leave the bullets in because it was too risky to operate. She later gave birth to two very healthy daughters and a very healthy son. All was fine for sixteen years, then one day one of the daughters walked into the kitchen in tears. "What's wrong?" asked the mother. The girl dried her eyes. "I was just taking a tinkle and this bullet came out. Her mother comforted her and told her it was okay and explained what had happened outside the bank sixteen years ago. About a week later, the second daughter walked into the kitchen in tears. "Mum, I was taking a tinkle and this bullet came out....." Again, their mother told her not to worry and explained what had happened sixteen years previously. A week later her son walked into the kitchen in tears. Before he could say anything, his mum said, "It's okay, I know what happened. You were taking a tinkle and a bullet came out". "No", said the boy, "I was playing with myself and I've just shot the dog".

Don't tell me you didn't smile!

"Who'd be a teacher" is a question which springs to mind when reading a story about one of the "old school" variety. Thirty one years in his profession, Michael Becker, is faced with a disruptive thirteen-year-old who, despite four requests, refuses to stop telling a joke in class. Mr. Becker hauls the lad from the class, down a corridor and into a storeroom. Can anyone tell me what is wrong with the story so far? In my day I'd have been sent outside after the first warning. There wouldn't have been a second, I would have got the cane. And where would my parents have been on this subject? Right behind the teacher, but that was then, and this is now. This thirteen-year-old's parents predictably cite that old standby "special needs", which seems like the panacea for all compensation and then complains to the police. The upshot is that Mr. Becker, who is now suspended, looks like losing his job. Not only that, but in court he was fined £1,500 (when a hoodie gets a caution for assault), is ordered to pay £1,875 costs, plus the government tax of £15, which comes under the heading of "Victim Surcharge". I'm surprised VAT isn't added to that. Wait until the next Budget.....

After thirty one years of dedication Mr. Becker's career is probably over. He then had to listen to the presiding judge state, "By a serious error of judgement, you have already brought upon yourself greater punishment than anything this court can impose". He also said that Mr. Becker came "perilously close to deserving custody". What about the special needs oik deserving what he got? Naturally, the parents have milked every tear of angst out of some document called the "Victim Impact Statement". I've never seen one, but you know it's just the sort of document that parents like these would be creaming over. All the attention, all the fuss. The boy's mother stated, "My son has been having nightmares for weeks and they have consisted of Michael Becker chasing him, or re-living the incident. He has had medication to help him

174

switch off. It has caused a great deal of stress in our family". Talk about over-egging it. The only good thing – and it really is a good thing – to come out of this case, is that the parents were refused compensation. Thank Christ for that! I mean, call me a cynic, but does one not think that behind all the grief, the anger, the humiliation and the paperwork, that the lure of ill-gotten gain was not highly prominent in the original complaint to the police?

Is it not indicative of our society that because we do not back our teachers on discipline we now have a situation where community cop-outs are escorting pupils home? Police "assistants" – similar to teaching assistants but armed with sub-machine guns, sorry, walkie-talkies – are travelling on buses and guarding "anti-social hot spots" due to an increase in knife crime and general assaults. Sixty-five local authorities have used these patrols over the last year covering both primary and secondary schools – what the hell are some people breeding? The problem is that we've allowed those who should have been sterilised to breed the most.

Which brings us neatly to a misguided police inspector called Andy Lewis, who feels that it would be a nice touch to take youngsters fishing in the Berkshire countryside in an attempt to keep them out of crime. What has Berkshire ever done to deserve this? I mean, it already has Reading – isn't that enough! Anyway, the youngsters are apparently vulnerable because they live in urban areas, in this case, Lewisham. Gangs there are prevalent and obviously three days of fishing could change all this. Not surprisingly the youths in question are Somalis. Inspector Lewis is about to repeat this little farce with a group of Afghans. The article concludes by stating that local white lads may go as well. An afterthought by the paper, or the policeman? Not surprisingly, these ethnic incomers have been caught by the namby-pamby-do-gooder social conscience hook, line and sinker. Well, it's their plaice now. There will soon not be a foreign sole left this side of Dover..... Sorry about that, you have borrowed this book from the library haven't you? You can't have paid for it, surely – oh, it's a birthday present. So who is it that doesn't like you?

There was a picture of a young girl heading an article concerning young drinkers and the havoc they are causing to both themselves and society, not to mention the bill to the NHS. This photo showed a female in short, black dress, knees together, lower legs apart, with pants straddling her ankles. She looked a real state, standing in the high street. Where is the dignity with these young women, one wonders? The questions were answered the following day, when it was revealed that the lady concerned was one Sarah Lyons, aged 20, who is a teaching assistant – which brings a smile. The full inane grin is complete when you learn that she resides in Cardiff. Apparently, when asked, friends said the knickers weren't hers, but a "joke" pair that was being handed – or legged – between the group of girls. Presumably an old Welsh custom, similar to holding aloft a giant leek and exclaiming, "Oggi, oggi, oggi". Oh, what fun the Welsh have! And whatever happened to Max Boyce?

What is this love affair with cyclists? I'm still in favour of mandatory abortion for any woman whose amniocentesis result looks as if she will give birth to any lycra-clad arsehole. They are very often the most arrogant of arseholes. Along the canal, either side of the bridge under Heath Vale Bridge Road, there is a sign, which states "Cyclists dismount". Do they ever? Do they buggery! I would just love to see two coming face-to-face and ending up (or down) in the canal. Now that would be a moment worth savouring. There always seems to be money available for cycle path development. Sustrans (Sustainable Transport) never seem to be at risk of recession or cutbacks. Paint for cycle paths is always available. We now have the ludicrous situation whereby cyclists can legally ignore one-way street signs. It seems that as they don't pay any tax or contribute anything towards the roads upon which they cycle, they still get all the perks not afforded to those who do pay, like not having to wait at red lights, cycling without lights and fear of subsequent fine, cycling on a pavement, wearing headphones, and being arrogantly unaware of passing traffic. However, should it not pass, due to the cyclists being at fault, the fault still seems to lie with the motorist. It would appear that the motorist is guilty until being proven innocent. I never realised until writing this just how similar a motorist's position is to that of an unaccompanied male in the presence of children.....

Whilst at school, during maths lessons , I never understood algebra. $X + Y + Z = ?$ It equalled bugger-all in my maths book. If only they had been able to explain the principle in language I understood – though more likely a language I don't understand, e.g. ethnic + religion + grievance = compensation. Here we have the case of a Sikh police officer, one Gurmeal Singh. His religion is patently more important to him than the conventions, traditions and working conditions of his adopted country. It has always riled me in that due to one of those pathetic little cults, Sikh followers are allowed to wear turbans rather than conform to the dress code or uniform of the profession they have freely undertaken to join. What they wear on their head outside of their workplace is neither here nor there, but at work they should remember that when in Rome, or in this case, when in Manchester, etc. etc. Mr. Singh was told to remove his turban and replace it with a helmet if he was going about his police business on cycling duty. Unhappy with this suggestion he was advised to wrap a turban around his helmet. He then felt affronted, about as affronted as the till bell of compensation could muster, and complained. He stated that he felt like Rodney Trotter in that classic "Only Fools...." episode, where Del Boy tried to sell 200 "crash turbans" to Sikhs in Peckham. That episode would probably no longer pass the zealous PC broadcasting panel. But never mind, Mr. Singh is "offended and humiliated". Well, he would be! They're all good ingredients when claiming compensation, as he did, £200,000 he asked for.

One aspect of Mr. Singh's complaint centred on the fact that he was "coerced" into walking through a petrol fire exercise, despite having informed his trainers that the substance used to keep down his beard was highly inflammable. I would have told him to shave it off or sod off. Apparently, it is considered a serious breach of the Sikh code of practice if the hair of the face or head is cut, or singed. I felt that if this was the case, he could always rename himself Mr. Singe! Naturally, as in the grand scheme of all compensation cases, the PC has been off work for three months due to sickness, but was well enough to appear at the tribunal. Once again, unsurprisingly, they found in favour of Mr. Singh, stating that he had fallen victim to an "offensive violation of dignity" and promptly awarded him £10,000 plus £710 interest for indirect racial discrimination and harassment, plus another £1,914.15 for loss of earnings.

This waste of taxpayers' money, which has done nothing for the greater good and everything for the dislike of minorities who come here and change rules that we abide by, has cost £200,000 in legal fees. Oh, and by the way, this PC also refuses to wear his police badge on his turban on religious grounds. But that's okay. I would have deported him on the grounds that he was "taking the mickey out of us on a grand scale and we are not having it any more!" What? You don't think that's a good legal defence? Well, it would be in my statute book – one that I'd have thrown at him the second he complained.

On a serious note, though, this type of isolationist action does have repercussions because, I tell you now, if I was stopped in the street, or in my car by a Sikh policeman, I would refuse to answer any questions on the grounds that he was improperly dressed.

We've given up on Sainsburys in Farnham. The never knowing whether there will be ham and egg pie is just too problematic to contemplate. We have started going to Morrisons, in Fleet. I know, I know, Morrisons. But I have to say, I think Sainsbury's layout is staid and extremely predictable. Morrisons have "market stalls" laid out in aisles, smaller portions individually wrapped and staff who are not up their own backsides. At Sainsbury's I have never seen so many female assistants strutting about – it's always those with headphones. They have the look of someone who has just been promoted to chief flight attendant. The general class of customer at Morrisons is very similar, but then, this branch has been built within the confines of one of the most expensive estates in Europe and offers magnificent views of the "Charles Church" development area. The blot on the checkout was the female customer in front of us, who spoke on her mobile phone all the way through packing, paying and exiting. I told the very pleasant lady cashier that there should be a sign stating, "Please do not make or receive phone calls whilst using the checkouts". I cannot stand bad manners, as you know. Well, you know what I'm like, always standing up on a bus – well, I would if I travelled by bus, obviously. Always walking on the outside of a pavement when a lady approaches. Again, I would do, if I walked anywhere there were large crowds, like a town centre, which I don't. But the point is that the thought is there.

On our return journey from Fleet we had to stop for roadworks, which are at the end of a bridge over the Basingstoke Canal. The bridge is typical of today's architecture, cheap metal sections, bland, unpainted though functional. We later passed over a beautiful Victorian bridge spanning the same canal but built of cast iron – ornate, green and cream in colour and so much more in keeping with its former, pastoral surroundings and just as functional. Why do we always have to use the benchmark of mediocre as standard?

Well, "Strictly" is flourishing, Joe Calzaghe went last week and this week it was Jo Wood's turn. My mum thought it should be "that blonde man, as he was awful". Having dissected all of the celebrity contestants we came to the conclusion that it was one of the professionals she wasn't impressed with. Ah, the joys of ageing.

I was not impressed with pictures in the "Daily Express" of Brendan Cole using a catapult in order to kill a chicken. He was on an antipodean travel programme learning to "hunt" like local native tribes. God how brave he must feel. I am sorry for Jo Wood as I liked her, but I am glad her partner is off – bastard!

Ben and I have just returned from our morning sortie along the canal. The cygnets are fast becoming quite flecked, white is showing through most prominently when the under side of their wings are displayed. It's the end of October and they say the country is in for an Indian summer, as it is in the mid-sixties this week. No surprise, really, as I am certain we have enough Indians in this country to make it so.

I see that the latest appeal by Gary McKinnon in his attempt not to be extradited to the US has failed. I think his mother has put it as succinctly as possible. She said, "No other country in this world would so readily offer its citizens to the US as sacrificial lambs merely to safeguard a 'special political relationship'". They are now to appeal to the European Court of Human Rights – I wish them well. How complex is world politics? We send back the Lockerbie terrorist to Libya, which hacks off the Americans – and rightly so – but then, presumably, a trade and oil deal would be deemed rich enough to ensure America's wrath – although not enough to damage the "special relationship". But we can always make it up with Mr. McKinnon's extradition.

I note that Premier League teams have reported swine flu amongst football players and that spitting on the pitch is considered a health hazard and a contributory factor in this matter. I've always considered it to be damn bad manners. Interestingly, the two teams concerned are Blackburn and Bolton Wanderers. Now, I'm not suggesting that spitting is confined to the north-west, as it happens frequently, I've noted, in north east Hampshire – Aldershot, Farnborough and Cove – although I've witnessed very little across our Surrey border in Guildford or Farnham. A few miles in distance, but a world away in society.

"PC meets DVLA" is today's April fool story in October. The DVLA were to sell two number plates at auction, but decided to withdraw them. The numbers are F4GOT and D1KES. Apparently they could upset homosexuals and lesbians. Stonewall, the stony face of all those batting for the other side, remarked, "It is regrettable that personalised number plates that could easily cause offence were made available". The only offence caused is to those with much smaller brains than their penises and breasts. You really do have to take issue with these humourless prolls. (Tried spell check on this, but it didn't come up with one or two "l"s so left it as I felt it should be spelt). If, of course you are aware of the correct spelling, please send answers on a postcard to someone who gives a toss! While we are on the subject of homosexuals, I see that Matt

Lucas's former "husband" has killed himself. There's a picture of them on their "wedding day". Please don't make me laugh! Wedding day! Anyway, Mr. Lucas is said to be "utterly destroyed" by the news and has had to leave the West End play he is currently acting in, or rather was acting in and will not be returning. I always thought that actors worked on the basis that the "show must go on".

Margaret Thatcher has a lot to answer for. I've said previously that history will look back on her regime and influence as being the greatest contributor to the corporate greed in this country. Her "free market" policies and the dissolution of this country's sovereignty through her signing of the Maastricht Treaty and the wholesale privatisation of our utilities, transport and education have brought this country to its knees. Whoever thought that Britain would be so totally lost in a sea of Europeanism? Mirroring health and safety, the EU is a cancer permeating its way through the veins of all that is decent and logical and replacing it with legislation and interference that was never required nor requested; it appears to sate the ego and justify the jobs of those in a distant land with motives far removed from the population they purport to serve. Is what we have in Europe really what we thought we were signing up to? I've no doubt that the corruption, expenses, fraud and jollies at our expense are on a scale that would make the present MPs' debacle seem like a lost receipt for a train journey. Europe is an even more closed shop than Westminster, which is now sadly reduced to the role of local government. Did anyone who voted to join the EU ever consider that in today's paper one reads that our retail rights regarding full refunds in shops is now to be challenged? Once again, we have to fall in line with other countries and we apparently have no legal redress as the proposals are given the okay by a majority of nations. I understand plans are afoot for a European income tax. No-one foresaw this, surely.

This comes hot on the heels of announcements that EU bureaucrats are seeking the right to be allowed access to UK citizens' bank accounts. Who and where are the people who are supposed to protect us from this invasion of our privacy? That there is to be a European president, be it that British traitor

Tony Blair, or any of his foreign chums, it matters not. The fact is, it's another nail in the independence of all sovereign states. An EU foreign minister is another unwarranted post to be filled. All this does is to feed the egos of those in national government not satisfied with their powerful lot, or so ambitious that only a post of similar standing to the US presidency will suffice. Do the populace of other countries suffocating within the strictures of EU legislation not realise that their nationality is suffering? Is it just we Brits? Surely not! Food is labelled as produced in the EU. Why do we not demand stronger labelling for our goods, why is there no greater support from our industries and government? Are they all colluding in the destruction of everything we felt solid, honest and not with a little national pride?

The common agricultural policy has, for years, favoured the French, Germans and Italians, so why do successive British governments still accept this situation? Probably because Britain is a nation of acceptors. I remember earlier this year, when there was an EU plan to label doughnuts, crisps and sausages as being "good for you". I suspect the main problem is that everything that comes under the EU umbrella is so totally unaccountable. Its freedom to distribute money to all and sundry is extremely worrying. I note that £1.4 million has gone towards a religious programme to "define God" at Oxford University. A London carnival must be very grateful for the £137,000 it received from an EU grant. Why? There's one very suspicious amount to The Centerprise Trust in London who are part of a consortium given £136,000 to celebrate people of African descent! Why? Here's a very devious way of promoting the EU – officials have been distributing pencils, computer mouse mats, clocks, key fobs, etc. at a cost of £68,000 when visiting schools in this country. Another brainwashing exercise for the young and vulnerable. EU officials seeking "media training" have been handed £460,000. Our Euro contribution is to rise from £4.1 billion to £6.4 billion next year. And for what? It appears to me that it's for Euro-arses to waste ever more on farcical and politically motivated causes. It's like a juggernaut, which is out of control. If it's not financial, it's idealistic – and that's worrying.

In conclusion, it says everything about the "democratic process" of the EU, when Denmark and Ireland, who did not conform with their free vote to the decision required, were later forced to have a second election. Interesting how much money was then spent in making sure they got the correct result. How can this be right, how can any organisation get away with a second vote, just because the first one didn't satisfy those in power? I suppose in the not too distant future, we will be remembering the days when we had a vote, as I have no doubt that option will be deleted from future legislation.

Well, yesterday was Hallowe'en, which heralds the start of two months' worth of fireworks. We had to give Ben two tablets to calm him down as the pyrotechnic display commenced sharply at 6.30 pm and continued through to near midnight. Chewy bones, marrowbones, choc-drops, all failed to quell Ben's nervousness and his tummy. The tranquilliser tablet, or two, made little impression either. It was a complete nightmare during "Strictly", trying to come to terms with those in the dance off, whilst attempting to get Ben off the settee with a "bugger off!" It was no laughing matter. I returned from the brewery, having taken three tours during the day, shortly before 5.30 pm. Just as I drove into our lane I espied adults walking alongside children dressed in Hallowe'en garb and about to cross the lane and enter our gate. I assumed the adults were parents and not paedophiles in the act of grooming. But who knows. Perhaps I should have asked if they had all been CRB checked. As I alighted from my car they started to walk towards me in hope and anticipation of a treat. "We're not into that tawdry Americanism", I exclaimed. My words were received and understood as "sod off you little bastards", which I am glad to say they all did!

I read with some amusement, as one does, that that odious cult, the Catholic Church, or more precisely, its head office in Rome, has criticised Hallowe'en as "anti-Christ and dangerous". That's rich coming from a belief steeped in pain, sexual abuse, hypocrisy and rosaries. Some so-called expert, whose name I cannot be bothered to remember, said, "Hallowe'en has an undercurrent of occultism and is absolutely anti-Christian". If they complained on the grounds that it's another chunk of American cheapery, which lines the pockets of retailers, I might agree with the lost souls for once.

Do you remember..... What? It's no good you shaking your head before I tell you. Right! Once again, do you remember earlier in the book I mentioned that East Sussex Police "Farce" was spending £10,000 on head massages for its staff who were under stress? You do. Good! Well, they don't learn, do they? They've just hired a fashion expert in an effort to increase female police officers' confidence. Surely a higher arrest rate would achieve the same level of confidence. Serving officers and other female employees will benefit (apparently) from "style makeovers". They will be offered tips on dressing in certain ways to improve self-esteem. There will be advice on "well-being, good health, confidence and personal development". All this is free of charge to the individual but at a cost of thousands of pounds to the taxpayer. This airy-fairy waste of funds is the brainchild of Supt. Jane Rhodes who says it is a "cost effective means of effectively training, retaining, informing, supporting and developing our staff". Well, she seems to have covered all aspects of justification with that little lot. It was, however, convenient not to mention that Sussex police are 250 front-line officers short in number, although I suspect this scheme will help no end.

I see that PC Malcolm Searles, now ex-PC Malcolm Searles, he being the young buck who killed a 61-year-old lady in Bromley whilst driving a police car at high speed, has been given 6 _ years imprisonment. No doubt, he'll probably be out in just over three. He'd have been given life if I had my way. He arrogantly abused his position by using a police car to drive at high speed with lights flashing and sirens wailing, and all to deliver a birthday card to his sister is not what you expect from a serving police officer, but sadly, our police are just not what they used to be. The only good news is that he is no longer a self-serving officer.

The worrying trend of corporate distaste for having your own views on any matter shows no signs of abating. I see that a lady, aged 67, posted a letter to her local council in Norfolk complaining that a local homosexual and lesbian march to be held was, in her opinion, "offensive to God". Now whatever one may think about her silliness with reference to a god, surely she is entitled to her view or beliefs. The council, on receiving her letter, appears to have then contacted the police, for it was their joint conclusion that her letter amounted to – wait for it – a "hate incident". Police officers were then despatched to her house to question her. Mrs. Howe, the lady concerned, has never been in trouble in her life. She is, in short, a law-abiding citizen. Not one, but two PCs interviewed her about the offending letter. As she said, "This sort of treatment makes us scared to speak out." It's not just you, Mrs. Howe, it's all the law-abiding folk of this ex-good country. To be fair to Stonewall, even they described the police reaction as "disproportionate". Norfolk Constabulary described it as a "routine check up". But then they would, wouldn't they.

Oh, how the police shoot themselves in the foot when it could so easily be a hoodie or an immigrant. New guidelines have been issued by Warwickshire police, which include the following.

"Do not assume these words for the time of day – such as "afternoon" or "evening" have the same meaning". The spoke (once again there is no name to identify the arse) said, "Terms such as 'afternoon' and 'evening' are somewhat subjective in meaning and can vary according to a person's culture or nationality". Ah, now the penny (soon no doubt to be replaced by the cent) has dropped. It's all about the others, incomers, foreigners. The spoke continues, "In many cultures, the term 'evening' is linked to the time of day when people have their main meal of the day. The point is, there is an element of subjectivity leading to a variation between cultures that we need to be aware of – taking steps as far as possible to ensure our communication is effective in serving the public". What absolute twaddle! This 53-page guide also dissuades one from the use of the term "boy" or "girl" as this may cause offence. To whom? The phrase "young people" should be used instead. Firefighters, not firemen, should be used. To my mind, they will always be firemen and if they are women, I think fireladies would be rather nice.

If I were in Warwickshire police force, I'd say, "Bugger the lot of them". Once again, you can never find out who wrote this rubbish, or more importantly, who instructed them to. The only certainty is that it's the faceless, unaudited, unaccountable, unelected committee of humourless, wasteful bastards who have been involved from page 1 to page 53. There, that feels better!

Still waters run deep, they say. Well, that's only half true if referring to the canal, they are still but not that deep. This morning's walk with Mutley took on a distinctly autumnal feel. The leaves are a beautiful golden hue, many underfoot. The coots scoot and the ducks swim as you approach with bread in hand. Sadly, Ben still hasn't understood the basic premise that I take him for a walk. It's now ten months since we collected him from the RSPCA and all who meet him comment that he is a very friendly dog with character. That's with the exception of Peter – you know, of Peter and Jacquie fame – who was nipped by Ben and now precedes every attempt to stroke him with the words, "You're not going to bite me, are you?" He was stroking the dog under the chin. Ben appeared to be lapping it up, when suddenly he yelped (that's Ben, not Peter) and took a nip out of Peter's digit. I've no idea what he did; perhaps he touched a raw nerve, so to speak. He's been all right since (that's Peter, not Ben) but he did roll over immediately and lick the bitten finger (that's Ben, not Peter, although maybe Peter did when he got home!) I never rang to check.....

We had a problem last week with wasps. They'd been nesting all summer above the porch. We could see them getting in by the guttering. They weren't causing a nuisance so we just left them to it. Last week, however, the inside of the porch was awash with them. There were probably more wasps between the inner and outer doors than there were would-be incomers at Sangette in its heyday. We called in a pest control company. The man appeared at the appointed time. We exchanged pleasantries and he opened the back of his van. Small talk on my part was met with, "oh, aye, aha, mmm, maybe" for he was a man of few words. He donned protective gear, pumped up something at the end of a wandering lead and proceeded to "dust", as he put it, the affected areas, both above the guttering and inside the porch where the little fellows could be seen loitering without intent. After a short period of time he knocked on the door for payment. Fifty-seven pounds fifty, including VAT. "You shouldn't get any more trouble after the weekend" (it was Friday). He pointed to the areas of dusting and then pointed outwards and upwards. There were more wasps. "It's the foragers returning", he added. "Once they put their noses to the dust, that's it". "What, they fly off, do they?" I enquired. "No, they're gonners – can't breathe. Weather would have killed them off, in time, but who can say....." "Pretty deadly stuff, this dust", I commented, seeking assurance that our visitors really wouldn't be seen for that much longer. "Oh, yes, as I say, after the weekend that'll be it". "Does it work on illegals?" I enquired. "Oh, that it did", he said, without the trace of a smile before bidding me good day.

"The Restaurant" returned for its new run this week, and what a joy it promised to be. However, at the end of the first episode I was completely taken aback by the ineptitude of most of the participants. If this is the cream of the one thousand hopefuls who I understand enter each year, gawd knows what the rest were like! The couple that impressed me the least was one of those retained, a husband and wife from London who sell flowers. They had to make a starter and decided on gravlax with trimmings. After the disappointment of not finding gravlax in Asda (surely they weren't surprised?) they plumped for a packet of smoked salmon, and not the best quality either. Gravlax in Asda? It's two syllables! Most of the shoppers wouldn't know of its existence, let alone that it swims about.

What a nasty piece of work that footballer Marlon King must be. Jailed for assaulting a young lady who rebuffed his advances, it appears he has had thirteen convictions for various offences. Wigan Football Club has rightly sacked him. What I find disappointing is that Gordon Taylor, Chairman of the Professional Footballers Association, has stated that they will support him. Why? How can, and why should, any organisation give support to someone who appears never to have learned from his many mistakes. This so-called professional, who was on £35,000 a week, punched a 20-year-old girl in the face, having rejected him in a nightclub. He is married with three children, by the way. He apparently said to her, after being turned down, "I'm a multi-millionaire, you are not in my league". What an interesting little chat up line. How pathetic to have him bring up money in an effort to make someone interested. Included in his thirteen previous convictions are two for assaulting women. I also wasn't aware that he'd served a previous custodial sentence for receiving a stolen car. So once again, could someone please tell me why such an arrogant, aggressive cove such as this should be supported by anyone, let alone the hand that has fed him somewhat royally in the past?

It is instances like this, coupled with the vitriolic abuse of referees by both players and managers, combined with the money paid by sponsors and paid out by clubs, that every year reduces my interest in football. I take an interest in the results of all divisions on a Saturday and I sometimes watch "Match of the Day", although not regularly. It was always the highlight of Saturday night television, "MOTD", a pint of beer and a pork pie! Now it's "Strictly" followed by a game of scrabble and hot chocolate. Mind you, the last few weeks' football results have been very worthwhile watching, not just because Charlton are second but because Liverpool have made losing almost a habit. I just hope it's one they can't break.

Getting back to "Strictly" for a mo, I see Alesha Dixon is whinging that it is young people who are discriminated against in TV. It has nothing to do with age, dearie, it has everything to do with the general lack of professionalism, experience and that which is so prevalent in the young, bad diction. And that Ms Dixon is why you grate on me every Saturday night.

I would have been spitting feathers if only I had remembered to pack some, along with the sandwiches and a drink on my way to a talk. The news came on the radio, and it was announced that,

"A British Muslim woman....." I shouted at the radio, "You can't be a bloody Muslim and British, it just doesn't work. I can't be a white Pakistani". I listened with teeth gritted as it was explained that this 41-year-old had entered this country wearing burkha, within which was concealed a computer memory stick. Within this stick were 7,000 documents, some containing plans for making bombs. She was given two years' imprisonment, which was reduced in actual time to bugger all as she had spent so long on remand. This divorced mother of six came to this country – which is why she can never be British – from Holland. The reason she left was because of the intolerance to her wearing the burkha, which is a bit of an irony. What a pity we didn't show that same intolerance. Her home, when searched, contained letters showing that she had volunteered herself and her children as suicide bombers. And she gets two years? The newspaper article I read gave no clue as to whether she was going back "home" to Manchester, where she lived with her offspring. And if she does and carries on a normal, peaceful life in our country, a country that she chose to adopt as her home, is she going to work and adopt the laws of this country as being reasonable, or are we, as I suspect, going to continue supporting those that "could have been and still could be suicide bombing children". What is wrong with this country? When will we wake up? Oh, and don't worry, whilst my teeth were gritted and my hands with knuckles white on the steering wheel, I sucked on a pair of Tic-Tacs, one orange, one green, and arrived at my destination the personification of peace and tranquillity – what an actor!

Every day is 1st April; it's like Groundhog Day. A Mr. Morris, aged 42, who hails from Bristol, rides a Suzuki motorcycle. Every day, on arrival home from work, he dismounts and pushes his bike over the kerb and across the pavement to his home. He's done this for nine years. He has now been told by that bastion of authority and public security, the police, or to be more precise Avon & Somerset Police, that he is committing an illegal act. Inspector Salmon stated, "No-one should push a motor vehicle on a footpath. If a person wants access to their property they must get planning permission for a driveway and a dropped kerb". They apparently expect him to carry his 400 lb motorcycle. Surely that's against local health and safety laws? The mentality is mind-boggling. He maybe Inspector Salmon, but he will always be PC Plankton to me.

Right! Time for a joke:

A loner walks into his local pub and says to the landlord, "'Ere, you know where I live, alongside the railway line, well, I was walking back home last night when I saw this young girl tied to the railway track. I untied her and took her back to my place. We had sex all night long, every position, in every room. She was on top, I was on top, it was amazing". The landlord seemed impressed. "Phew, weren't you the lucky one! Was she pretty?" "Dunno", came the reply, "I never did find her head!"

You know me, never been a supporter of the Royal Family, although Prince Charles's concerns for architecture and using local materials always struck a nerve of sympathy. Sadly, I now understand that he proposes to demolish a farm near Bath and build 2,000 houses on fields. What is wrong with this man? A spoke stated that, "Residents' views will be taken into account". Cold, distant, uncaring and arrogant – and not to be believed for one moment. So now, our Charlie has ruined his chances of survival and will have to be shot (metaphorically speaking, of course) along with those who will be named closer to the end of the book.

I see that £3 million is to be wasted on replacing Imperial measurement road signs with those of a foreign metric disposition. Once again, this move is aimed at reducing the damage caused by foreign drivers confronted and confused by feet and inches. WELL, LEARN OUR LANGUAGE AND OUR MEASUREMENTS. Why should we always have to change our history and practice to accommodate those from a foreign field? I'm sure this won't be the end of it. We know of a family whose surname is Acre. I suppose they will have to change this under the

Lisbon Treaty to Hectare. Winston Churchill's trusty servant, Inch, and all the other little Inches around the country will no doubt have to become Centimetres. And anyone called Yardley – will they have to be changed to Metrely? Miles Kingston – would he now have to be Kilometre Kingston? Will Michael Foot and any other Foots have to be called, Michael Just Over Thirty Centimetres, although it would be hyphenated, of course. Whimsical, but you know where I am going.

Here we go again, and the do-gooder, open border supporters wonder why the natives are despairing. There is a pet food plant in Acton, Suffolk, which is advertising for applicants at the rate of £5.80 per hour. However, one stipulation raises its Euro head. The applicants must be able to understand Polish, as that is the mother tongue of the supervisor. Following complaints to the company, "Supreme and Nutrition", the advert has been amended to, "Polish language would be an advantage but is not essential". Once more, I ask you. Is it me, or.....?

Talking of slippery slopes, which we were, this continuing erosion of historical rights is worrying. Now, by historical I mean they were common sense ones, not to be confused with new rights, which are merely there to promote some cause or agenda. The historical rights in question concerns the every day involvement with children. I learn that over-zealous council officials in Watford have banned parents from being in the same playground as their children on the spurious grounds that they might be paedophiles. This move involves two parks, which are controlled by Watford Borough Council – Harwoods and Harebreaks. Rangers patrol these sites which cater for children aged 5 to 15. The Council claims that Ofsted regulations gives them no other choice than to ban parents, unless they have been vetted and undergone a CRB check. The good news in this case is that unlike most articles, which describe the information as coming from a spokesman/woman or source, this article identifies the mayor, one Dorothy Thornhill. She is probably old enough to know better, but limply says, "Sadly, in today's climate you can't have adults wandering around unchecked in a children's playground. We have reviewed our procedures so although previously some parents have stayed with their children at the discretion of the playworkers, this is not something we can continue to do". Unbelievable. A chink of light, however, came in the response from Ofsted, who said it was not necessary to have all adults on the premises checked. Claude Knights from Kidscape summed it up. He said, "They are encouraging a climate where parents and children are rendered suspicious without proof of wrongdoing or guilt. Caring parents should not be viewed as a threat". Perhaps the mayor should have had a word with Ofsted first, and then put herself out to grass, possibly in a pasture very close to the children's playground. She may, of course, look suspicious with that gold chain dangling from her neck, but most local people would know why she was there.

It's stories like the following that frustrate Middle England and lay disdain at the door of the (in)equalities and race brigade. Classifying gypsies as an ethnic race gives them rights beyond their wildest dreams (normally one which involves a lot of tarmac and caravans.) In Essex recently a number of caravans arrived in a field close to a small village and which overnight had been turned into an eye sore. There are now twenty caravans resting on newly laid tarmac (some dreams turn into reality very quickly). Six feet high fencing shrouds all this activity. The field in question is part of the green belt. An injunction has been taken out, but being above the law they ignored it. The local council stated there was to be a court hearing shortly and that every available legal means would be used to resolve the dispute. And at what cost to the poor taxpayer? How can it come to this? Why were they not just thrown off by force? The trouble is, this would involve the police being used to do something useful for society as a whole, and let's be honest, that is not their priority. But it shows just how soft we are on those that continue to take the Michael.

The same situation happened a couple of months ago in Cambridgeshire. After a six-year battle, costing £400,000 in legal costs to evict a group of gypsies, another lot moved in just down the road. The process of removal has now to start all over again. Throughout this country local councils are spending horrendous amounts of money conforming to government legislation concerning the housing of travellers, whilst also spending fortunes evicting those they are legally obliged to remove from illegal sites. All this was put into perspective by Robin Page, an independent councillor who stated that the government was "too politically correct to act". (Gutless, I call it). He said that the law in Great Britain should be the same as in Ireland (irony or ironies, huh!). There, illegal occupation is regarded as a criminal offence, not a civil offence, so it is much easier to sort out the problem. Police have powers of arrest and the confiscation of caravans.

If it's not in the country where gypsies cause anger and resentment through their "unsocial" actions, shall we deem them, they don't fare any better in the towns. A couple and their seven offspring have been housed in a £1 million home in the leafy suburbs of North London. They have failed to enamour themselves within "Totteridge society". It costs the taxpayer £600 per week to house this family. Why? The property has five bedrooms and three bathrooms. The landlord has accused them of causing thousands of poundsworth of damage and surrounding neighbours state their lives have been made a nightmare. Barnet Council approached the landlord with a view to her helping them with this "family". What I don't understand is that Barnet Council was forced to find them accommodation. Why? Do they have a legal duty? This couple, as I said, have seven children. Why? Does no-one have personal responsibility any more? The patriarch of this Irish family denies his children have been intimidating and threatening, although he describes them as "cheeky". Bless, eh! It makes you laugh (well, it would if it weren't so miserable for those living close by) that he describes the landlady as racist, saying, "She doesn't like travellers, and "I'm going to get her done for harassment". (Such excellent grammar and composition of sentence!) The last word is from the landlady, who pointedly commented that she has run into problems with paperwork whilst trying to evict this family of travellers, because they "seem to know the system". I bet they do, all the way to the Benefit Office. What fools we are.

If they are not harassing you from the west, then they are harassing you from the east. A jeweller in fashionable Altrincham has had problems with Romanian gypsies snatching jewellery, while other members of the "family" distract staff. Despite reporting these thefts, which happen on a five to six week basis, to the police, no arrests have been made. Frustrated by the lack of results, the loss of stock and therefore potential sales, Mr. Plant, the owner, put up a sign in his window, which stated, "Sorry, we do not serve Romanian or Eastern European gypsies". Yup, you've got it! The police were down on Mr. Plant before you could exclaim "Ethnic cleansing". The police said Mr. Plant had fallen foul of the Race Relations Act, which recognises gypsies and travellers as ethnic groups. They also said his sign contained writing that was deemed to be offensive (obviously more offensive than the crime of theft). They also stated, "We take all complaints of this nature extremely seriously". (Again, far more seriously than some foreigner taking advantage of our hospitality and the do-gooders' charter). I despair. What's that? You do, too. Oh, we despair.

Okay, time for a couple of throw-aways:

I see that a report has come to the conclusion that beer contains female hormones. I fear they could be right, as after eight pints I talk crap and can't drive properly!

Two blondes walk into a building..... You'd think at least one of them would have seen it! Only joking!

CHAPTER NINE

Fireworks and Ben Do Not Mix

Maureen was supposed to come with me to a talk I was giving in Hextable at an eightieth birthday party. However, she had to stay at home, as Ben could not be left on the Saturday after Guy Fawkes Night. It seems that every night is Firework Night during the early part of November, with no-one taking notice of the 11 pm time limit. But then, it's not profitable for the police. I really do feel that fireworks should be banned from sale to the public and that all displays should be organised. Sadly, one takes this view as the great unwashed appear incapable of reasonable action and responsibility for same. It's very similar to pubs where children are allowed in, but as we've said before, everyone has to be responsible for the children, except the parents concerned.

Firework displays were always contained within a framework of 5th November and subsequent weekend. Can't wait for Christmas and the New Year when it starts all over again. The fifth of November was awful for Ben. We had the televisions on in three rooms, but that still didn't settle him. You try watching "The Restaurant" with a collie draped across your shoulders in the manner of someone wearing a stole. And it's not as if he is restful when he is lying there. Friday night was even worse. Two sedatives, a chewy bone and all we got for our trouble was diarrhoea (not us, obviously) so come Saturday night, and the proposed buffet in Hextable, Maureen decided it was easier to stay with the dog. It would have meant him being six hours by himself, normally not a problem, but who knows what we might have come home to – actually I think we do know!

In the event, I returned about 11.40 pm and so watched "Strictly" which Maureen had seen and recorded. We got to bed at about 2 pm. Somewhat jaded on Sunday we watched the Remembrance Parade on TV and no-one could help but feel immensely proud of those who had served and died, or served and still lived. It just makes one feel so bitter about the waste of

British lives in Afghanistan. It's not a war we can ever win, we have our own Vietnam. Why is it that Middle England, and Middle Britain to be fair, can see this? But those in authority appear blind to the situation. An unseen enemy will never be broken down. Protect this country from within, I say. Make Britain safe. We're never thanked for our efforts wherever our noses have been poked. However, be that as it may, I did wonder just how necessary it was to have the Archbishop of Canterbury waffling through his spiel, spouting his Christian nursery rhymes. I would much prefer it to be a completely secular occasion. I did grin as the voices of youngsters sounded and the camera scanned the choristers in red and gold uniforms. At the end of that part of the service they walked away in file, followed by their older brethren. I said to Maureen, "I wonder how many of that lot have been CRB checked? And has the Archbishop of Canterbury?" They should be, all of them. No member of those combined cults should be exempt. If a parent in Watford can't go into a playground with his or her children, well.....

Now here's a country whose laws we could follow with a renewed sense that justice had been seen to be done. Saudi Arabia doesn't stand any nonsense. This week, a man has been found guilty of raping five children, aged between three and seven. The 23-year-old was entitled to appeal against his original conviction. He did. It was rejected and he is now to be beheaded. His body will then be displayed on a wooden beam in a public place. To date, this year's tally of those beheaded, and therefore unable to continue whatever unlawful acts they were committing, number about forty. How refreshing. No taking them on fishing trips to see if they will do better in future and of course, it all helps towards the housing market.

When, with the help of my parents, I bought my first car, it was considered a privilege to drive. I was seventeen. I felt as if I had become a grown up overnight. Oh, how things have changed. Ben Gammell passed his driving test three weeks before he killed a 14-year-old girl. He had girls in his car, so he decided to show off. His extremely adult idea of impressing those on board was to "frighten" some children by swerving in front of them. How brave is that? Sadly, for a young lady called Eleanor McGrath, Mr. Gammell hit the kerb, lost control and ploughed into the group, pushing those in front into a brick wall. One lad, aged 16, suffered severe head injuries and is still in hospital months after Mr. Gammell's pathetic actions. Oh, that Saudi law was enacted here.

We bought a new TV from a local retailer last week. We tried both Comet and Curry's, but were not overly-impressed when they would not "throw in" the HD lead they both assured us was so essential for a good picture. Apparently, the scart lead is no longer sufficient. I remember when just an aerial was sufficient, but whatever. We trundled off towards Farnham and found an unknown make of TV at a reasonable price (how reasonable, of course, will depend on whether it's still working the day after the warranty expires). This little chappie we acquired from one of the smaller independent retailers. Once again, though, we were confronted with the information that we really did require an HD lead and no, they wouldn't do a deal either. By now we had both lost the will to live and we gave in to the inevitable. We were going to have to buy one from somewhere. We were shown an assortment of HD leads, ranging from the cheapest at £15, the one that was described as "not lasting you a month", and you did feel that if you bought it you were rather a non-person in the TV viewing league, to the most expensive at £89.99 (always sounds so much cheaper than £90).

Back home we unpacked, positioned and admired the new TV, along with the new DVD/video player/recorder, and the £89.99 HD lead. I mean, who wants to look as if you are at the lower end of the league table? William called in during the afternoon and with his help – actually I made the tea if I remember rightly – it was up and running within a very short time. It was, to be fair, a brilliant picture on every channel and all done without the aid of the HD lead. So yesterday, we trundled back and received a grudging refund. "But you can't believe what a difference this

HD lead will make", said the same youthful assistant, as he threw one last dice into the mix in an effort to retrieve the sale, and his commission. Slightly irritated by now I commented that as it was me that would be sitting in front of the TV, and me who was happy with the picture, that was an end to it – and it was!

Trundling once more, we decided to do some Xmas shopping. Ah, the store was packed with goodies. Maureen perused the shelves like a child not knowing where to look next. "That's ideal", "Oh, look at this", "He'll love this", "Isn't this sweet, I can see him with this now". The basket was full to overflowing at the checkout. "Mmmmm", said the assistant, sporting trinkets pierced through her lower lip. "Someone's in for a special Xmas". We both looked at each other sensing the pleasure our purchases would bring when opened on Xmas day. Yes, Ben would be in his doggy heaven. Mock rubber sausage roll with sesame seeds, bright orange rubber quoit, and a stocking made out of pig hide filled with seasonal chewy biscuits - ah, the list was endless. What's that you ask? The children? My mother? Oh, Maureen will get them something when she's in town on Xmas eve! Bound to be something in the pre -Xmas sale. Okay, okay, I'm only joking. I'll probably give them vouchers as they are easy.

I never thought I'd ever feel sorry for Gordon Brown but today is that day. I wasn't aware that he sends hand-written letters to the bereaved relatives of soldiers killed in the line of duty. (Let's be generous on this occasion). Mrs. Janes, whose son Jamie was killed in action, took exception to the bad spelling, mis-spelling, tone and everything else it seems to me that was uttered within the sentiments written by our man at the top. It seems he couldn't do right for wrong in this matter. If written on No. 10 headed paper and pp'd, it would appear as clinical and impersonal. If handwritten, then any oversight is misconstrued as "an insult" to her child, in this case. To be fair, Gordon Brown is partially sighted. I accept that Mrs. Janes is feeling more than slightly fragile, to say the least, but surely, if you are going to grind your axe, then it should be ground in private, in confidence. Sadly, this lady decided to go to the "Sun" – the "SUN"! How demeaning is that? Mr. Brown then rings to apologise for any hurt caused and the conversation is recorded. Who stands by when answering the phone with a recording device? This is then played out once more in the "Sun". From letters to Ceefax and comments made in other papers it seems that I am not alone in this view, that the woman has shown no dignity whatsoever and even the "Sun" readers, however crass they may be for the majority of their lives, are in agreement.

They all gathered last night, thousands of them to "celebrate" the anniversary of the fall of the Berlin Wall. I said at the time it was one of the worst things that could happen. Before its symbolic destruction, the east (Russia) was a powerful entity and so was the west (America). The reunification of Germany heralded the demise of the Soviet Bloc and the enlargement of a federal Europe that took its place. With that enlargement came the mass immigration we shall rue over the next generations, as the chickens come home to roost, should there be any room for them to perch.

Interesting to read that we, us, the taxpayers, workers within these Isles, have paid out £3.4 billion since 1997 looking after foreign prisoners. There are, apparently, 11,350 of the buggers in our jails. That's a fair old percentage and goes a long way to the indigenous population's gripe that this country is the dumping ground for all that is rotten in this world. Of course, in many cases, the little loves cannot be sent home due to the fear that their human rights could be violated. Britain is looking to do a deal with Nigeria, whereby prisoners could be sent back to complete their sentences. Why are we "looking at it"? Just send them back. One Nigerian prisoner is reported to have commented, "In British prisons I can get three meals a day, I have right (sic) to medical care, I can complain if my rights are violated and I can't be beaten". Doesn't it make your blood boil? These people know their very British rights, all right. There are currently 765 Nigerians in our jails, by the way. That compares with 627 from Ireland, 523 from Poland and 564 from Vietnam. What a pity their boat didn't sink – bugger!

Politics and allegiances to the various parties never cease to amaze me. There was a bi-election held last Thursday in Glasgow, the seat once held by that odious and infamous Michael Martin, the ex-Speaker of the House and personal investor of taxpayers' contributions, all of which were no doubt very gratefully received. Twelve thousand plus voters put their "X" alongside Labour's name on the ballot sheet. Labour was returned with a thumping majority. How can this be? The Conservative vote was abysmal. SNP must be wondering what the hell happened. And the Lib-Dems came behind the BNP, which I find more than slightly amusing. But then, the Lib-Dems would do well to reflect that sitting on the fence and being all things to nobody gets you exactly where they are in British politics. Even their leader is a clone of the Conservative Party's marketing man, just less well known.

PC Mark Johnson who left his two Alsatians in a car where they died from heat has finally decided to show up in court. He has failed to appear on two previous occasions. The district judge has obviously become slightly peeved by his tiresome antics, as Johnson was "ordered" to attend and make his plea. He did – "not guilty". Can't see how myself, it's an open and shut case, which is more than you could say for the windows in his car. His solicitor successfully applied for a pre-trial review. Why so? Ah, well, two, not one, but two, psychiatrists, a psychologist and his missus will all give evidence. His solicitor said that, "The case will turn on medical issues. There is evidence that my client was suffering from a medical condition at the time". Somewhat less suffering than that experienced by his dogs, no doubt. It is said that PC Johnson had a compulsive, obsessive disorder and a depressive illness. So good to note that mitigating circumstances can be found appropriate for most ills and errors these days. It all smacks of making sure that someone, anyone, is to blame except the one who had the key and locked the door on the poor animals.

The subject of compensation from a new source or wheeze, depending on your view, reared its very ugly American head when a 47-year-old decided to sue the Highways Agency for failing to protect him by not gritting the highway sufficiently. The man concerned was injured in a crash on the A30 in the West Country earlier this year. He was on a life support machine for two days. The Highways Agency maintains that the roads were gritted, but heavy rain had washed much of it away. The water on the road then froze. Claims solicitors must be rubbing their hands with glee once more. No-one is more aware than me that this cove has rights, but does he not also have responsibility for his own decisions? In this case could he not have asked himself, "Should I travel knowing what the weather is like?" I think there should be a system whereby tests can be done when the patient is on a life support machine to see what action he or she may legally take should they get better. If it looks as if they will sue all and sundry, just turn off the machine – that's my view! Only joking – well, almost.....

Just a quickie – it wasn't so much the outcry that MOD personnel were to share millions of pounds in bonuses, it was the news that there are 85,000 MOD staff who don't fight for their country. What the bloody hell do they do all day? Please tell me. Surely, there is flotsam which could be jettisoned from this department. Another job for Michael O'Leary!

I find it hard to credit that a mother could be issued with a £75 litter fine by a council for feeding ducks. The lady concerned was by the lake in Smethwick Hall Park in the west midlands with her 17-month-old lad. A female warden approached and after a brief admonishment issued a ticket. Seventy-five pounds is totally out of context for this "heinous" offence. There were no signs telling anyone not to feed the ducks, a pre-requisite surely when attempting to extract money for the council coffers. It smacks of being no different to those who clamp where no sign of private property is obvious. The council concerned is Sandwell. Their spokesman, one Mahboob Hussain (obviously a local) who no doubt glories under his title of Council Cabinet Member for Neighbourhoods and Housing, defended the fine. He said there were many people upset by the feeding of wild life. Added to the council comments and indicative of the quality of its employees, I suspect, is the following from a council spoke. "As the woman (lady would have been nicer) was being issued with the fine, the kid (child, surely?) was still throwing bread". The "kid" was apparently too young to be issued with a ticket as well. I'm sure Sandwell will soon amend the law to accommodate those still in the womb, but with known intent. The lady is not going to pay and will be taking it further. Good on you, gal!

Nice to see that Cornwall Council is making an effort to keep the knowledge of the Cornish language alive. All road signs when being replaced are to be bi-lingual. There are naturally those who think it a waste of time, but we have road signs in parts of this country in languages far more foreign than Cornish, so why should we not protect our own heritage. There are approximately 300 people who can speak Cornish. Unless a language can be supported in everyday usage it will always be left to the few who wish to see their heritage protected. Good luck to them, I say.

It's been a good week for good news. It was really a case of Georgina Blackwell versus Belway Homes, or Georgina versus the Dragon, some might say. I wouldn't, obviously, as it smacks of a tabloid headline. It's always nice when the ordinary chap, or chapesse, in the street manages to slay the corporate business arseholes. In this case it was the arrogance and money of Belway Homes (boo now). They took Sandra Blackwell, Georgina's mother, to court after she refused permission for the developers to use her land in order to access their newly acquired profit centre, or housing development. The access meant the destruction of her garden. Georgina read the case notes, which led to an appeal, which she has just won and landed her mum with £75,000 compensation. There's always the exception and for once, compensation was right and proper. Oh, joy.

Ah, ha! We're having one of those 1st April moments. A government-funded report on education is suggesting that teachers should be more "flexible" on behaviour and homework when dealing with gypsy children. The report says that schools should "meet parents half way". I suspect that this is educational speak for "give in to their every whim", if only they could attend school long enough to spell it. Secondary schools, it adds, should adopt a "flexible attendance policy". What did I say? It's a slippery slope.....

If it's not a slippery slope, then it's a wedge with a very thin end, I tell you. Were you aware that £550,000 has been allocated to a pilot scheme called the Open Madrasah Network. This funding is to help Muslim under-achievers attend lessons in Arabic, Urdu and religion. They are taken out of our mainstream schools for this special attention. There are already four of these Madrasahs in Bradford, and no doubt there will be more. I wasn't aware that there are 1600 Madrasahs in this country, with some 200,000 children attending and studying the Koran. If ever there was a reason to keep religion, all religions, out of schools, it's because of the dangers that come from areas that are unaccountable and subject to terrorist indoctrinations.

I note with dismay that a company called VT Critical Services have been awarded a 10-year contract to repair Metropolitan Police vehicles. What a pity that maintenance isn't done in-house, but that's the way of the world. Part of this contract, however, is to replace tyres that are punctured – even when the vehicle concerned is on patrol! This force's farce is highlighted when the vehicle in question, with two policemen, is seen on double yellow lines awaiting repairs for two hours. That's two policemen sitting in a car with a punctured tyre because they are no longer allowed to change the tyre themselves. I can't imagine they minded for a moment – two hours doing nothing. What a scandal. Peter Smyth, Chairman of the Metropolitan Police Federation, described the policy as "ridiculous", while a Metropolitan Police spoke stated that, "As police vehicles are maintained to a very high standard tyres are changed by specialist contractors". Stuart Middleton, who is the Met's Director of Transport Services (there's important!) said, "Outsourcing (he means contracting) much of the Met's vehicle repair and maintenance to VT provides good value". To whom? Certainly not the Ministry of Common Sense – or the taxpayer in other words.

Well, it's mid-November and Ronnie Biggs is still with us – an amazing recovery story. Such is the extent of his recovery, that far from his knocking on death's door, he now hopes to watch Arsenal play at their new stadium in Ashburton Grove. I read that he has a "wish list" of things to do before he dies. He says that he would like to visit the scene of the train robbery. Is that to rub salt into the wounds of the Mills family? He'd also like to visit his home area of Brixton and buy a pint of beer (from taxpayers' money obviously) in Margate. Such wishes. Mine is that he doesn't live long enough to fulfil any of them. He's costing us enough already in his Barnet care home. I wonder what that gutless Justice Minister, Jack Straw, thinks when he reads such stories. I'd like to think that he winces just a tad.

Just getting back to Arsenal for a moment, I mentioned their ground in Ashburton Grove. I am aware that their ground is actually called the "Emirates Stadium" but I find it hard to accept these sponsored names. Big money, with no history. York City always played at Bootham Crescent. Under sponsorship, it's now renamed "Kit Kat Crescent". Bolton Wanderers play at the Reebok, whilst Coventry City is at the Ricoh Stadium. How sad is that? Newcastle United is looking to sign a long-term contract with a company. It could, of course, be any company from anywhere in the world, as long as they have big money. It has always been St. James' Park and hopefully the Geordies will rise to the occasion and protect the interests of fans over fad. If "The Valley" is ever renamed, my affair with Charlton will be over. Souls are sold so cheaply these days. PS – if conversation ever dries up between courses during one of your little dinner parties, you can always ask if anyone knows the name of the only Tube station to be named after a football club and the answer is – Arsenal. The station concerned changed its name in 1932 from Gillespie Road under the auspices of their then manager, Mr. Herbert Chapman. There! Thought that would interest you.

The "Sunday Express" must be desperate for headlines. Under their banner are two free offers – one for roses and another for shaving gel. The main story is "Charles's Amazing Republic Gaffe". When turning to page 9 – a fair way in for its lead story – one learns that Prince Charles had a discussion at a dinner party, which centred on Australia becoming a republic and his agreeing with that option. This conversation was thirty-two years ago, in 1977. Is this really the best it can do? Now you know why I only buy a newspaper when I am writing a book or CD. Well, when I say buy a newspaper, I actually collect it from my mother's, the day after she has read it. I can't ever see me spending eight shillings on a newspaper. STOP PRESS: I've just looked at Saturday's and Sunday's, which I am throwing out, having cut out the relevant articles which we will be discussing shortly, and it appears that Saturday's edition is fourteen shillings, while the "Sunday Express" works out at a somewhat costly one pound and six shillings.

There were two winning tickets in the Euro Lottery – one belonging to a syndicate of seven from Liverpool (I'll say no more!), the other a couple from Newport in South Wales. Forty-five million pounds per ticket! Now, between the seven, dubbed the "Magnificent Seven" in the tabloids (how original is that) it works out at £6.5 million each, or thereabouts. But for the couple, £45 million is an awful lot of money, far more than is needed by two people, especially living in Newport. And, frankly, I stand by what I have always said, and that is that no prize should be larger than £1 million. I mean, that would keep most of us in a manner that we'd never been accustomed to and with the added benefit that forty-five people could share a much more enhanced lifestyle, rather than just one with more money than they could shake a stick at. Maureen asked me what single thing I'd do, or buy, if we won a vast fortune. I hastily add here that it will never happen, as I've no intention of ever contributing towards the Olympic Games. Well, not by this route, anyway. I would love to buy my own steam locomotive to run on a preserved railway and hopefully give pleasure to many people (sounds soft, I know, but you know me). Maureen said she'd start a wildlife hospital for injured, and if I know Maureen, unwanted pets. Well, at least she didn't suggest a toy boy!

I'm off with the boys to Birmingham on Friday morning. We will be leaving for the NEC at approximately 10.30 am all being well. Our model railway, or train set as William calls it in an attempt to wind me up, has been invited by the Warley Model Railway Club. It is the largest exhibition in the country. Last week, Simon and I took the decision to retire the layout from the exhibition circuit after what will be nine years and some twenty-five odd exhibitions. We are all getting older and I think we sometimes expect too much in the way of support from our fellow operators, who very kindly organise their social life and holidays around the layout's travels. We are hoping to find a permanent home for the layout, where it could be used without setting up and taking down, which takes two hours each time.

I rang one of the Committee members to ask where we are to be billeted. A very pleasant chap, responsible for accommodation, informed me that we are booked into the Premier Inn, Hockley Heath. I've heard of the place but couldn't pinpoint it on a map. He explained that it's about ten minutes from the NEC roundabout, before adding that it's about half an hour to get to the roundabout from the NEC hall No. 5, due to walking to the car park – several light years away from the hall apparently. You then wait in the queue of traffic before life is seen moving on the M42. Brilliant! Even more of a downside to this conversation was that I had to endure his West Midlands accent. Unavoidable, I suppose, considering the geographical location of the exhibition. But did he have to say "Hockley Heath, that's Haitch-o-c-k-l-e-y Haitch-e-a-t haitch". It's an "aitch"! He then helpfully, but irritatingly added that, "The Premier Inn is situated on the Solihull Road, spelt S-o-l-i-haitch-u-l-l". I know how to spell Solihull! We've been to all manner of exhibitions, small, medium and large and they've all had their characters and their characteristics. We've enjoyed them all, well, nearly all. My favourites are often the smaller ones in small schools, where people stop and chat for half an hour at a time, reminiscing about an incident or memory they wish to share, and you are ever so glad they did. Those moments are then shared with the rest of our layout members over a pint and dinner later that evening.

The Warley Show, being large, is I fear going to be less personal. The public are often up to five deep, I'm told, bulging against the barriers that stop people getting too close to the layout. The barriers also stop little ones exclaiming, "What's that?" whilst poking their fingers into the roof of a building, which has taken me several hours to make. The good news about the show being this weekend is that I will be able to miss "Children in Need" without making any special effort. I really do find the whole proceedings obnoxious. All these wannabe celebrities from banks, shops, hospitals, all doing ridiculous stunts to acquire your money through guilt, hype and pressure. It leaves me cold. I mean, who the hell wants to sponsor somebody sitting in a bath, up to his or her neck for ten hours in cold porridge? Where is the thrill of spending money to watch someone bungee jump off a tower block to save some little oik who will probably end up stealing a charity box by the time he's seven, the irony being that the charity box he has stolen will probably be for the charity that saved his neck in the beginning. Me? I just hope the rubber band breaks. I'd sponsor that! What do you mean – miserable git!

Getting back to exhibitions and barriers, I remember a couple of years ago, we were invited to the Blackburn Model Railway Exhibition. One of the best for hospitality and friendliness – and a free curry for anyone who was in the pub that night. It had nothing to do with the exhibition, we just happened to be in a pub watching rugby and the landlady and staff issued free curries with chips to anyone who was in the pub at the time. What a lovely gesture. Anyway, I made up, or rather Maureen made up, a sign to be put on the front – that's the public side of the layout. We often have to put up "Please do not touch" signs, but this time the sign read, "This is a mosque free layout". I thought it would go down well in Blackburn. To be fair, there was no reason to fear an outcry, as model railway exhibitions are a very white hobby. Not too many burkhas or niqabs to be seen perusing a model representation of an English seaside town in the fifties and sixties. It was at this show where, on the Sunday morning, a lady in her sixties was standing leaning on the barrier which protected our layout. Alongside her was a man in his late twenties, or early thirties. He wore a permanent monk on his face – no expression, no humour. He was always going to be either Lancastrian or German. He was Lancastrian, in fact, they both were. Both very local, with Ribble Valley rolled "r's". Yes, them again! Anyway, I was affixing a newly purchased "privy" to a back garden when Ribble Valley lady said to Ribble Valley man, "But Kate's a lovely girl". His eyes were staring at the ground as he replied, "Aye". She continued to look at him. "So how long is it now you've been going out with Kate?" "Four year", came the reply. She asked, "So what's Kate got that no other girl in your life ever had?" He then looked up, straight as a die, and replied, "Kate's only girl I've ever met who can change drive shaft in under one hour, twenty minutes". Classic! Absolute classic! If Victoria Wood had written that, you couldn't have got better. It's a very northern thing; it wouldn't work if written by a southerner. I couldn't wait to come home and tell Maureen. Well, as you know, I don't get out much - and when I do, it's only to play trains.

I read that some complete arse of an academic, who has more money than sense, is to give a million pounds to something in order to save lives in developing countries. What is the point? Does he wish all wildlife to become extinct? We need to lower the population, dear. Has he not looked out from his academic windows recently – it's full of people in the streets, and not many are local. He is also encouraging others to give 10% of their income to his cause. His first disciple, it is stated, is his wife. Slightly sycophantic, I felt, prompting me to stick two fingers down my throat. I said complete arse, I really should have said completely misguided arse. It's more appropriate.

Hot on the heels of stating that I never thought I'd ever find myself in the position of defending Gordon Brown, I now find myself defending a new ruling by the EU. They have decreed that displaying a crucifix in a classroom violates religious and educational freedom. This ruling is initially affecting schools in Italy, known, of course, for their somewhat Catholic taste of wearing crucifixes. Schools have been told that they have to remove these religious symbols for fear their presence could disturb children who are not Christian. Not sure about this bit, as you start to smell a sop to Muslims appearing at the door. Providing it's the same for all schools of all faiths then I am all for it. I just hope the system whereby some pigs are more equal than others does not apply in this instance.

It's funny how headlines one day can concur with your feelings so fully, and two weeks later you shake your head at a newspaper's leader. On Wednesday, 4th November, the "Daily Express" ran with a picture of Big Ben and the headline, "BRITAIN: THE END as Lisbon Treaty becomes law, we've been sold down the river". A statement and sentiment shared by all who love her, I would have thought. Today, Tuesday, 17th November, the front page reports, "OUTRAGE AT 'PARASITE' ATTACK ON THE QUEEN. Labour candidate's hurtful jibes". It appears that while a Tory MP suggested on his web site that there should be a public holiday to "celebrate" the Queen's 60 year reign in 2010, Peter White, a Labour Party candidate, retorted, "What is the point of celebrating the diamond jubilee of someone who is born into a position of privilege? She is a parasite and milks this country for everything she can". Is this man not entitled to his view? Quite how this little spat could become headline news is beyond me.

Of far more importance was the page 7 article concerning the possible appointment of the Belgian Prime Minister to that of EU President – a post none of us were allowed to air our views on, let alone vote upon. He wishes, it is stated, to replace the national flags and anthems with that of the EU. This, to me, marks the worst excesses of the vile, insidious cancer that is federalism. Licence plates, identity cards, EU sports events – an EU army? EU taxation? EU financial controls and budgets for member states? This federalist movement never stops. They gnaw away at the edge of individuality and heritage in a quest to provide a clinical, sterile, controlled, docile race of humanoids devoid of hope, power or expectation. As I've said before, I can see the time approaching when the idea of voting for the masses will be completely eliminated on the basis that those in power know best. I don't know just how far these nameless wonders can push the residents within the EU before a little more backbone is shown by the populace, but I look forward to a time when there is mass demonstration against everything that flies an EU flag.

Time for a trio of international jokes:

A man boarded a plane at Sydney Airport and, taking his seat as he settled in, noticed a very beautiful woman boarding the aircraft. Sitting comfortably, he realised she was heading straight towards his row. Bingo! She took the seat right next to him. Eager to start up a conversation he blurted out, "Business trip or holiday?" She turned towards him, smiled enchantingly and said, "Business. I'm off to the Annual Nymphomaniac Convention in the United States". The man swallowed hard. Here was the most gorgeous woman he had ever met, and here he was sitting next to her and here she was heading to a meeting for nymphomaniacs. Struggling to maintain his composure he calmly asked, "So, what's your business role in this convention?" "Oh, lecturer", she responded, batting her eyelids. "I use my experience to debunk some of the popular myths about sexuality". He cleared his throat. "Really? And what myths are those?" "Oh, well", she explained coolly, "one popular myth is that African-American men are the most well endowed, when in fact it's the native American Indian who is most likely to possess this trait. Another popular myth is that the French make the best lovers, when it's actually the men of Greek descent. We've also found that the best potential lovers in all categories are the Irish". Suddenly the woman became uncomfortable and blushed. "Oh, I'm sorry", she said, "I really shouldn't be discussing this with you. I don't even know your name". The man smiled, "Tonto", he said, Tonto Papadopoulos, but all my friends call me Paddy!"

Which leads us neatly to a supermarket in north London at the start of the joke and New Zealand at the end. We then shuffle continents and relax in a bar at a casino in Las Vegas.

A man walked into the produce section of his local Tesco supermarket and asked to buy a half-head of lettuce. The student working in that department told him that they only sold whole heads of lettuce. The customer was insistent that the boy asks the manager regarding his request. The student walked into the back room and said to the manager, "There's some old bastard out there who wants to buy a half-head of lettuce". As he finished the sentence, he was aware that the customer was standing directly behind him, so he quickly added, "and this gentleman has very kindly offered to buy the other half". The manager agreed that a half-head could be sold and the customer happily went on his way. Later that morning the manager said to the student, "I was very impressed with the way you got yourself out of that situation earlier. We like people who can think on their feet. Where is it you're from, son?" "New Zealand", replied the student. "So, why d'you leave New Zealand?" the manager asked. "Well", he said, "there's nothing but whores and rugby players there". "Oh, is that right", replied the manager, "my wife is from New Zealand". "Really", replied the student, "which team did she play for?"

Okay, got your passport stamped? Been checked through the new body search controls? Spent three hours in WH Smith's buying a paperback you wouldn't normally read? Then fasten your seat belt.

A very confident James Bond walks into the bar in a casino in Las Vegas and takes a seat next to a very attractive woman. He gives her a quick glance, raises an eyebrow and casually looks at his watch. The woman notices this and asks, "Is your date running late?" "No", replies James, "Q has just given me this state-of-the-art watch. I was just testing it". Intrigued, the woman says, "a state-of-the-art watch, eh. Tell me, what's so special about it?" James explains, "Well, it uses alpha waves to talk to me telepathically". "My", says the lady, "this is interesting. What's it telling you now?" He looks her in the eye. "It says that you're not wearing any panties". The woman blushes slightly and puts her hand to her mouth and giggles, "Well, it must be broken because I am wearing panties". James smirks, taps his watch and replies, "Bloody thing's an hour fast". (I'd love to have been that smooth!)

I see that the police officer accused of hitting a lady during the G20 demonstrations in London earlier this year is to stand trial. He has denied common assault and been released on unconditional bail. I did smile when I read his name, Delroy Smellie. I mean, with a name like that surely his solicitor could use it as mitigating circumstances.

Getting back to that well-off, but misguided, academic wishing to dispose of £1 million to the developing world, he could do worse than spend it on the protection of elephants. I read with dismay that the illegal trade in wild life is third only to drugs and arms. In the African state of Chad the elephant numbers have now declined from 3,885 in 2005 to just 617. Those greedy, selfish bastards who kill to gain have killed at least eleven rangers. Surely £1 million would be well spent there, sir?

Forgot to mention it, but when we had problems with Ben and the fireworks we rang the vet, who suggested a CD (two actually, but in one pack) entitled "Sounds Scary", which includes fireworks, thunder and gun shot noises. It cost £25. We've had it for over a week so far and he's not asked to listen to it once..... Talk about ungrateful!

Meanwhile, back in the world of government unreality, they never seem to realise that they should be seen to lead their public through times of recession. Having spent £3,380 on a new "Department for Communities and Local Government" logo, the word "Department" was then dropped. This, naturally, required a new logo for both the web site and headed paper. Now this little exercise cost £24,765. The home information packs initiative logo cost £22,000. Twenty five thousand pounds went on "creating an identity for community builders". These are people who encourage community projects, if you were wondering about it and doubtless you were. Are you also aware that the title "Her Majesty's Chief Inspector of Fire Services" has been renamed "Chief Fire and Rescue Adviser". This new and somewhat downmarket name cost another £3,520 to alter. The "Cleaner, Safer, Greener Communities" logo cost £33,400. Here's another couple. The "Code for Sustainable Homes" logo, £7,260, whilst the "National Housing and Planning Advice Unit" ate up another £10,000 of our money. Their arrogance is stupefying.

You know I've never been in favour of our country hosting the Olympics. I've always considered that (a) the cost is too high and (b) the impact on ordinary life is too overbearing. Businesses have had to move in order to facilitate the stadia and training facilities. Areas of outstanding natural beauty have had to be bulldozed in Dorset to make way for major roadworks in order that Weymouth can play its part. What takes the monetary biscuit is the use of lottery funding being taken from heritage and conservation projects. It is an abuse of the public's goodwill in supporting the lottery, as this was not as intended.

Okay, some will find the above acceptable. I never have, because we basically never have a say in anything. It's only for those with their single-minded personal gratification and those who will "make" out of it. The taxpayer is shelling out £3 million a week to finance private consultants and managers. That's a heck of a lot of money – and for what? The budget for this farce is £9.4 billion and rising by the day. So no fear of recession here, then? The sad aspect of all this hope and glory for Great Britain (as was) is that while the Olympic funding eats up more and more money in admin and fees, our athletes are left without funding if it doesn't look as if they are in with a chance of medals. Certain sports have now lost all funding. I can understand there will be disappointment for individuals somewhere down the line.

The pit is not bottomless, although it seems bottomless for admin and management. And that is where the unfairness of it all kicks in. For instance, there's a young lady called Francesca Jones, who is nineteen. She is a rhythmic athlete. She has taken the British title three times, but has just lost her funding because she is 55th in the world. So if there's not a hope of a medal the discipline is dropped. On the other hand, however, the Olympic Development Agency, has spent £16 million on consultants in a year.

One hundred and fifty one million pounds has been paid to project managers – not an inconsiderable sum – and sadly, £60 million of this figure was paid in bonuses (and during the week they probably work in the City. Well, it makes you think!) Since the project started, consultants have pocketed £55 million. Ernst & Young, the accountants, have been paid £12.4 million for their advice so far. Fujitsu Services have gladly accepted £5.8 million for computer systems. There are over one thousand Whitehall civil servants involved in the games' scrutiny – and so it goes on. It really does seem on a par with the EU gravy train, Westminster expenses and City greed. And all at the expense of the very people the Games were there to promote – the athlete. And there was me naively thinking that it was the taking part that counted.

Well, the good news is that once again, as ever, Carol looked her lovely best when telling me of the weather this morning – which was nice. It's a great start to the day, continually fantasising as to whether she is wearing anything under that raincoat – other than a basque, stockings, suspender belt and six-inch heels, obviously!

Maureen has introduced me to the delights of "Goldenballs" – no, not mine, I'd have noticed! I speak of the gameshow. I'd never seen it before, well it is on ITV and I really haven't seen it now. I was, however, passing from kitchen to office with a cup of tea when Maureen said, "Just watch this a minute". It was right at the end, when there are only two contestants left. This is the bit where you split or steal. Maureen explained the rules and remembered that on a previous programme both contestants had agreed to split, only to find when the balls were opened that one of the two had stolen, thus collecting the full £16,000, which was on offer. The lady who would have split the winnings was not only left penniless but distraught. I know that's the game, but I couldn't have done that. I would have been just so happy to have copped £8,000. How could you leave the studio knowing what a heel you'd just been? How could you look the other contestant in the eye in the Green Room afterwards? Or even on your way to the bus stop, though I suppose if the other contestant was from Dudley, Liverpool or he/she was foreign, swarthy, well, yes, obviously.....

It's now later on this evening and I have been giving more thought to "Goldenballs". I've come to the conclusion regarding what is best for both parties at the end of the programme. If it were me, I would now "steal". If the other person had also stolen, then they would have shown their true colours and we would both walk away with nothing, but then I would have, irrespective of my choice in the matter. If they had shown the "split" ball and I had stolen, they would then have shown themselves to be a "proper" person and I would still be able to offer them half of the prize money, having explained why I chose to steal.

Teletext revealed that £1.5 million of British taxpayers' money is to be used in Asia to help with pot holes in roads, as one person is killed every thirty seconds. The money is apparently being spent on repairing them and there was me assuming that we were going to make more of them and increase the death rate! I mentioned this to a mate of mine who was fairly stunned and said, "Asia, they could start with bloody Leatherhead!" But then as we both know, charity never begins at home, let alone the mundane mending of our potholes!

My mother is "doing me 'ead in" as they say in modern parlance. She has the irritating habit of responding to any question with "Eh?". I start to repeat the question when halfway through she answers it. I was visiting her one day last week when the phone rang, and she was obviously struggling to hear the person at the other end. I suggested I took her to the doctors for a hearing test. After the obligatory "Eh" she informed me that she wasn't deaf, but that her telephone was "funny". She added as a rider, that everybody else seems to speak more softly these days.

It was two years ago that I had to call in Guildford Borough Council Social Services Department. A lady called Angela visited my mother to assess her and suggested various additions to her home. What prompted this call to GBC was a phone call mum made to Maureen, when Maureen was working. People who have retired for some time tend to forget that if they ring you at your place of work there could be ever such a small chance of you actually working. Maureen was there, and was interrupted to be informed that mum was stuck on the loo. Our daughter-in-law in waiting was despatched to help mum. DILIW sorted out my mum, but it wasn't the sort of thing anyone should face on a regular basis, so that became the catalyst for help to be summoned. Within the month Angela had had installed two handrails by the front door, a key safe, a trolley on wheels, a pendant with associated box and electrical plug and a toilet seat with adjustable legs that sits over and inside the toilet itself. This piece of equipment has the benefit of doubling up as a home gymnasium! Having signed for all these labour saving and safety-first devices we duly shook hands and Angela sailed off into the sunset. To be fair, she actually walked to the car park and drove off at precisely 3.17 pm. But no matter.

At 3 am the following morning our phone rang. I jumped out of bed. "Hello". It was the midnight Albert. I don't know why, but all those retained by Social Services for this sort of care work seem to be called Albert. He explained that my mum's newly fitted alarm had gone off. They had tried phoning her but had received no reply. By the time I put the phone down, Maureen was up and dressed and we were down by the front door within a minute. Top bolt undone, bottom bolt undone, Yale on catch we hastened to the car. Three minutes later we arrived at my mother's. Torch in hand we scrambled the key safe number, extracted said keys and let ourselves in. The place was in darkness. Maureen turned to the right to check downstairs for security before going to the back door to make sure nobody had broken in. (Note: it was better for Maureen to check for burglars, as I suffer from a stomach complaint – no guts!). I went to run upstairs. Sadly, however, my mother had sent the Stannah stairlift back empty – why? If you've ever confronted one of these in the dark, you will know they are heavy buggers. I went arse over tit, catching my shins before continuing upstairs, shouting, "Mum! Are you all right, Mum?" Blood was pouring from my shins, through my jogging bottoms and onto my trainers. A weak voice emerged from the darkness, calling my name. "Are you all right, mum?" My mother replied, "Yes, I'm all right, it's ever so late, what are you doing here?" "I'm here because your alarm has gone off". "Eh?" "I'm here!" I said". "Has it?" On entering the room and turning on the light I found my mother still to be wearing the said pendant around her neck. "Angela told you to take it off at night". "Oh, no she didn't". "Oh, yes she did". I had to finish this panto-like farce. "The point is the alarm has gone off, they phoned you and you didn't answer, that's why they phoned us. Did you not hear the phone?" "Oh, yes", said my mum, "but I didn't think it would be for me at this time of night". I find the pendant to be very helpful; the problem is you can only tie them so tight.....

When my parents moved down to be near us nine years ago, we took them shopping every Saturday at 9.30 am, and every Saturday at 8.10 am my mum would ring to see what time they, and latterly, she, was being picked up. As I said, my mother's hearing isn't getting any worse, it's just that everyone else is speaking more softly, and this was very evident when one day she rang to ascertain the pick-up time. Maureen stated, as always, "9.30". My mum replied, "Turkey?" "No", said Maureen, "9.30. I'll pick you up at 9.30". "Turkey?" my mother stated once more. "What about a turkey?" Maureen, now realising this conversation was going nowhere changed tack. "Mum, I'll pick you up at half past nine". "Oh, right", said my mum, "you can tell me about the turkey then"! It doesn't get any better.

More recently, because my mother's knees are not as they were, she has taken to staying at home while we do her shopping.

What happens now is that I go round on a Friday, have a cup of tea and then collect her shopping list, Barclay card and Nectar card. As my mother always says, "Don't forget the Nectar card, I want to contribute to Christmas". What that means in reality is "Don't forget me at Christmas". As if she would allow me to!

Recently, my mother required some cash. She had to pay the papers, the window cleaner and the great-grandchildren were due to visit with our daughter, and I know she likes to give them a bit of pocket money. "Could you get me out £100", she enquired. I passed this information on to Maureen, who was doing the shopping by herself as I was taking a tour of the brewery. As you know, I'd love to help with the shopping every week, but sadly, some of us have to work.

Off trundled Maureen to Sainsbury's for my mother's shopping. She had in previous times collected cash for my mum and thought she could remember the PIN. In went the card, digits on pad, reject came the response. Maureen tried a different combination on a similar theme – rejected once more. Now, as you know, you can't do it three times as it will swallow your card. Back went Maureen to our house to deposit our shopping first before nipping round to my mum's with hers. Maureen rang my mother and explained that she couldn't get the money out as she couldn't remember the PIN. "Oh, right", said mum, "it's 4400". Off trundles Maureen once more to the BP Service Station in Mytchett where she enters the newly acquired PIN, only to find the same response as the one at Sainsbury's. She repeated the motion, same response. Now although it didn't swallow the card, due to the fact that Maureen had attempted withdrawals at two separate cash machines with three different PINs in a space of forty minutes, it informed her that she would now have to ring India for a new PIN number and, as you know, that is three years out of your life! You can't understand a word they say any more than they can understand you. The only constant in all this is that the chap's name who you are talking to in Bangalore will be Kevin, and he will know everything there is to know about Coronation Street. Sadly, he is unable to transfer you to your branch, or even England. Maureen did what anyone would do in the circumstances and withdrew £100 from our bank account, on the basis that mum would write her a cheque.

Having arrived at my mother's, Maureen put away the shopping and whilst the kettle boiled informed my mum that she had given her the wrong PIN number. "Oh, no", mum said, "it's the right one – it's 4004". "Well, that's not what you told me", said Maureen, "you said 4400". "Oh, I know", my mum said, "as we were on the phone, I couldn't give you the right combination, someone might have been listening". It's like living with Thora Hird!

You remember I mentioned our awful weekend in Derbyshire, almost a year ago now. For several months prior to that weekend, Maureen had been making frozen meals for my mother – broccoli cheese, cauliflower cheese, vegetable bakes, fish pies – you've got the picture. Round we would go, every Sunday, with another five or six. Because Maureen was retiring from full time work, handing over and getting ready for our weekend, time seemed to be of the essence. We bought my mum some M&S, Waitrose and Be Good To Yourself Sainsbury's ready meals. About a week after our weekend away, when they had all been devoured, I asked how they had been. Just a question to pass the time, really. When you are visiting someone who appears to be living in a care home for one, conversation can be at a premium. "They were like muck", my mother retorted, "your nan and I had better in the war". Oh, great, I thought, there's gratitude. A year on, if I ask the same question, I receive a very different answer. "Oh, they're lovely, there's nothing like home baked". What my mother doesn't realise is that we still buy M&S, Waitrose and Be Good To Yourself ready meals – we just repackage them in foil containers and write the contents on the lid in time-honoured fashion. If you see my mum, don't let on, eh!

I think I've also mentioned that my mother has never listened to me in 62 years, and when she does, she doesn't like what she hears. She goes into what we consider to be the "meerkat position", which in action means she hunches herself up and places her hands in front of her before staring blankly ahead.

I mentioned it to our children and you saw them come alive, because it struck a chord that they had never been able to put a name to. It was somewhat of a relief to know that it wasn't just me that suffered this dismissive notion to every suggestion from meals-on-wheels to a rise and recline armchair.

Right! Time for a little Irish light relief:

There are five Englishmen in an Audi Quattro. They arrive at an Irish border checkpoint. Paddy, the customs officer, stops them and informs them, "It is illegal to have five people in a Quattro. Quattro means four". "Quattro is the name of the car", retorts the Englishman disbelievingly. Look at the log book – it's an Audi Quattro and it's designed to carry five people". "You'll not be pulling that one on me", replies Paddy, "Quattro means four, you have five people in your car and you are therefore breaking the law, and that's an end to it". The Englishman becomes angry. "You idiot, call your supervisor now. I want to speak to someone with more intelligence". "Oh, I can't do that", responds Paddy, "Murphy is over there, busy with two guys in a Fiat Uno".

CHAPTER TEN

Of Brummies and Flat Vowels

Well, I've returned from our weekend at the NEC. The Show was excellent. The interest in our layout was very encouraging, with lots of people asking lots of questions regarding scenery, construction, signalling, turntable operation, etc. Our rooms at the Premier Inn were clean and the staff was extremely friendly. To be fair, the staff at the NEC and those associated with the Warley Model Railway Club, who organised the Show, was extremely polite and helpful. In fact, the only local who wasn't friendly was the waitress who served (I use the word loosely) our meal on the Saturday evening, but to be fair it was a Harvester restaurant. I know, I know, I'd never set foot in one normally, but sadly, circumstances dictated otherwise. I'll explain. The Premier Inn at Hockley Heath – remember it's spelt "Haitch".. – served evening meals as well as breakfast – which were excellent by the way - mass catering at its most edible and efficient. The Friday evening meals were okay but not exactly what you would call stimulating. You got what you expected, but without any real sense of excitement. You went through the motions of eating.

At the bar, one could buy almost every foreign-named lager you could wish for. Our eyes, however, were firmly fixed on the two traditional hand pumps. Both displayed Bass clips, although only one was working. The temperature of the beer when served was that of lager – freezing! Perfectly acceptable for lager, as there's no taste anyway, but freezing is not the temperature at which beer should be served. It should be room temperature or thereabouts, though I am aware that this is subjective and taste is very individual. It was due to the fact that the Premier Inn had no real ale at all on the Saturday night that we moved down the road to the Harvester. I mean, Premier Inns are a bloody great chain. How can they not get their orders for real ale right? The place was awash with model railway enthusiasts. Surely somebody has told them that steam and beer go together, like Astaire and Rogers, sausage and mash, Liverpudlians and benefit.

So, because of their inefficiencies on the alcoholic liquid front Premier Inns lost the thick end of £100 worth of food sales. The Harvester sold Marstons Pedigree – cold! It was still a reasonable pint, once warmed over the radiators, and glass rubbed between hands. A pint or so was downed by each of us before the meal was served by that waitress, whose tone was mono and enthusiasm akin to someone used to waking up every day knowing that she lived in Birmingham – which she undoubtedly did. The meal was distinctly average and I am being generous at this point. The bill, for six, came to £43.94, and we still felt we were robbed. The table was sticky, the seats covered with crumbs and the noise from the extraction fan above the kitchen area was overbearing. Still, I am sure they know how best to run their business. It did, however, serve as a reminder never to go near a Harvester again, beer or no beer.

Our arrival on checking in on the Friday night at the Premier Inn was very pleasant. A well-rounded, but flat vowelled, local lady with ready wit and smile welcomed us. As did a life-size cardboard cutout of Lenny Henry, who stood by the door to greet us. He smiled also. The three of us shared a twin-bedded room, Peter, Mr. Henry and myself. He seemed to be everywhere. He is obviously the face of the Black Country, or should that be the Black Face of the Country? A booklet entitled "A Premier Welcome....." appears on your dressing table. It opens to Mr. H grinning broadly as he appears to be checked in by a dark-haired lass who smiles in accordance with the photographer's wishes, no doubt. Turning the page, you find Mr. H in robe, testing the bed – luckily for us and those who haven't eaten – without sight of Dawn French. A further turn of the page finds him grinning inanely in bed snuggling up to a teddy bear. You can't see clearly but perhaps the bed isn't big enough for both Mr. & Mrs. H. and a bear. Another page we see him awake and on a further page accepting a breakfast from the very same girl who checked him in at the start of his visit, if I'm not mistaken. Turn again, and oh how hilarious. He has a sausage, from his breakfast presumably, as it would be rude to take it from someone else's, held on a fork in front of his mouth, with the sausage bent in such a position as to replicate his smile. Such fun! Turn again, and we see the bedroom door handle and a "Sshh..... sound asleep" sign. Presumably Dawn is now around. Either that, or the teddy bear is attracting even more attention.

All in all, a good weekend. I really and genuinely couldn't understand why the locals seem to be so happy with their lot. Are they not aware of how they sound to others? Still, their accent is our amusement. What did you say? Pompous? Surely not!

It's been a good week so far. Roger Federer beat Andy Murray and Liverpool were knocked out of the Champions League. Thursday night's television epitomises all that is good with the BBC and everything that is wrong with the commercial stations. "The Restaurant" was followed by the new series of "Gavin & Stacey", which was followed by "QI". "The Restaurant" is now down to four couples and I have to say that I would despair if it were my money going into business with any of them. If I am honest, I am a little disappointed in this series. I think it's the fact that there's no-one I can say I am particularly fond of. One likes to root for a favourite – a bit like in "Strictly" – but we will plough on to the end. With regard to "Gavin & Stacey", Series 3, Episode 1, the jury is out. One continuous gripe, and it's a gripe I've had since Episode 1 of Series 1, is that the actor who plays Gavin is, to me, somewhat wooden and I don't think he looks right. His hair and stance don't help, either. I always see him in a 1970's space uniform, strutting about the Star Ship Enterprise, though "beam me up, Gavin" doesn't ring true somehow.

The week has continued in good form. I have just read that Gordon Ramsay is facing winding up orders against two of his restaurants due to unpaid Inland Revenue bills. Perhaps he should have put some or all of the money he spent remodelling his face towards his tax fund. It's an old-fashioned way of looking at things, Gordon, but I've always found it best to pay one's way in order of priorities. There, I'm sure that will help him in the future.

You're not going to believe this but that last story reminds me of yet another.

A father walks into a market with his young son. The boy is holding a 50p coin. Suddenly the boy starts choking, going blue in the face. His father realises that his son has swallowed the coin, starts panicking and shouts for help. A well-dressed, attractive but serious looking woman in a blue business suit is sitting at a coffee bar in the market, reading her newspaper and sipping a cup of cappuccino. At the sound of the commotion she looks up, puts down her coffee cup, neatly folds the newspaper, places it on the counter, arises from her seat and makes her way very unhurriedly across the market. On reaching the boy, the woman carefully takes hold of his testicles and starts to squeeze, gently at first and then ever more firmly. After a few seconds the boy convulses violently and coughs up the coin, which the woman deftly catches in her free hand. Releasing the boy the woman hands the money back to the father and walks back to her seat in the coffee bar, where without saying a word, she resumes drinking her cappuccino and reading her newspaper. As soon as he is sure that his son has suffered no lasting ill effects, the father rushes over to the woman and starts thanking her. "I've never seen anything like that before", he says, "It was fantastic. Tell me, are you a doctor?" "Oh, no", the woman replies, "I work for the Inland Revenue"!

Also glad to read that the Supreme Court saw common sense and decided against banks having to refund thousands of customers who were charged for unauthorised overdrafts. I never did understand the campaigners' argument. Surely, if you go overdrawn without authorisation, you must expect to pay charges. It's not difficult to understand. If the Supreme Court had upheld the Office of Fair Trading and the campaigning support groups, the cost in refunds would have totalled some £22 billion. The banks would then have had no choice but to recoup that money by charging the poor sod that is not profligate and wasteful. Once again, it's not often you'll ever find me on the side of big business bastard PLC, but fair's fair.

The "Daily Express" highlighted the case of one of those crying over their bank balance. Jason Walsh, a psychiatric nurse, admits that he repeatedly exceeded his overdraft limit over a two-year period. He even accepted that he was "a typically bad bank customer and I just didn't look". Didn't look? He was being charged £25 on direct debits and a £150 for being over his limit. He even states that at some stage he was paying £200 a month in fees. It seems that once again these people wish for everyone else to be responsible for their own stupidity and lack of attention to not a lot of detail. It wasn't hidden in the small print, Mr. Walsh. Perhaps he should see a psychiatrist, I mean he should know of one, what with him working in the industry, an' all! What never ceases to amaze me (though perhaps it should) is that those who feel the rest of us owe them an easy living are supported by such institutions as "Which", "Moneysupermarkets.com" and Martin Lewis who founded "MoneySavingExpert.com." The Chief Executive of "Which", Peter Vickery-Smith, states "It's a bitter blow for the millions of people who have been patiently waiting to get their bank charges back". Have these people lost sight of the fundamentals of borrowing? I suspect it's symptomatic of the times we live in. Those who err, be it legal or illegal, must be indulged, while those who try to play a straight bat pay for it. Still bloody good news, though.

I read a letter on Teletext where the writer was bemoaning the number of "touts" who stopped him or her in the street in order to sell gas, electricity, Sky, mobile phone deals – and no-win, no-fee compensation. These sharks who, as you know, tend to be on the lowest rankings of humanity, along with football agents, seem to be doing good trade in the north-west, which somehow doesn't surprise me. Ten councils, I note, in the Manchester area alone, have paid out fortunes to people apparently injured whilst slipping or stumbling over uneven pavements. Salford Council has lobbed out £1.78 million. Bolton Council wrote a cheque to one woman for £66,000. She injured herself falling over a sunken grid. Good news for all, if you can get it. Bad business for the taxpaying masses.

I'm reminded and I can't think why, but I am, of the story of two women out playing golf. One teed off and watched in horror as her ball headed directly towards a foursome of men who were playing the next hole. The ball hit one of the men. He immediately clasped his hands together at his groin, fell to the ground and proceeded to roll around in agony. The woman rushed across the green to the man and immediately began apologising. "Please allow me to help you. I'm a physiotherapist and I know I can relieve your pain if only you will allow me". "No, it's okay, I'll be all right, I'll be fine in a few minutes", replied the man. He was obviously in agony, lying as he was in the foetal position, still clasping his hands at his groin. At her persistence, however, he finally allowed her to help. Gently she took his hands away and laid them to his side. She loosened his pants and placed her hands within. She administered tender and artful massage for several long moments and asked silkily, "How does that feel now?" "Great", he replied, "it feels great but I still think my thumb's broken".

When passing the vicarage with Mutley this morning, I noticed that the lean-to has been replaced with a boat – not one you sail on a pond, but a full sized one. I'll have to be especially vigilant of a morning, just in case I espy the vicar trying to import Ugandans by way of the Basingstoke Canal. Well, you never know!

As I write this, Somali pirates are holding a British couple hostage. The couple, Paul and Rachel Chandler, were sailing their yacht across the Indian Ocean when they were abducted. It now appears that a British war ship was close by and saw everything, but was unable to help. It must be rather rotten for them, but I have to ask, why were they there? Have they not heard about these Jack-the-lads who are taking bloody great oil tankers on a weekly basis? I suppose you could say they sailed into the face of adversity. The Chandlers hail from Kent, I understand. If they do ever get out of it and back to Blighty, I implore them to stick to the Medway in future. It may be less adventurous, but I'm sure it's for the best in the long run. There, that should be of comfort if they read this – you know, if ever an extract from this book is reprinted in the Somali Times.

Nice to know that our money is still being frittered on those who appear to have received more than their fair share from the taxpayer. A 67-year-old tenant, who weighs nearly 40 stone, is having a home built solely to house him and his wife. Norwich City Council are sadly legally obliged to look after him, as he has – yes, them again – needs. What with his being a registered disabled tenant, a housing association called Flagship have received a grant from the government's Homes and Communities Agency for this special sized home. It will enable him and his wife to sleep in the same room! He spends eleven hours a day watching TV. It makes you laugh, he says "They came round with a plan and we changed a few things and asked for different things for our own needs and any future needs". Notice the needs? I wonder if he turned off the TV when they were there.

Interesting to read that ITV are being sued by one of their ex-news presenters – Lisa Aziz. I remember her and she always came over as being very professional and pleasant. She's taking them to the cleaners for a not inconsiderable £5 million, alleging that she was removed due to her age – she's forty-seven. Well, it won't be the first time. Thus far, my sympathies are with her on the grounds of ageism, though I fail to see how she, or any of her co-presenters, is worth £160,000 per annum. I would have thought £30,000 plus a stocking allowance would have been more than reasonable. Where my sympathies falter is when you read that she claims another presenter impersonated Trevor Macdonald, a fellow black weatherman, as well as mimicking Pakistani and Irish accents. What has that got to do with her case, or the price of eggs? Does she feel the need to bring in the race card? Presumably she does. What worries me is any suggestion that mimicry or impersonation is now an offence, or maybe just an offence if the object of that impersonation is black, blackish or Irish. Anyway, she's now on sick pay and obtaining counselling at the Priory Clinic for work-related stress. Well, it all helps to build up the case, I suspect.

If anyone out there ever queries my dislike and distaste for the Royal Family, one only has to realise that the monarchy cost us poor sods £41.5 million last year. When you add security and policing the price rises to £180 million. The Queen is to seek a rise in her allowance as her funds are becoming severely depleted. The Royals' travel costs for the year were £6.2 million. When will these lapdog supporters of such an archaic, lack-of-value put their collective hands up and accept that the mixed race inbreds should be drummed out of London and given grace-and-favour tenement dwellings in Glasgow. Well, she's always liked Scotland, hasn't she! And it's not just us. There's going to be rumblings in Canada next year when the Queen's visit is expected to cost the host country £2.07 million. Charles and Camilla have just returned from a visit to Canada and this 11-day jolly cost the good citizens £1.5 million. Seventy-eight thousand pounds was paid in hotel fees, £182,000 for media staff and £359,000 for officials..... Who are these hangers-on? I mean, that is an awful lot of money to be spent for an 11-day official visit. I wonder how much Saga could have done it for? No wonder polls show that Canadians want to replace the monarchy with a republic. Princess Beatrice, who performs no royal functions whatsoever, has just cost the public over a quarter of a million pounds. This tidy sum is to refurbish her flat. Not for her, nipping down to B & Q to get her bits and bobs.

Interesting that not long ago the head of Tesco said that finding suitably educated school leavers was a problem. Stuart Rose, the head of M&S, has now stated that school leavers cannot read, write or do any arithmetic. Amazingly similar to previous situations we've discussed, whereby the reality check is dismissed by those responsible for failure. Iain Wright, the Schools Minister, reflected, "Mr. Rose's comments were sweeping generalisations". He laughably added that our school and college leavers are "better equipped for the world of work than they have ever been". I'm shaking my head as I write this. Does he really believe the party line he has to utter? He must be aware that no-one believes him. Look at their poise and dress and listen to them talk, the evidence is there for all to see and hear. Oh, and witness their struggle to answer any general knowledge question on a quiz show!

Hot on the heels of the news that the police inspector in Sussex, who decided to give free head massages, etc. has retracted her offer in the face of public criticism, a Cambridge hospital is to offer advice and a twenty-minute massage. These are part of their de-stressing days to be offered to employees. Apparently, health staff in the NHS takes over ten days a year sick leave, but then they get paid. I've been self-employed for over thirty years and have had two days off when I had flu and couldn't crawl out of bed. But then, being self-employed, you find you never have a bad back.....

If it's not Children in Need, it's National Aids Day, starring Annie Lennox on Breakfast TV. Do we all have to catch it, or something? She was being interviewed this morning and she was wearing a top emblazoned with the words "Aids Positive". Why? Why do people want to champion the survival of the species? Surely all these epidemics help to keep down the population. Can't the do-gooders grasp that fact?

Nice to read that the French are doing their best to help immigrants reach the golden grail, i.e., England. A new camp has been set up for would-be illegal entrants near Calais. This centre will provide beds, food, washing facilities, plus medical and dental care. Advice will flow as dozens attempt to reach our shores and the benefit of, well, benefits. French charities are "inviting" migrants to spend up to two weeks at the camp. This is the second, as another was recently opened close to the last major truck stop before Dunkirk and Calais. I had to travel round the M25 last week and as I passed Clacket Lane Services, and the sign announcing Kent became close, I am sure I could still smell the remains of Sangette!

The Asylum Seekers Charter shows no sign of abating and do-gooders would benefit from reading this in their quest to understand why Middle England bemoans the situation we find ourselves in. There's a family of Somalis who have been treated at our expense to a five-bedroomed home in fashionable (though now becoming less so) Maida Vale. However, Mummy Somali and her seven dwarfs, or children, have outgrown their cost-free haven. Westminster Council have rehoused them in a central London flat, a stone's throw from the shops and lights of the West End. Their pad in Maida Vale cost the tax payer £800 a week. Their new apartment, with balconies giving unparalleled views across the road, is double that rent. Hands up all those who think it's fair. No, I didn't see a hand go up either. It gets better. I've just read on. Apparently Daddy Somali doesn't live with his wife and their already enormous benefit-receiving offspring. He lives with their eighth child in a two-roomed council flat in Camden. Naturally, he doesn't work. Last word goes to Mummy Somali, who stated that the new flat is in a nice, quiet area and they rather like it. Speechless, bloody speechless!

You can always rely on the Keystone Cops to bring some light relief when the only alternative is a cup of tea – which I am just going to make. Figures have just been released showing the top ten police forces in the "car smash premier league". The past year has shown some five hundred cars to be written off. Top of the premier league is the Met, with one hundred and twenty five, West Midlands, unsurprisingly second, Merseyside in third, and very surprisingly, Surrey, in fourth place with twenty-five..... and so it goes on. One can understand the top three places, but how we've lost twenty-five in our revered county is quite inexplicable. I can only assume it's been in the course of duty, attempting to rebuff common people at our borders. Seriously, though, the write-off value of these vehicles is £2.6 million, with nearly double that amount being paid out in compensation to those injured in the pursuit of whomsoever they were pursuing. The number of police car related deaths has also risen from twenty-four two years ago to forty last year. Still, with dark glasses, a uniform and flashing lights being such an aid to fashion, machismo and a go-faster lifestyle, it's bound to turn a chap's head.

It's interesting that Switzerland, not part of the EU, has held a referendum and decided to abide by the decision of its people who have voted. The fact that they are not going to have a second referendum proves they are not part of the EU. Four towers, or minarets, have already been built on mosques in Switzerland, calling people to arms – sorry, prayer. The Muslim population wished to build more, many more. The Swiss have always been a canny nation and decided to nip the problem in the bud before Islamisation, as they call it, takes hold. How sensible, how democratic. The vote was 57% for the ban on further minarets, although the four that are in existence will be allowed to remain. You'd never think that out of a Swiss population of 7 _ million, some 400,000 would be Muslims. But there it is. And while they heed the warning signs and take steps to retain their sovereignty and traditions, our government is examining plans to set up the largest boarding school this country has ever seen. It is, of course, a Muslim school. A charity called Islamic Help is looking to fund raise £1 million to purchase a building which would house the school, a teacher-training base and counselling centre. This would be in Lancashire and would take up to 5,000 Muslim girls. When you consider that Eton has 1,311 places, this is quite some concentration of a single faith. Gordon Prentice, the Labour MP whose Pendle constituency will accommodate the school (soon to be a part of England that will no longer be a part of England) has expressed his concern over the "undermining of community cohesion". Another step on the slippery slope, I say.

After eleven months with us Ben's ability to understand the basis of a walk is still lacking. We decided to buy a haltie. Once unpacked we read the instructions and unlikely as it seems, English was the first language on the menu. We scoured the photos and drawings and try as we might, we didn't quite get to grips with the instructions. Slotting the haltie onto the dog's head was not as easy as we thought. Having called Ben into the kitchen, where he sat quite happily, we tightened and then loosened strips over his nose, under his chin, behind his neck, but without success. William has a haltie for his dog, so we'll wait until we visit him next time and he can show us what to do. Maureen commented on "what a good boy" Ben was, as he sat while we struggled. It was only when I sat in front of him to get an idea of what was wrong that I noticed his willy was poking out! "God", I exclaimed, "the reason he's being so good is because he likes it! I think it's the smell of leather!" He's the only dog I know (though there are probably several in Aldershot) who's into bondage! By the way, Ben has now listened to the CD a couple of times and has shown no fear of the firework and thunder noises that have emanated from our stereo for forty-odd minutes, but as Ben said, "A recording is never as scary as the real thing". Sarky git!

You never know where political correctness and equality is going to strike next, although you know it is inevitable. It seems that genuine need comes a very poor second (vying with common sense) in many cases. There is a refuge for battered women in Weymouth which is to close next year, or this year as you are reading it. It houses six women and their children. Council officials are ignoring the good it does and are to close it. Why? Because it doesn't cater for men. A spoke for Dorset County Council said, "We want to make sure men and women are both helped". The shelter costs £82,780 per annum to run. It is to be replaced with an "outreach service". Doesn't that very title smack of some unaccountable, cheap alternative that will be of no use to anyone except the council budget fixers. What does make you think, however, is that men need shelters in the first place. Try as I might, I cannot contemplate the embarrassment of knocking on a refuge door and saying, "Can I come in? My wife keeps beating me". What sort of men do this? I'm not suggesting for one moment that the man should retaliate and assault the woman in return, but I do feel that he should hold his head up high and leave with dignity, not go skulking away to a male refuge. The story did remind me of a joke, however.

My missus has just gone to hospital with two black eyes and a broken jaw. It seems we were on different wavelengths when she said she wanted decking on the patio!

Taxpayers' generosity shows no sign of abating. I see that nearly £40 million is being spent providing methadone and drug addiction treatment for convicts. This tidy sum is plucked from the NHS budget. Why? Prisoners can no longer be forced to go "cold turkey" as was the method, as opposed to the methadone, in days of yore, as it breaches their human rights of care. It is a ludicrous situation whereby a drug addict, who steals, assaults, burgles, and in some cases destroys people's lives to feed their habit, ends up with these rights. Since a test case was found in their favour, 200 prisoners have successfully sued the authorities for failing to provide medical care for withdrawal of drugs. Each case has won the complainant £4,000 in compensation. I'd love to discuss this with the Howard League for Penal Reform. I wonder if they have a spare year in their diary.

When will the principle be applied that those who get themselves into that mess have a duty to pay their debt to society, not the other way round. As soon as there is a conviction all rights should be lost.

This one will make you laugh, but in a mocking manner. Paul Brown, known as the "Bird Man of Sheppey", is to be transferred from Swaleside Prison in Kent to an undisclosed new location. He has been keeping a budgie company for five years but may not be able to take it with him. You can imagine his response. Yes, you've got it. "What are my human rights?" Mr. Brown is a former bouncer serving a life sentence for killing a chap outside a Rochester pub. He said, "I have had my budgie for over five years and any pet owner will tell you how close you become to your animal. To be told you have to abandon it is very distressing, cruel and stressful for both the animal and yourself". It's probably a bit like the distress, cruelty and stress suffered by the chap who was stabbed, but I'm only guessing.

Mind you, it gets better with this little story to end the trio of prison woes. Kirkham Prison near Preston in Lancashire, which is category D, has one of the country's worst records for drug use and escaping. So, it's only natural that the prisoners are being asked to pay £1 each to enter a draw, the prize for which will be a day out unescorted. I know, it's another one of those April

Fools, but not in April. In order to qualify for the prize the governor, one John Hewitson, has informed prisoners that they must help cook a Christmas dinner at a nearby care home, with the entry money going towards the cost of the meal. With Blackpool less than ten miles away, one can imagine where the winner will be headed. The assistant secretary to the Prison Officers' Association said, "What is happening here is abhorrent. There are ways and means of arranging for prisoners to be allowed out for a time as part of their rehabilitation, but the decision should not depend on the outcome of a raffle. The public are funding this because the prisoners are paying to enter from their prison wages, which are paid by the tax payer". This raffle was arranged under something known as the "Incentives and Earned Privilege Scheme". This was introduced in 1995 and the idea is to encourage good behaviour by allowing privileges such as wearing personal clothes or watching TV in cells. You might like to know that the inmates at Kirkham enjoy a range of leisure facilities, including salsa classes and a putting green. If only we could put the money available to prisoners to support the same activities in care homes one would feel that justice was being seen to be done.

Now here we have the case of Amjaid Karim whose name would indicate quite strongly that he is of foreign extraction, i.e. not one of us! He is one of those who have failed to learn respect for others or our laws, and doubtless never will. Since 1997 he has clocked up thirty-five convictions, many of them for motoring offences. He was disqualified at the age of 18 but still managed to crash a stolen car. Karim is very brave and has high moral values, as he left a friend covered in blood in the wreckage. He gave himself up four days later, his friend died. Three years on, and he was caught again for dangerous driving, given a four-year jail sentence and banned from driving for a further ten. If he had been made to serve those four years he would still be in prison. But by August, 2009, the police saw him driving erratically, this time having stolen a Mercedes. They chased him at speeds of up to 140 mph. It ended when he crashed into railings. Sadly, for the public at large, he survived, unlike his ex-friend, of course. Once again, he ran off but was found hiding nearby in a pond. There should be a by-law that says that if you run away from the scene of a crime, take refuge in a pond, therefore confirming your status as pondlife, you should be made to end your days there – death by drowning! There – sorted!

Sad to see that another young lad, this time a four-year-old, has been killed by a so-called family pet. This follows on from a five-year-old being killed in similar circumstances. Between these attacks the police started to track down those owning dangerous dogs, and more than eighty illegally held or owned dogs were taken from their owners. This is just in Liverpool and Lancashire. Is it a north-west thing to own a bull breed of some description and of such aggression? I can only presume that in that part of the world the dog is seen as a fashion/macho statement. I am aware this mentality is universal though, as we have owners like that just over the border in Aldershot and Farnborough. I find it's the underclass's way of coming to terms with their own inadequacy – and that's really the nub of it. I suspect there's more of that "underclass" in the north-west than elsewhere. As I take Ben along the canal, we regularly come into contact with owners whose dogs have names such as Pip, Poppy, Bonnie, Daisy and Alfie. So much less aggressive than Spike, Sabre, Satan, Debo, Ty (after Mike Tyson, I understand). Such hero worship! But pet names do tell you a lot about the owners.

This is a good'un. A 22-year-old Brazilian English language student confronted a 57-year-old drug addicted burglar outside his home. The Brazilian hit the burglar with a vodka bottle and was then charged with causing grievous bodily harm (as opposed to grievous bodily fluids!). Anyhow, the charge was dropped when the burglar declared that "being attacked was a hazard of his chosen profession". Nice to see that burglary now ranks as a profession. However, his attitude was unusually candid and noble, I felt, but here we have the rub. Having been convicted and given five years, four months' jail for his troubles, the burglar appealed on the grounds that his injuries had caused him significant money problems, impacting on his ability to manage and organise his life. Mrs. Justice Rafferty, the appeal court judge, stated that the vodka bottle, which by the way was of the 3-litre variety (or big-bugger, in common parlance) caused two serious internal brain haemorrhages, two fractures of the skull and multiple fractures of his facial bones. She added that "equally as importantly, neuro-psychological damage cannot be ruled out. We think it is arguable that insufficient account was taken of the severity and effect of these injuries". Nice to see so much concern for someone who costs the taxpayer a fortune through his own misdemeanours. If anyone was a victim of his own failure, then it was this chap. The upshot of it is that his sentence was reduced by ten months to reflect the injuries sustained. What a joke, though I well recall the kleptomaniac who, whenever things looked bad always took something for it!

Only in this festering sore of a country such as ours could a judge let someone who has admitted to over 650 burglaries off on the grounds that he felt the offender had "turned over a new leaf". Not only did Judge Christopher Ball not lock him up, but also he arranged for the offender, one Bradley Warnham, aged 18, and his girlfriend, to be rehoused, rent free, in a new town. I don't even have to tell you the aftermath of this story, do I? Yes, that's right, he has been arrested on suspicion of two more burglaries. Eighteen years of age, over 650 to his name, and the presiding representative of the Crown thinks he has managed to change his ways. What a joke, too, the sequel.

I read with dismay that due to a major change in the European Agricultural Policy the principle of farmers allowing fields to be left as grassland, or "set-aside", has been scrapped. The upshot in this country is that barn owl numbers have plummeted. All the hard work over decades to increase their stock are to no avail, and all due to the faceless, pointless bastards in Europe (do I sound ever so slightly aggrieved? I do hope so). Two-thirds of the barn owls in Suffolk were unable to produce offspring this year. The rate of success of those that did hatch is much lower than previous years, and all because there is insufficient food. Still, I'm sure it will all help Barratts and Wimpey when the next round of housebuilding starts again in earnest.

For every negative, there's a positive. Two burglars who robbed an outdoor pursuit store in South Wales were both killed when a train hit their mode of escape - a quad bike - shortly after 4 am in the morning. Apparently, they and two others on another quad bike used the railway line to gain access to the site. They entered using bolt cutters before ramming the store with said bikes and driving off with £40,000 of stolen goods. Usually, the railway is devoid of trains at this hour, but for once an unscheduled train happened to be in the right place at the right time. The other quad bike was also hit, but the burglars managed to get away uninjured. The police at the time of writing are still searching for them. More fortunate, is that all of the goods were retrieved. I really do hope they were still in clean and tidy condition. There may not be a God but I'm not so sure that St. Christopher isn't overseeing justice as the Patron Saint of Travel.

They never stop coming, do they? I've just happened across another miserable scrote to add to the list of miserable scrotes. Once again, it's a politically correct miserable scrote. This female, a Ms who works for the University of Alberta in Canada, goes under the name of Shauna Wilton. Apparently, after watching an episode of Thomas the Tank Engine with her 3-year-old daughter (note she's not a Mrs) she became concerned. Now, most people just enjoy it for what it is – childish escapism. Not our Ms Wilton, oh no. She, a "political analyst" by trade – please, someone, can they tell me what she actually does – started her journey, or mission, by reviewing twenty-three other episodes. At the end of her analysis, she spoke at a conference on political science in Canada. She thinks that the programmes expound "conservative political theology, with stories portraying a rigid class system with a lack of women". She sees Thomas, Percy and James as representing downtrodden workers, slaving away for their rich boss, the Fat Controller. She also counters that the "themes" of the stories are not "constructive" for children.

Her final comment is "eventually these children will attain full political citizenship, and the options and world outlook they develop now, partially influenced by stories like Thomas, are part of that process". Really! People like her should get out onto a real steam railway and just enjoy the scenery. I pity her 3-year-old growing up with someone who analyses every nuance or inflection within a children's television programme. I think there's a case for the child to be taken into care, on the grounds of her mother's obsessive feminism and miserable scrotism. PS - telling the Wilton woman that all engines are "she's" might have helped Thomas's case, though somehow I doubt it.

Here's a group Ms Wilton would feel at home with. There's a worryingly ghastly gaggle of people calling themselves "Pink Stinks". They are a pressure group whose cause, or issue, is with girls playing with "pink" toys. They want people to boycott shops and stores that sell these "sexist" toys to girls. What is their problem? Boys are in blue, girls are in pink. Please don't tell me it's going to mar their future careers, or lack of them should this state of affairs continue to exist. Even more disturbing is the news that the Justice Minister, Bridget Prentice, is backing them to the hilt. She added her four-pennyworth (plus VAT!) by stating that "It's about not funnelling girls into pretty, pretty jobs, but giving them aspirations and challenging them to fulfil their potential". And this woman is not only in politics but she's a Minister. Presumably there are a few votes to be had from the radical left, then. It would be interesting to know if the Minister was told by her parents not to play with anything pink on the grounds that it might impede her career. Somehow I suspect not.

Just a quickie – nice to read that the French Justice Minister says that Muslims who force their wives to wear burkhas are not welcome in France. Oh, to hear Jack Straw being that brave. I remember seeing Jethro on stage in Aldershot a couple of years ago, live. Well, he would be, no point paying good money to see a stand-up comic lying down dead! Anyway, I loved his gag about going to a Muslim birthday party. He said he had never played "pass the parcel" so quickly in all his life. He received a good response from the audience for that. Which reminds me – did you have that Muslim lady call on you last Saturday? No? Oh, she called here. Full niqab, the works. Could only see her eyes. She rang our bell and waited. I didn't answer. I just looked through the letterbox and said, " See how you like it".

The "let's use health and safety as a panacea for all ills" bandwagon is rolling on rather nicely. The Grand Arcade shopping centre in Cambridge, not unreasonably, has a "no hoods policy". It has security officers to enforce this rule, though they appear reluctant unless the occupier of the hood is over 80-years-of-age. Witnesses had stated that youngsters in hoods had not been challenged by security staff. However, Peggy Harden and her husband, Desmond, both 84, were walking through the Centre when a security officer approached them and asked her to remove the rain hood from her jacket. Mrs. Harden is 5'2" and walks with a stick. Hardly the type to cause mayhem, but an easy target for those wishing to make an impression. Interesting, then, that while the security officer advised the Hardens that the "no hood" policy is for security reasons, a spoke for the shopping centre said, "It's more about health and safety than security", (please tell me how?). No mention of burkhas being a risk to H & S or security then! He then came out with the following meaningless bull. "Grand Arcade has a 'no hood' policy to ensure a safe and enjoyable shopping experience for everyone. However, it is not our intention to cause any upset and we apologise for any stress that may have been caused. We are reviewing our policy to ensure the safety and well-being for all our customers". Why didn't he just say, "Someone should have used a bit of common sense. Sorry".

I see that the number of people driving whilst on the phone has doubled in the past two years. It's really not surprising, surely. The fine may have risen from £60 to £1,000, but I witness the arrogant morons on their phones every day of the week. Motorways, main roads, B-roads, country lanes..... Suits in BMWs, mother plus children in 4-wheel drives – they couldn't give a monkey's. Make the fine hurt and disqualify everyone for one year for the first offence, five years for the second. That might start to make an impression and would certainly help me with traffic when driving around the M25.

The insurance company, Endsleigh, has released figures as to where the safest and worst driving areas are to be found in the UK. Belfast, Bangor (north Wales) and Swansea were the safest. Slough, Bradford and Birmingham were the worst. I wonder if being areas of high immigration has anything to do with their league position? I can hear the Race Relations Board bleating before the Biro ink is dry on this page. But, of course, any statistic showing a negative factor for the minorities would be hastily lost within the filing system.

CHAPTER ELEVEN

Magi, Mistletoe and Misery

So, Terry Wogan bows out of radio broadcasting after several decades. I can honestly say, hand on heart, that I never heard him once. I thought I was listening to his show many years ago, but it turned out to be Ken Bruce. Did the bosses at Radio 2 decide on Chris Evans as his replacement in an effort to decrease the listening audience overnight? I cannot see his style being commensurate with the leisurely, homely style that I am sure Mr. Wogan brought to millions of households.

I like Sarah Kennedy as she is far more unpredictable. We need mavericks, as you know, and she fulfils this broadcasting role admirably. But then, anyone who publicly declares that Enoch Powell was the best PM we never had is always going to be all right with me – and the rest of Middle England, I suspect.

I was driving home from a talk yesterday afternoon when the PM News spent some considerable time on the current trial of Peter Tobin, who is now found to have committed other rapes and murders. The accounts of how he picked up young girls, drugged them, raped them and then disposed of their bodies in rubbish sacks showed just what a callous person he is. Awful as it was to listen to, I continued without feeling any great emotion. There then followed an interview with his ex-wife, who from her account, appeared lucky to still be alive. The mental, psychological and physical torture he put her through was truly horrific. It was when the ex-wife got to the point in her story where she mentioned that he had once bought a dog for her as a pet that I turned the radio off. I never did find out what happened, but from her voice and the way the story was going, I knew it wasn't going to be a happy ending. Strange, the point one gets to, where you don't want to hear any more – but there it is. Emotions are like everything else – very subjective.

There is a picture of Mr. Tobin in this morning's paper which jogged the memory of last night's listening. It shows a very ordinary looking man, one you could imagine serving you in a hardware store, but then, people like him don't go around with the words "evil bastard" in neon lights across their forehead. Sadly, even if they did, you would never be confident that the police would spot such signs.

Getting back to animals for a mo, there was a two-page article in the "Daily Express" concerning the slaughter of horses during World War 1. Over 1,000,000 were transported to France and over half that number never returned. Accompanying the article were two photographs, one of which was very large and very explicit, showing soldiers amongst the debris of war. In the foreground there were dead horses and a now horseless wagon . I really don't know how I could have coped seeing this senseless slaughter if I had been unlucky enough to have been born when this atrocity of a war was being fought. I never read the article as once again, my anger and emotions from that story would have ruined my day. The picture told me everything I needed to know and feel. They stay with you, as have the ones of the elephant and the polar bears being shot for fun. I see the black Russian bear is now a very endangered specie, shot by hunters for both fun and money. The money emanates from the Chinese food market that appears to have an appetite for paws and the medical market that requires certain innards for its potions. In the same way as the Chinese have destroyed the tiger population for body parts, they are doing the same with the bear. But obviously there are no sanctions as trade and money always prevail.

There was an article in the "Daily Express" a few days ago stating that the government was to introduce aspects of Sharia law into UK legislation. It concerned the financial sector. Today, there are two pictures in the newspaper, one showing a man in Somalia buried up to his waist in a field, having been sentenced in court to die. His crime was adultery and murder. The second photograph which was digitally altered so as not to reveal his head, shows the stoning to death of the same man. What a pity it wasn't this part of the law that we are introducing into ours. The bugger wouldn't be doing it again.

There is definitely a "them and us" when it comes to race and religion. A Muslim woman walking along the road, wearing the full head gear, eye-slits only, has had her veil torn off her. Not for one moment am I condoning this behaviour, but when you read of the price paid by the culprit, it seems to be out of all proportion when compared to the many vicious attacks on members of the public, leaving them severely injured. But then most of them have been white. This case does not mention any form of physical attack, so whilst the "assault" was really not on, a 16-week jail sentence, suspended for a year, 150 hours Community Service and a £1,000 compensation package, is surely a tad over the top. Naturally, the victim talks of feeling "invaded" – a bit like we feel in England. She talks of being "emotionally and psychologically hurt". She now feels scared to walk down the street. Well, that all seems to add up to £1,000. The charge, by the way, was of "religiously aggravated assault". I have to tell you that I wouldn't mind a grand for having my titfer knocked off, though it wouldn't be a religious hat, obviously. D'you know, I've never seen a Calvinist trilby, a Wesleyan homburg or a Baptist bowler on sale in Dunns. Perhaps I've missed them!

What a bloody cheek! The Payments Council, which I believe to be a relatively new organisation/quango set up by the banking industry, has decided that cheques are to be phased out by 2018. I have absolutely no doubt that whilst it is time and money consuming for them, it will be a grave disappointment to millions of us. The cheque was/is one of the finest inventions ever. The banking industry will no doubt be rubbing their hands with glee, as they excitedly look for ways to narrow and control the public's ability to pay for goods. This, in turn, will extend the amount of profit they can extract from each transaction. Please tell me who benefits from these decisions. Is it us? Never! It's always Greedy Bastard plc.

What an indictment on our society when one reads of two 10-year-old boys being charged with the rape of an 8-year-old girl. The days of innocence with the phrase "you show me yours and I'll show you mine" have long gone, I know, but these two children knew right from wrong at their age and I am always of the opinion that leopards rarely change their spots. God knows what they will be like when they grow up.

Nowhere is that last observation more appropriate than the 5-year stretch just handed out to a burglar who preys on the elderly. He is now 28 and has shown no sign of change after a lifetime of crime. At the age of 15, Social Services took him on a boating holiday in the hope he would see the error of his ways. That £13,000 trip just taught him how to stick two fingers up to society.

Good news! All our Christmas cards have been posted. I've checked all those that we have received just to make sure we haven't missed anyone out. The really good news is that so far, I've extracted seven unfranked stamps from the envelopes, which have either been restuck, or Pritt-stuck, onto new envelopes – well, I hate waste. I've also learned the lesson of buying non-Christmas stamps this year. Last year I was over enthusiastic as to the number of friends we actually had and eventually got rid of the last of the colourful Christmas chappies at Easter. Anyone receiving such a stamped envelope from me would be of the opinion that I am Tony-No-Mates. Well, I am an only child and an ex-trainspotter.

As I mentioned earlier with regard to the cost of newspapers, one way I manage to hold back or check before purchasing anything is to revert in my mind as to the price of the goods in LSD. That way I can see what I am actually paying for anything. The Royal Mail has decided in its finite wisdom to increase the price of a second-class stamp from 6 shillings to 6 shillings and 5 pence. The cost of a first class stamp will rise to 7 shillings and 10 pence. That is the seventh rise in seven years. Well, at least they are consistent, but it does give you some idea as to why I become so happy on espying an unfranked stamp.

Just occasionally one reads a story that, not for the first time in this book, warms the cockles of the coldest of hearts. A lady – I don't know her, but I like her – Beth Tyler-King, looks after injured and homeless animals. She took in a fox cub which had been chased by mindless thugs. Now, the lady in question is deaf and Beth (if I may call her by her first name) didn't take long to realise that the fox cub was also deaf. Over the past eighteen months she has managed to get the fox to understand hand signals. The picture in the "Daily Express" of Beth and fox sitting on the windowsill (that's the fox, not Beth) encapsulates all that is rewarding and satisfying about our relationship with animals. What one person would kill for, another would devote time to. I don't think it takes too much thought as to which one is the nicer person.....

Well, it's snowed. The pundits are even forecasting the possibility, not to mention the pissability, of a white Christmas – which will be nice. Everything has stopped, of course – schools are closed, shops are closed, factories are shut and there's a run on milk and bread. I remember the Big Freeze in 1963. Now, that went on for some time. We were not sent home from school or made to stay at home on grounds of health and safety. Like workers, we walked to school if the buses were not running. I think the big problem today is that everyone under thirty has been cosseted and the younger you are, the worse it gets. It seems that everybody has to be cocooned by health and safety from being exposed to any form of perceived danger – from falling conkers to a three-rung ladder. The problem will be that when a major disaster happens, few will be mentally prepared and that's a lot different from being practically prepared. During the Second World War no-one had experience of finding themselves in an Anderson shelter, only to emerge at the end of the raid and discover they no longer had a house, or sometimes a loved one, but they learned to survive, cope and make the best of it. It became known as the Blitz Spirit – it was a very British thing and I seriously doubt if it could be resurrected in the multi-cultural society, such as it is now. But, it's only snow and what for the north of England is winter, for the south is a disaster.

I am airing the first of my New Year wishes now. Please, please, spare me from personalities wanting to "come out" in public. After Stephen Gately's long goodbye we (and it can't just be me, surely) are suffering from Gareth Thomas's long hello, as opposed to "Hello, sailor". He's a rugby player, apparently, which makes him the quintessential macho-man. GT has been leading a double life for twenty years. His fizzog and story are all over the papers and TV chat and news shows. Being 6'3", sixteen stone, representing Wales and the British Lions, the news of his throwing an odd-shaped ball for the other side has been met with respect by both players and fans alike. But then it would be, wouldn't it! It's like having the Jeremy Kyle show on every channel's news. "It's been really tough, hiding who I really am". "If it helps someone else, then it will have been worth it". Please – why not just tell a few friends and let it rest. It's all becoming a sort of celebration.

Now! Let's get this straight, we take in foreigners because we are too gutless not to, they then abuse our unbelievable hospitality and commit crimes, before being cared for in our prisons. At the end of their sentence, or about four weeks whichever is the shorter, they are now being sent from whence they came with a goody bag, courtesy of you and me. This "goody bag" consists of cash-loaded cards worth £454 to use once back on their home soil, plus support packages worth up to £5,000 in order for the criminals to start up their own business, or enter training – or buy drugs or pimp or..... Phil Woolas, a man not fit to be an immigration officer, let alone the Immigration Minister, is responsible for this disgusting waste of our hard-earned money. So, we pay to say goodbye. How long will our border control, or should that be lack of control, be able to repel the "boarders" under EU laws?

It is a sobering thought that as the cash machines in foreign climes jingle with the sound of our discontent, Mohammed Ibrahim, aged 32, who ran down and killed a 12-year-old girl is allowed to stay. He is another failed asylum seeker who has never held a licence, yet has a host of motoring offences to his lack of credit. He was on bail and disqualified when he ran down Amy Houston. You can see what sort of man – or lack of it – he is when you realise that he then ran away from the scene of the crime, leaving her fatally wounded beneath the wheels of the car. This complete waste of her life happened in 2003. Ibrahim is an Iraqi Kurd who has staved off efforts to deport him for six years – and he has won on the grounds that to be sent home would be too dangerous for him. Not as dangerous as it was for Amy Houston. Fourteen months ago he was finally to be deported but, hey, our Kurd has married an English lass and fathered two children! So now an asylum and immigration tribunal judge has ruled that he can stay on the grounds that – wait for it – "deportation would harm his right to family life". What about the right to life that he took from Amy Houston? Her parents must have been going through hell this last six years but then, as we all know, he has rights. Who is this judge who is so blind and out of touch? You shake your head in disbelief.

Right! Let us lighten the mood. Here we have some silly throwaways reminiscent of, if not from, the Tommy Cooper stable. These are jokes that can be told in mixed company and enjoyed by all, even those you invited for Christmas dinner but hoped would have passed away before the event arrived.

I went to the butcher's the other day and I bet him fifty quid that he couldn't reach the meat on the top shelf. He said, "I'm not taking your bet, the steaks are too high!"

I went to a seafood disco last week. D'you know what – I pulled a mussel.

My friend drowned in a bowl of muesli. It was a strong currant that pulled him in!

A man goes to a doctor with a strawberry growing out of his head. The doctor says "Don't worry, I'll give you some cream to put on it".

Another man walks into the same doctor's (I'm trying to keep down the cost of travel!) He says "Doctor, I've hurt my arm in several places". The doctor says "Well, don't go there any more".

A third man is at the same doctor's (It's been a busy day!). He says, "Doc, I can't stop singing the Green Green Grass of Home". "Mmmm", says the doc, "that sounds like Tom Jones syndrome". "Is it common?" "Well, it's not unusual!"

A man walks into a doctor's surgery (It's the last patient of the day) "What seems to be the problem?" asks the doctor. The man looks sheepish. "It's, mmm, well....., mmm, I have five penises", the embarrassed man finally blurts out. "Blimey", says the doctor, "how do your underpants fit?" "Like a glove", said the man, "like a glove".

And lastly, a couple to put you in the mood for Christmas, or possibly to wish it was over. Why was Santa's helper feeling down? Because he was suffering from low elf-esteem.

I don't know whether you're aware, but Santa's helpers are merely subordinate Claus's.

I went round to my mother's today. Once more, it was like visiting Miss Haversham when she was having a really bad day! I think mum was asleep, as there were a couple of mumbles before she replied, "Ooh-oops". That's her usual reply to my "morning" as I open the front door. She hadn't opened her post, although she had picked it up off the floor, which was a start, I suppose. I suggested that she begin writing her Christmas cards but, as last year, she doesn't seem particularly interested. What she really wants is for me to write the cards, address them, put stamps on them and then post them. The first thing one has to do is to look through the address book to make sure that everyone who is anyone has not been overlooked. In reality, it means that she doesn't want to forget anyone who sent her a card. I've just realised how much "like mother, like son" that sounds – bugger! I offered to make her a cup of tea . She always replies "oh, yes please", but she is never in the process of making one for herself when I arrive. She doesn't seem

248

to be interested in doing even that, as it involves getting up and walking to the kitchen. Or, in short, making the effort. She said she had been crying the day before as she had awoken and thought my dad was still there in the chair opposite. I'm not unsympathetic. I know how awful that feeling can be. I woke up this morning and thought Ali Bastian was still in "Strictly Come Dancing", until I remembered that she had been knocked out last night. It really wasn't fair, she was so much better than Chris Hollins but then, that's what happens when you give the public the chance to decide. And they do decide on personalities, not performances. But, hey-ho.

Apart from this setback in fairness the weekend went extraordinarily well. Charlton won, Manchester United lost at home to Aston Villa. Liverpool lost at home to Arsenal. Not that I have a lot of time for Arsene Whinger but it is all a question of priority. Just getting back to "Strictly" for a moment, what was the point of introducing "Barcy Dussell" for the last three weeks? As there are now five judges, one tends to be missed out for comment in order to save time after each dance. Darcy brings nothing more to the show, other than her beautiful looks, of course – oh, and her speech pattern and diction. Is she there to test the public's reaction as a potential replacement for the dictionless Dixon? I wonder.....

I've just received a letter from one Marshall Monks, who is the director of customer care for EDF Energy – with whom we obtain our gas and electricity. The first paragraph extols the virtue of paying by monthly direct debit. We do – and now will be receiving a 6% discount, which for a typical customer will mean a saving of £70 per annum. The second paragraph informs us that their dual fuel discount will amount to another £8 being saved each year. The last paragraph contains the vomit-inducing line, "We're trying to help you save today, to save tomorrow". This is followed by the words "Yours sincerely" which I felt sure was a mis-spelling, or shortened version, of "insincerely", probably part of the company's cut-backs. Why do I see the face of Hughie Green when I read the name "Marshall Monks"?

Having read that youth crime is reducing and that youth offenders will no longer be called youths because the word has "negative connotations" and never believing the lie for one second, what still shocks is the level of violence used by the perpetrators. I see that the police in Birmingham have arrested six males aged between sixteen and twenty-two, plus three girls aged seventeen to nineteen. They were all involved in the death of a 57-year-old man, kicked to death outside a shopping parade. It appears that he refused to hand over a cigarette when requested. Some or all of the men also hit him with bottles. The bottles were handed over by the girls who collected them from a nearby bottle bank. The man's wife, or girlfriend, screamed for them to stop, but they continued until he died. Six young men, one 57-year-old. Such bravery. It's for scum such as this that hanging should be reintroduced.

Where does this hatred and violence stem from? Is it from films, Internet? I'm sure it all contributes. Not to mention the drugs. The only way to stop those with this mentality is to put them down. They have to be taken out of the system for ever. It is the only sure way you know that they will never re-offend. Earlier this year I remember the case of three yobs who assaulted a passer-by in Redhill for refusing to give them a cigarette. Tom Wayland, who appears to be the ringleader of this gang of three, was the one who knocked Mr. Craven, a 42-year-old, to the ground. He had a beer can (though more likely lager) smashed over his head before being hit on the back of the neck and smacked in the ribs. The second member of the gang, a girl of sixteen, then stamped on his head, before a 17-year-old joined in the attack. And what was the punishment? They were all subjected to a 3-year supervision order and made to pay £400 each in compensation. If it had been me, they would have all got the birch and ordered to pay several thousand pounds in compensation. Oh, and the minimum imprisonment would have been ten years each in my newly constructed Newgate Prison. Again, what was the judge thinking of? As he passed sentence, he actually said, "The public will ask what on earth am I doing". Well, if he doesn't know..... And while the victim and his family have to come to terms with such an awful ordeal, Wayland's mother wrote on some website, "We can now enjoy Christmas, now that my Tommy's home. Thank you very much everyone for your support". What sort of person supports such thuggery? Even if she is family, can she not see the wider picture as to what sort of thug her son is and show a touch more thought and compassion for the victim.

I remember the case of a driving instructor and her pupil being surrounded by a gang of yobs on a housing estate in Bristol. One smashed the back window of the instructor's car and stole her laptop. Another opened the glove compartment and started rummaging through. She was then punched repeatedly before they ran off with her mobile phone. The main culprit, who has a history of such crimes, pleaded not guilty. Once at court Judge Jamie Tabor stated that the driving instructor was "too believable". He described the lady as being of "good character", and said that her courage, clarity of thought and undoubted honesty "would sway the jury against the defendant". So the case was dismissed. How in the name of sanity and fairness are you ever to believe in our judicial system? For me, it stinks! You have gun gangs posing on the web, the police letting off child rapists and judges saying that they wished to give harsher sentences but their hands are tied.

I have to tell you that I have a pile of cases extracted over the year concerning assaults, robberies, drink driving, etc that have been sitting on my desk whilst I have been writing this book. The sheer depth of the pile shows how unfair our system is. Not one punishment has been seen to fit the crime. I've now decided to file them, rather than mention them in detail – save one.

This is from last January and concerns a young man called Paul Midgley, aged 23. He and his girlfriend, Chloe Morton, aged 22, had just moved into a house together. Mr. Midgley, an accountant, was walking back to his parents' home after a night out, when Lee Swales, who was sixteen at the time and drunk, felled Mr. Midgley with a single blow. He died four days later – manslaughter, not murder, was the charge. Swales was sentenced to 2 _ years in a youth offenders' institution. He took the life of an ordinary, law-abiding member of society, ruined his family's life, his girlfriend's life and for what? Two and a half years, although probably less.

Please don't tell me that life is fair. There are photographs of both the victim and the aggressor. The former looks an open, fresh-faced lad, the other, pure evil. I wonder if they are born that way?

From those who err to those who enforce – but sadly, often err themselves. Having just read that a Surrey Chief Superintendent and a Superintendent are soon to be making a trip to court in connection with speeding fines which appear to have been unpaid, mainly because those involved are members of Surrey Police, the following should be a sobering thought. It was back in January that a glazier was banned from replacing a police station window because he had committed a motoring offence. I know – but read on. Paul Kerfoot, aged 55, was told he could not work on any Nottinghamshire Police Station as he had accrued three points within the past five years. Detective Chief Inspector Mike Windmill-Jones (there's posh!) stated that, "All contractors were vetted in line with national policy". What does that mean, when it's at home? Paedophiles have rights, left-handed black lesbian asylum seekers have rights (obviously!). But a glazier with three points doesn't! I'd like to know exactly what "national policy" says about those of us convicted of minor motoring offences. I've had three points on my licence within the last five years. Do we all pose some sort of threat – and if so, what? Just a thought, but is there not such a thing as "deprivation of livelihood"?

An interesting statistic showed that over half of all Metropolitan police gross misconduct cases involved community cop-outs (Community Support Officers). Many have been sacked or reprimanded for criminal offences – drink driving, motoring offences, misusing police computers, behaving inappropriately, etc. It's no real surprise, is it. They are not "proper" police. The wonderfully named Martin Tiplady, who is Director of Human Resources for the Met (I wonder at what cost) said, "Boredom and reduced motivation were partly to blame". He said that some felt like glorified security guards. Not that high in the professional pecking order, surely.....

Mind you, so-called "proper" policemen aren't whiter than white anyway. Some are gun-running! Two police constables, one of whom has been in his force for over twenty-one years, the other, eight, have both been arrested and suspended. The allegation is that they resold guns handed in for destruction. Someone's pension isn't going to be all it was cracked up to be!

I am sure fraud, theft and corruption have been prevalent in all police forces since Dixon ruled Dock Green. It was just covered up more back then, more secret, more of a secret society really. A bit like the Catholic Church and child abuse, but with different uniforms.

What PC Lauderdale never witnessed was colleagues being allowed time off for pagan ceremonies or to become members of the trans-gender police association. In the escalating drive for equality and religious correctness police who worship heathen gods are to be allowed up to eight days per annum in order to celebrate their chosen festivals. The "Pagan Police Association" is now officially recognised by the Home Office and will be attracting funding from you and me. The picture accompanying this article shows a police constable who is a follower of paganism. His name is Andy Pardy, only one letter away from Andy Pandy – so close, yet..... But then, we subsidise the Black Police Association. Why? The trouble is, where do these associations stop? At least we now know why we won't be seeing the full complement of police on our streets during the summer solstice or Hallowe'en. They'll all be buggering off to worship Wicker, Thor or Arthur or Uther Pendragon (that should save at least one e-mail telling me I got it wrong!) So we should find a few of them downing speed cameras and donning face paint and weird clothing. Christ Almighty, they're only a set of bells away from becoming fully paid up members of the Morris Dancers' Association (if there is one). They'll be next in line for public funding. As always, there was an unnamed Home Office spoke who said, "The government wants a police service that reflects the diverse communities it serves". That statement would, of course, include the NTPA – or to give it its full title – the National Trans Police Association. This all-embracing collective appeared in public for the first time at the three-day trans-gender festival – or Away Gay, as I prefer to think of it – in Manchester's Gay Village.

Naturally supported by Greater Manchester Police, the NTPA currently consists of approximately fifty members. This includes male and female police officers who have either had sex change operations or are on the waiting list. Not to be excluded are those who dress in clothing of the opposite sex, but are not going ahead with "gender reassignment surgery". Does that mean, then, that we could soon all be having our collars felt by someone dressed in a skirt but sporting a large Adam's apple and speaking with a deep voice? Let's hope they don't mistakenly raise their sausage instead of their truncheon – could be painful! You see, once again, it's not that I have a problem with them being police officers, it's reading that the group communications co-ordinator, Martha Hand, comments that NTPA will be applying for public funds to promote their work. Bloody cheek! What work? And why should it be paid out of our funds? On a footnote, Ms. Hand, who used to be a male custody officer and is currently a civilian worker with Lothian and Borders Police Force, is hoping to complete her sex change. The report doesn't specify when, but it's presumably some time before she leaves this mortal coil. Wouldn't be surprised if we pay for that as well. I note she changed her/his name to Martha. With a surname like Hand, surely it would have been more appropriate to call herself Fanny!

And if it's not enough for police constables and sergeants to cross-dress on duty, they are donning burkhas, niqabs and full Muslim garb. It could only happen in this race-petrified country. Three policewomen went out onto the streets in Sheffield, two covered entirely, except for the eye slits. They were accompanied by four Muslim women. In return, Muslim women were taken on a tour of Sheffield police station's custody suite and CCTV office. All very cosy and no doubt costly. The force's farce came under the heading of an "In Your Shoes Day". Even more cosy! While representatives of groups such as the "Centre for Social Cohesion" and the "Taxpayers Alliance" plus the local Tory MP all condemned the "must get out more" day as a waste of public money, political correctness got even madder. A sycophantic spoke for South Yorkshire Police stated that the force was keen to, yes you've got it, "celebrate diversity". Do they read this crap from a pre-set speech? Sergeant Deb Leonard, one of the gang of three who donned burkhas, said – and I warn you, get the sick bucket ready - "I have gained an appreciation and understanding of what Muslim females experience when they walk out in public in clothing appropriate to their beliefs". For me, it beggars belief! What? There was no sick bucket handy – well, I did warn you!

The report didn't comment as to whether the Muslims felt any greater appreciation as to why so many of their kin folk are in custody suites or under CCTV surveillance, but then, not all porkers are equal.

It's not just in South Yorkshire that this latest round of "diversity culture" is costing the taxpayer. Oh, no. In Avon and Somerset the police are issuing headscarves for their female front-liners when entering places of ethnic minority worship. There are two colours available – black for fully qualified professional police officers and blue for the pointless community cop-outs. The force's Assistant Chief Constable, Jackie Roberts, who, by the way has issued herself with one (black presumably?) commented from the PC hymn sheet, or Koran – whatever! – please read that last word in the manner delivered by Catherine Tate, i.e. dismissive. She said, "Producing head coverings for our officers and staff to wear in places of worship is part of our commitment to engage with all communities (that word again!). It recognises the cultural and religious practices of our communities (that word again, again!) This is a very positive addition to the Avon and Somerset uniform and one which I am sure will be a welcome item for many of our officers". I wonder what those officers would say in "real life", if free to speak their minds.

There's an article, plus photograph, of Rowan Williams, the Arch Twat of Canterbury, which is headed, "Williams: Labour Think We're Oddballs". Shall I put him out of his misery? It's not just Labour, dearie. He feels that the political classes are out of touch with most ordinary people who still have God in their "bloodstream". The Welshman goes on to say, "The trouble with a lot of government initiatives about faith is that they assume it is a problem, it's an eccentricity, it is practised by oddities, foreigners and minorities". I see no assumption about it. Pots and kettles spring to mind. I cannot think of any other business so out of touch with ordinary people than that of religion, with its broad church of extremists, obsessives, innocents and mute sheep-like followers – and that is not to mention the sexual abusers. No finer point of the naivety aspect can be made than from the following - and let's face it, there's been enough examples of the abuse.

A vicar in York has hit the headlines this morning. Father Tim Jones, who looks after what from the photograph appears to be a very pleasing church, told his flock that stealing from supermarkets is okay if it's a last resort. He said it is often "the best option" for Britain's poor. He made an interesting comparison regarding what is acceptable and what's not when you are without money. He states that it is far better to shoplift than turn to prostitution, mugging or burglary. Well, he's right about the latter two as no violence is involved, but I do question placing shoplifting above prostitution. At least with prostitution everyone gains. No-one gets hurt and no-one loses money. With shoplifting, the shop automatically loses and customers everywhere pick up the tab through increased prices. Dear, oh dear, Father – do get a grip!

You know, before I put these two articles to one side, I have just taken another glance at the photograph of Rowan Williams. I was nearly going to say Atkinson. Now, no-one can help their looks, especially being bald. Just ask my cousin, Simon! But you can do something about your appearance, and his appearance does come over as being slightly scruffy, with that wispish hair and full beard. I can imagine the photograph being shown to a child and the parent mentioning with pride that this is the leader of their religious group. See how generous I am not using the word "sect" or "cult". I can just see the child weighing up the options and contemplating the possibility that perhaps Satan is a safer alternative after all.

Anyway, time for a couple of gags on a religious theme:

C of E joke: A vicar books into a hotel and asks the Receptionist, "Is the porn channel in my room disabled?" "No", the Receptionist replies, "it's just regular porn, you sick bastard!"

Catholic joke: A drunk staggers into a Catholic church, enters a confessional booth, sits down and says nothing. The priest in the next cubicle coughs a few times, but the drunk continues sitting and saying nowt. {A sop for our friends in the north!} Finally, the priest knocks on the partition three times and the drunk eventually mumbles, "It's no good knocking on my booth, there's no paper on this side either!"

I think I may have told the following on my latest CD but it's too good to ignore, and the last thing any author does is to re-read or listen to his own work.

A retired Italian wine maker went to the village church to make his confession for the first time in many decades. When the priest slid open the panel in the confessional the man said, "Father, during World War Two a beautiful woman knocked on my door and asked me to hide her from the enemy. I then hid her in my attic". The priest replied, "But that was a wonderful thing you did, my son. You have no need for a confession". The man continued, "Father, it is worse than that, for she quickly started to repay me with sexual favours". "Ah", replied the priest, "people in war time sometimes act in ways that they would not during normal circumstances. If you are truly sorry for your actions, my son, then you are forgiven". "Oh, thank you, Father", implored the wine maker, "that is of great relief and a load off my mind, but may I ask a question?" "Of course you may, my son". "Should I tell her that the war is over?"

Okay! Just to even them up we have another C of E one:

Elsie Golightly, the church organist, was by now in her eighties. She was admired universally for her sweetness and kindness to all. One afternoon she received a visit from her local vicar. She showed him into her quaint sitting room. He was invited to have a seat whilst she prepared tea. As he sat facing the old Hammond organ the young fresh-faced vicar noticed a cut glass bowl sitting on top of it. The bowl was filled with water and in the water floated, of all things, a condom. When Elsie returned with tea and scones they began to chat. The vicar tried to stifle his curiosity about the bowl of water and its strange floater, but soon it got the better of him and he could no longer resist. "Miss Golightly, I wonder if you could tell me about this", he enquired, pointing to the bowl. "Oh, yes", she replied enthusiastically, "isn't it wonderful? I was walking through the park a few months ago and I found this little package on the ground. The directions said to place it on the organ, keep it wet and it would then prevent the spread of disease, and do you know, I haven't had so much as a cold all winter".

Oh, the joy of being a non-believer, unsullied and unshackled from the restraints of faiths, but then, as you know, atheism is a non-prophet organisation.

Well, it's Christmas Eve and for the first time in our history Maureen is not cooking a turkey this year – to be precise, she's not cooking a whole turkey – we've bought a crown. We tend to buy most of our meat from a company called Farmer's Choice who hails from Segensworth in Hants – and no – they are not sponsoring this chapter – or our Christmas! I am mentioning them off my own bat. We pay a standing order each month and obtain meat and fish as required. It's free range, very tasty and you know where the animal has been reared – no jokes please! Last year we ordered a complete turkey, several pounds in weight, and sixty-three in money. My mother then announced as we sat at the table, "Of course, I don't eat turkey myself". Funny that, because when my dad was alive she ate turkey. In fact, she ate all meat. Now, aged 92, she is a martyr to cauliflower cheese, as I alluded to earlier. Other than my wife's sister, who has moved from Southfields, near Earlsfield, not far from Wandsworth and Putney – or, in other words, South West London – that's the total number for Christmas dinner – four! And she doesn't eat turkey either! Debbie's in Wales, at her in-laws, Glyn and his wife are home with a chicken, while William and his other half are between her family.

William is borrowing Maureen's car on Christmas Day and

Boxing Day, as their VW Golf is a bit iffy for overlong journeys – basically, anything in excess of five miles from Aldershot! He is taking Karen to Portsmouth in order to propose. He has bought a ring. When I say Portsmouth, it's not just as you get there and you see the sign exclaiming "Portsmouth" and all the pointless places it has been twinned with. It's more specific than that. Apparently, so legend has it, on their first date they sat on a seat on the pier overlooking the Solent, and the Isle of Wight, although knowing William's geography he could have been overlooking the Panama Canal and the Isle of Skye for all he was aware! Still, he's very good with children, animals and lawnmowers.

That crown of turkey is costing just over £30 and I suspect we will still be finding ingenious ways to eat it come New Year's Eve. We were up early this morning. I've taken Mutley for a walk so its orf to Morrison's in Fleet to buy what we need for the annual siege. It never fails to surprise, not to mention amaze, that so many people purchase food as if there will never be the opportunity to shop again. What? Okay, coming! Maureen is calling me, so I had better go. The quicker I'm back, the quicker I get to A'shot to buy her Christmas presents.

Not bad, having left at 7.50 am, we called in at the PO Box in Aldershot, picked up the last of the post that was waiting, did our shopping, called in at my mother's with her groceries, had a cup of tea and we were home by 11.20 am. I wonder if "Bargain Hunt" is on.

Just getting back to the shopping for a minute, I had a lovely warm feeling asking for new carrier bags at the checkout. One feels such a maverick. I suspect the offer will have stopped by the time you read this but Domestos is half price at 49p.

It's now 5 pm and I've just finished wrapping Maureen's presents. Luckily, she had some spare paper. I did check before I went into A'shot. It doesn't get any better in that town. Even when the festering lights are in full glare, you still get the feeling that they are using long-life, low-energy, can't-see Euro bulbs. Anyway, other than veering into WH Smith to buy the latest copy of "Heritage Railway", my only other foray was into my "one-stop

Christmas shop" – Boots. Maureen gives me a list of perfumes and I buy a selection – easy! The assistant remembered me from last year – which was no doubt nicer for me than it was for her. She wasn't just making it up, she really did remember me. As I shoved Maureen's list under her nose, she smiled and asked, "I suppose you want to know what's on special?" I nodded in eager anticipation of a discounted fragrance. I don't know of any industry that can charge so much for so little and never receive any more abuse than a sharp intake of breath from the customer or at worst, a "how much?" No man wants the assistant to think that the person he is buying for is not worthy, be they wife, partner, girlfriend, other-half, associate, cross-dressing gender-bender, etc. and I'm no exception. One of those fragrances is being kept separate and will now be handed over in the form of a belated birthday present.

I did give Maureen a present on her birthday but a household presentation of a Tiffany lamp isn't overly personal. Mind you, I remember when our friend Peter gave Jackie a George Foreman grill. She did smile, almost. Actually, Maureen has just stopped typing this to tell me that the Tiffany lamp was actually a present from my mother and I hadn't got her anything at all. Glad I kept one perfume back!

Right! We've moved on to teatime and I have been called to the table, so if we don't talk before or during Christmas, I wish you a very Happy Christmas and I will see you on Boxing Day. But before I do, I will leave you with a couple of seasonal jokes.

Firstly, there's an Englishman, a Scotsman and an Irishman, who all arrive at St. Peter's Gate on Christmas Eve, i.e. today. St. Peter says, "You do realise that as it's Christmas Eve you can only get in if you have something Christmassy with you". The three, almost in unison, reply, "Well, I didn't plan to die today". St. Peter says, "I know, death's a bitch, isn't it?" With that, the Englishman fumbles in his pockets and retrieves a set of keys. He jangles them hopefully in front of St. Peter and says, "Well, d'you know, they sound very similar to jingle bells, don't they?" St. Peter says, "Yes, they do. Go on, you are in". The Scotsman says, "Well, all I have got is a serviette, but if I do this (at which point he hastily re-arranges the serviette into a party hat), voila". So St. Peter says, "Well, that's very good. I like initiative. You're in". He turns to the Irishman, who brings a pair of stockings out of one pocket and a pair of girl's panties from the other and holds them up to St. Peter and says, "Well, I'm all right, then". St. Peter says, "Well, what have they got to do with Christmas?" And the Irishman says, "Well, they're Carol's!"

A Russian couple were walking down a street in St. Petersburg the other night when the man felt a drop hit his nose. "I think it's raining", he said to his wife. "No, that felt more like snow to me", she replied. "I'm sure it was just rain", he said. Well, as these things go, they were just about to have a major argument as to whether it was raining or snowing, when along came a minor communist party official. "Let us not fight about this", the man said smilingly to his wife, "let us ask Comrade Rudolph whether it is officially raining or snowing". As the official approached, the man said, "Comrade Rudolph, please tell us, is it officially raining or snowing?" "It is raining, of course", he answered in a stone-faced manner before walking on. But the woman turned, insisting, "I know that felt like snow", to which the man very quietly replied, "Rudolph The Red knows rain, dear!"

Happy Christmas!

So, how was it for you? Oh, of course, you can't say, can you. You can always e-mail me, but please don't! I hope you got what you requested from Santa. Maureen got her perfumes, plus a date for a weekend away, anywhere of her choice within a hundred mile radius of Ash Vale! I got a book on Britain's coastline, a colour picture book of the Great Western Railway in Devon and Cornwall and a large book on dead footballers.

William and Karen came round to pick up the car yesterday at about 10 am. Now, she thought he'd been asked by us to deliver presents to Portsmouth on our behalf and that is why we'd given him our car for two days, as a sort of sop. They were off to her father's in Biggin Hill for dinner afterwards. It could have all been a bit frosty if she had said no, but she didn't. We received a text saying, "The girl from Del Monte, she say yes". I will confirm here that Karen does not work for Del Monte, but a local authority. However, saying the girl from Surrey Heath Council, she say yes, doesn't have the same impact. Anyway, good news – the last of my children is about to be settled. They live together at the moment in A'shot, so it's not going to be the biggest of upheavals, but it means she is now on a more equal footing and no doubt will enjoy paying the mortgage. (Karen, I'm only joking. As your prospective father-in-law, you should be aware of my sense of humour, or lack of it by now).

I picked up my mother at 11 am, Glyn and Kate arrived shortly beforehand and my wife's sister trundled north-west from Godalming (GU7) arriving at mid-day. She's not staying overnight as her next door neighbours are away and there is no-one to look after her cat (bloody thing). If you see her, don't say I said that. It purrs all the time she strokes it, sits on her lap, preens and does all the things that cats do, but is completely dismissive of all others. Downright rude, really, no social graces, but then it is a cat – selfish, self-interested, self-important, self-centred, independent, prickly..... What a prissy pussy. I've long come to the conclusion that all cats are female in temperament, irrespective of gender. (I've now got to get Maureen to type this last bit without receiving a clip round the ear).

It's funny how your mind wanders, but I remember mentioning corporal punishment at a talk once. I considered, in front of an all female audience, that being caned at school had never done me any harm. I then went on to add, jokingly, that I now had to pay good money in London for that sort of pleasure! As the audience guffawed – all right, laughed – okay, okay, tittered, I added, "Only joking, I've found a really nice lady in Eastleigh". The talk in question was to a national ladies association at county level. At the end of the talk, when everyone was milling about, a lady came up to me and asked, "Were you in earnest about the lady in

Eastleigh?" I replied that it was only a gag before asking, "Why?" "Oh", she said, "because that is what I do for a living, I'm a madam and I deal with naughty boys like you". The lady looked like anyone else in the audience, smartly dressed, in her late forties, I would have thought. "Does anyone here know what you do for a living?" I asked. "Good Lord, no", she replied, "I would be drummed out of the regiment. Anyway, must go....." We shook hands, she turned to walk away, glanced back and with a coquettish smile and a real glint in the eye, said, "You'll find me on the Internet, East Reading". I never did, not sure Maureen would have been overly impressed.

Back to Christmas Day. My mum tends to get anxious these days, about the dark, her next door neighbour being away, not leaving lights on, etc. so she asked me to take her home before 5 pm. In previous years she has stayed well into the night. She has this strange view about lights being on in the house when she is out. Presumably, she feels she won't be burgled if there are lights on. I think she sometimes feels that there will be burglars actually in the house when I take her home. It's not as if I leave her on the doorstep. She is escorted, more helped in, actually. Her coat is taken off and I then help her into the chair and make her a cup of tea if she wants one. I check the back door is still locked and then make my way upstairs to search for any hidden miscreant (or scoundrel, malefactor, ne'er-do-well, wrongdoer, reprobate, villain, rapscallion, foreigner) – haven't found any so far! Boxing Day turned out to be the same, except that she got fidgety by 4 pm and asked if I could take her home "just in case"..... Just in case of what I never enquired.

When I collected mum yesterday I also brought the "indoor gymnasium" which I referred to earlier. Today, she told me that she would "hold it in". Glad to say that for us, our armchair, our dining room chair and the carpet, she did!

Two Christmases before my dad died, or five years ago, Maureen and I went away for our one and only Christmas without the family. We decided that, for once, after thirty-five years of preparing Christmas dinners (that's Maureen, not me) and wine pouring for the masses (that's me, not Maureen) we'd have a break. We booked a cottage in a village close to the north Norfolk coast and reserved a table for Christmas dinner at a hotel near Cromer. It was a lovely week, we visited Fakenham, Holt, Cromer, Norwich. It was a delight. No parents, no children, just us. The only problem, and a problem that loomed from the July when we made the booking, was telling my parents. Maureen would often say, "You've really got to tell them". I said I would, but when the time was right. The time was wrong from July until October. There was never a good time. One afternoon, when Maureen and I were both round at my parents', my mother enquired if we had seen anything of Glyn recently. "Saw him last week", I said. The following tumbled out in a manner reminiscent of a child guiltily admitting some misdemeanour. "Actually, you'll be seeing a lot of him over Christmas", adding quickly, "and William and Debbie". My admission trailed off. My father sat upright, his hands pressed firmly on his knees. "Why is this?" he asked in the manner of a preacher delivering a sermon. "Well, we, Maureen and I, that is, are going away for Christmas. Just us. A week in Norfolk". There, it was out! There was a dull silence. "I see", said my father at length. My mother came to terms with the announcement by sloping off to the kitchen and putting on the kettle. (Please don't ask if it fitted). The silence in the room was deafening. At length my father said, "Of course, it is your choice". An even longer and duller silence reigned before my mother reappeared with a tray of mugs and an announcement befitting a play. "Your dad and I will have to share a duck then....."

My confidence returned as did my usual irritation with both of them. "What's that?" I said, sniffing the air theatrically. "Is that the smell of burning martyr?" Silence. Over that Christmas they came to our house. In fact, everyone came to our house. We were the only ones absent. It was a lovely break. The grindstone resumed the following year. And that was the problem, really, there was an order to things that were followed by us all, although generated by my parents.

Before they moved down to live near us they would leave their home in Hackbridge and wend their way via various relatives where they would consume alcoholic drinks and light refreshments. The problem was, we expected them for tea. The last port of call was usually a cousin of mine who would then ring and tell us they were on their way. This meant we had about forty-five minutes before their arrival. It's not unreasonable to expect that when someone says they will be down at approximately 7 pm, for them to arrive within a time frame surrounding that figure. But often, we didn't get the phone call until 8.30 pm, which meant an arrival of quarter to half-past nine. This also meant that we didn't eat until they got to our house. In the latter years we ate regardless, when we were hungry, but they always expected a full meal on their arrival. And that was just Christmas Eve.

When I look back, what actually used to happen was that whilst the three wise men brought gifts of gold, frankincense and myrrh, my mother arrived each Christmas Eve bearing pickled onions, puddings and pies. As far as she was concerned the words "Christmas" and "food" were synonymous. They would arrive in their ageing Vauxhall Cavalier, its suspension complaining under its load, my mother sitting in the front seat like Lady Bountiful, surrounded on all sides by presents and bags of food. And just wait until they opened the boot! She was obsessed with food, not for herself, you understand, for as I said, she now pecks at it like a bird. It was the providing that counted. I put her fixation down to the privations of the war – that's the Second World War, not the Napoleonic. She took great delight each year in organising the rations for the festive period. The telephone line between our house and hers was extremely busy during the months prior to the Great Event, co-ordinating rations. The months, by the way, covered the period January to December. Dad and mum sallied back and forth between Dover and Calais every three to four months during the year, stocking up on their Yuletide provisions. They loved those over-sized bags of nuts, truffles and Belgian chocolates. Sadly, they believed we loved them too. As I think I have mentioned in previous books, we were never that fussed on the French wine either, and on more than many occasions felt we had made our feelings clear. My mother, however, was never receptive to criticisms of food she felt we should like. Therefore, we always received our quota of Chateau

Pee, whether we liked it or not. Quantity has always rated higher than quality and my wife's enthusiastic acceptance of a tin of Jackson's tea was her starter for another eleven to join it over the coming years. They still sit in their seven colours of the rainbow and beyond along a shelf in the conservatory.

Many years ago, my mother became very excited because someone had given them a cash-and-carry card. The telephone line fairly hummed. "Don't worry, dear, I'll get the Christmas pud this year – catering size". Maureen wondered how she would get a pudding the size of a beach ball into an already over-burdened fridge. We needn't have worried, however. When it duly arrived on Christmas Eve in the Cavalier, it was only four inches in diameter. Although slim in girth it was nigh on five feet in length and reclined along the width of the rear parcel shelf. Our two sons carried it from car to kitchen, wrestling it as though they were fireman desperately trying to control an errant hosepipe. Difficult attempting to get a snake of a pud into the fridge. You can't. Debbie's suggestion that it would make an excellent draught excluder was met with a very dismissive sniff from my mother. Eventually it was laid to rest along the window ledge, where it reclined, shrinking daily, until such time when even the dog turned her nose up at her daily helping. And so it came to pass that the last two feet were relegated to the dustbin in late March – and so close to Easter!

The foray into the cash-and-carry didn't stop at the pudding section. We had two three-gallon jars of pickled onions the size of cricket balls to contend with that year. As you have gathered, mum's maxim has always been "big is beautiful".

I have committed many indiscretions in my life but the most heinous was back in 1995 when I inadvertently let it slip that I quite liked her homemade cold beef pies and asked if she would provide one for Christmas Eve supper. Maureen could just about cope, both with the size of the pie and the insinuation that her pies were not quite up to scratch. If only it had remained at just the one pie. True to form, we couldn't just have the one, we had to have three – one beef, one pork and one lamb. And sadly, every year up until my dad died mum would sit and watch her only child, now approaching sixty, devouring those very pies, her eyes twinkling with maternal affection, and each year I would cringe as she asked me, "Is it up to its usual standard?" her eyes ready to acknowledge confirmation of her expected reply.

Christmas day dinner would consist of turkey, plus roast pork, with cold meat and fried potatoes on Boxing Day. However, come the glorious 27th, Maureen would once again find herself in the kitchen cooking the largest joint of beef the butcher had been able to muster. Now, we were not responsible for this joint of beef or the pork. We'd had no say in their purchase whatsoever, as this was another one of my mother's "treats". They had a friend who knew a butcher and every year this friend provided the pork and beef that my parents would bring with them. We were then expected to marvel at it in its uncooked state, marvel again as it was extracted from the fridge just prior to being cooked, marvel as it crackled during cooking, and then salivate at its juiciness and taste throughout the meal.

The Christmas Pudding – everlasting or ordinary – was never an easy matter either, as my father insisted on overseeing the production of the brandy sauce. Maureen could never put in enough brandy. Whenever we thought there was enough brandy in it, my father would always add another bottle to the sauce cooking in the pan! On occasion, the effects were that everyone slept for the thick end of four hours after dinner and there was great demand made upon our supply of paracetamol during the evening.

There was an order to opening presents as well. When my parents arrived on Christmas Eve there was always one present given to each of us that had to be opened in their presence, but not until after midnight. Because this ritual persisted long after they had moved down to Ash Vale, we never had the pleasure of an early night. Everybody's presents, that is our three children, and us two adults each had a pillowcase from my parents, plus bran tubs. For those of you who don't know what a bran tub is, my father commandeered crisp packet outer boxes from his local supermarket, as they had a round hole at one end. Six wrapped presents were then placed at random inside this box, the rest of the space being taken up with polystyrene chips. My parents watched glued to the action as we all unwrapped our presents from both pillow cases and bran tubs. The problem was, they couldn't look at all of us at once, so we all had to open them in turn. My father then gave my mother her presents, and then my mother gave hers to my father. No presents were allowed to be opened before the children were up, which meant that by the time everyone had opened their pressies, it was then time for dinner. The problem was that my father always enjoyed and requested – nay, expected - a cooked breakfast, which then put dinner back by at least another two hours.

On one occasion Maureen managed only to find five presents within her bran tub. My mother insisted there were six and was not happy until Maureen went outside and rifled through four black bin liners of Christmas wrapping paper and polystyrene chippings – and all to find a two-inch-by-one-inch key fob. Dinner was put back another half an hour.

We never had spare bedrooms, as the children were all still at home and every Christmas for over thirty years my parents took our bedroom and we divided ourselves between the two sitting rooms, each languishing on the settee at night. Cramped with bad backs we resumed our standing position, only to find that after four nights of this my parents showed no signs of going home. They sometimes even commented that it probably "wasn't that comfortable" before the conversation appeared to tail off with a request for me to provide a gin and tonic.

Many years ago, when we lived across the road from where we are now, Boxing Day seemed to have long gone, although in reality it was only two days previous. I had started back at work and had to go to London. This particular year my parents had not driven down and I had gone to Hackbridge to collect them. I thought, quite reasonably, that as I was going to London it would be the perfect opportunity to take them back with me. You should have seen the look on their faces at this suggestion. It was as if I was asking them to move into a care home. They had no conception of what it is like to be out of your bed and on a settee, year in, year out. They huffed and puffed and I overheard my father say, "I think we expect too much". I think they did. It didn't stop them next year, mind. So maybe we can be forgiven for wanting that one week away in Norfolk, where we had a lovely meal and were very kindly invited back to partake of drinks and coffees in the home of a local couple who were sitting at a table nearby. We never saw them again, it was just a lovely one-off.

What was I saying about cruelty and kindness at the start of this book – or a year ago, whichever is the most recent! It only seems like last Christmas that I enjoyed "Wallace and Gromit" and I have just been enjoying them all over again. Very disappointed in "Gavin & Stacey", one more episode to go on New Year's Eve. I recorded, or should I say Maureen recorded, the second part of "Cranford" – still to be viewed. Highlights were the "Royle Family", which was back to its best, though my cousin thought it was poor. Strange! The other highlight was "Outnumbered". I have never seen a poor episode yet – or indeed one that was ever-so-slightly sub-standard. Victoria Wood was turned off after ten minutes. I haven't seen such drivel since the last time I saw such drivel, although the "Daily Express" reviewer found it immensely amusing, but then comedy, as life in general, is very subjective.

Maureen's just been on-line ordering more delicacies from Farmer's Choice. A box containing fillet steak, rump steak, lamb cutlets and haggis should arrive within the next week or so. There is now room in our freezer. They also supply goose stuffed with chicken and pheasant, but I've always blanched at the thought of one bird being stuffed with two from differing flocks. It's a bit like mixing races with a necro theme, if you get my drift.

I've just finished off their free-range Orkney hand-filleted smoked salmon, which I consumed whilst I watched Neil Oliver discovering the delights of life on the Faroe Islands, with their very blonde and attractive women folk.

Talking of water, it's time for a jolly jape, I think. This one concerns a father ringing home to talk to his beloved.

Ring-ring: Ring-ring:

"Hello?" "Hi, darling, this is daddy. Is mummy near the phone?"

"No, daddy, she's upstairs in the bedroom with Uncle Paul".
(There's a brief pause)

"But, darling, you don't have an Uncle Paul".

"Oh yes I have, and he's upstairs in the bedroom with mummy right now".
(Slightly longer pause)

"Uh, okay then, this is what I want you to do. Put the phone down on the table, run upstairs and knock on the bedroom door and shout to mummy, 'That's daddy's car just pulled up in the driveway'"

"Okay, daddy, just a minute".

A few minutes later the little girl comes back to the phone.

"I did it, daddy".

"And what happened, darling?"

"Well, mummy got all scared, jumped out of bed with no clothes on and ran around screaming. She then tripped over the rug, hit her head on the dressing table and now she isn't moving at all!"

"Oh, my God!!! What about Uncle Paul?"

"He jumped out of bed too, with no clothes on. He was all scared and he jumped out of the back window and landed in the swimming pool. But I don't think he knew that you had taken out the water last week to clean it. He hit the bottom of the pool and now I think he's dead".

(Long pause)

(Even longer pause)

Then daddy said, "A swimming pool? Bugger, wrong number!"

CHAPTER TWELVE

I've Started So I'll Finish

Yesterday I took Mutley up the ranges as usual. They are closed for firing during the Christmas break, so one has the freedom of the land, so to speak. As I approached the road entrance, having passed "The Swan" Public House, I was aware of a tannoy system announcing nothing that was decipherable. In fact, it reminded me very much of Waterloo or Paddington Stations. There was, however, the largest gathering of Lycra-clad arses that one could come across outside the Tour de France. There were hundreds of the buggers. Fortunately, they were not cycling anywhere close to where we were headed. Ben and I came across a very friendly and very large Husky that wanted to play. Ben was not sure. We came across a black Lab puppy that wanted to play. Again, Ben was not sure. We came across a Staffie terrier and a greyhound. Ben was definitely sure and growled as I smiled unconvincingly at their owners and said, "He's funny with....." before adding the breed in question. We came across Alfie and his daddy near Great Bottom Flash. Neither dog took any notice of each other.

Back along the canal and opposite "The Swan" were three fisher arses (does the season never end?). It was cold but there they were, one hand holding a cigarette, the other with rod, well, two of them had rods. The third had a weight attached to a chain in his hand, which he used in an attempt to crack the ice on the canal. I had to take a second look at the rods. They were so long that I swear that if they tried really hard they could have hooked "The Swan" (that's the pub, not the bird). Are they for show? And all to catch something you can't eat. Pointless, absolutely pointless.

The walk must have taken its toll on Ben as when we came back he went into our bedroom and found a pack, which contained five paracetamol. To be fair, he never mentioned he had a headache.....

Since they've introduced the wheelie bins – one for the landfill, one much smaller for food waste – we also have purple see-through plastic sacks for recyclable waste. As you walk up the side road to the canal, it's amazing to see how many people have such common taste. It surprised me just how many buy goods, which have the words "basic" or "value" on them. I think I would have hidden those! Also, to be seen are small, dumpy, brown French or Belgian beer bottles, which are 10% alcohol and 90% gas. How do people manage to consume so much chemical rubbish?

So, what's the news in the paper over the last couple of days. Ah, yes, to no-one's surprise I read that the cost of the compensation culture is growing considerably, as more "no-win, no-fee" firms vie for the business of turning an accident into a windfall. Interesting to note that the number of compensation companies has risen from five hundred to two thousand, three hundred in eighteen months. Seventy have been struck off for breaking industry rules. It really is a tacky trade to be in. Apparently, "claims introducer" companies sell on details to legal firms who then contact the victims hoping they will sue for compensation. We all suffer from this scam. I put these companies on a par with those involved in wheel clamping. Oh, and add banker – oh, and estate agents. There would be more but we have to finish the book before I die.

Interesting to note different people's priorities. The "Daily Express" afforded two pages to famous people who had died in 2009. Each month is marked in column form, starting with a colour photo, plus short synopsis, followed by a list of names, ages, what they did, and exact date of death. January started with John Mortimer, February with Wendy Richard. March, Natasha Richardson and April – oh, yes, April had Clement Freud. May had Cyril Freezer. Who? you may enquire. Well, Cyril Freezer was very well known in model railway circles, but to put his fizzog and testimony covering half the column with Danny La Rue as a virtual one-liner seemed a bit out of balance. June saw

Michael Jackson top the list of those who had fallen and for July it was Harry Patch. August, Simon Dee, a man who thought more of himself than was good for anyone. September, Keith Floyd. Again, Keith Waterhouse would have been my top personality death of the month. Now October, oh, how I remember October. Not for my birthday – a Libra by birth, a Libra by nature – but for Stephen Gately's death. It is he whose mugshot appeared above all other deaths. He commanded top news ratings for successive days following his demise. His funeral, his mourners, his testimonies, the floral tributes from people who had never known him, it was like a re-make of Jade Goody, or Princess Di's funerals. Was he really so popular? Or was it because he was a homosexual icon? Norman Painting, who played Phil Archer for decades and died in the same month, received two lines and that included his name. Al Martino, the first man to top the UK singles chart, accrued just three lines. It might not make you wonder, but it does me. Just for the record, November was Edward Woodward and December rounded off with Maggie Jones, the actress who played Deirdre Barlow's mother in Coronation Street. Once again, I would have thought that Richard Todd, one of our all-time greats, should have been awarded more than the four lines that he received for his ninety years. But each to his or her own, I suppose.

The Christmas sales looked good enough to justify an increase in VAT and also looked good enough to miss. I watched the opening of the Boxing Day sales on the TV news. Unbelievable! Security staff, shop assistants, management, standing, waiting, sweating for the bewitching hour, or 9 am, to arrive. The keys turned, the bolts were unbolted, the locks unlocked and then it was bloody mayhem. They ran amok. I heard the breaking of glass and crockery as the melee ensued. Talk about headless chicken syndrome. I cannot understand how anyone with any sense of dignity and decorum would want to be involved in such an unseemly manoeuvre. Even if the goods were free, you wouldn't find me joining in the scramble. I take it most of those involved were from foreign climes as they certainly looked the part. In fact, I'm just looking at a colour photograph in the "Express" and an awful lot of the faces looked Japanese – or thereabouts. It must be their culture, or lack of it.

Interesting little article in the paper concerning parking fees in hospital car parks. Everyone I know feels that the charges are a complete rip off of the most gigantic and unfair kind. And a recent survey states that eight out of ten people feel it is wrong to charge cancer patients. Have I missed something? Why should one form of illness be exempt? The route of selective exemption dilutes the main problem that it is inherently unfair to charge anyone.

Bearing in mind what has been said regarding compensation, as we know, there is always the exception to the rule. I am not a Libra for nothing! Potholes have caused most of us grief in our lives – even if it is just a case of trying to avoid them. A lady named Deborah Hill has been landed with a bill for £290 for a replacement wheel and tracking when her car hit a pothole close to where she lives in Durham. I suppose the invoice could be called a Hillbilly! Anyway, the council refused to pay on the grounds that a utility company had been repairing that stretch of road. Surely overall responsibility for highways is that of the authority. Do they not make sure that repairs made by any utility or private company are up to the standard commensurate with that required for driving? It's totally unfair. I do hope the lady in question takes the council to court and wins, although I don't want her receiving compensation for stress and trauma, you understand.

Talking of which, I see that a stress helpline has been launched by the NHS. What a bloody waste of money. If you have a problem, sort yourself out or pay privately. Why should those with money and non-health worries be given help from some namby-pamby, woossy-pussy get a lifeline?

Some chap who nobody knew about until the weekend, when it became panic stations, has just been executed in China for smuggling in drugs. What really pigs me off is that he is being described as the first European in over fifty years to be executed in China. He's also been described as British. He's not British, he's not even European, he's Asian. It just so happens that he lived in North London. We've been subjected to two days of following his family as they travel to China in an effort to get the authorities to change their mind and allow clemency. The Chinese Ambassador was summoned to No. 10, diplomatic noises were exchanged, and all the usual interfering do-gooder groups, who should have known better, rolled out demands for his stay of execution. They used the grounds that he was mentally unstable. Well, he managed to get from here to there quite easily. I have read talk that he was ill-equipped mentally to deal with the situation in which he found himself. Well, how do you get to China in that condition without a carer, without support and presumably without taxpayers' assistance? The good news is that despite all the meddling by the British authorities and the human rights lobby, the Chinese are not easily moved. In fact, their resolve showed absolutely no signs of weakening and at the appointed time his execution took place. If only we showed the same resolve as the Chinese in such matters with those who err. But sure as eggs is eggs, this particular chappie won't be taking any drugs across the border again.

I see that a DJ on BRMB radio has been sacked. BRMB covers the west midlands, Hereford, Worcester and Warwickshire – you know, flat vowel and manglewurzel country. Tom Binns, the offending DJ, apparently cut off the Queen's speech on Christmas Day saying, "Two words – bor-ing". It doesn't say whether the complaints made by listeners which caused his demise were due to the unscheduled termination, or because he used the phrase "two words" when it obviously should have been "two syllables", which for me, is a far more cut and dried case for dismissal.

Okay. Time for a little light-hearted irrelevance. Question and answer time.

What's the difference between a bitch and a whore?
A whore sleeps with everyone at the party, a bitch sleeps with everyone at the party except you.

Which sexual position produces the ugliest children?
Suggest you ask your mother!

What makes men chase women they have no intentions of marrying?
Basically, it's the same urge that makes dogs chase cars they have no intention of driving!

Who is the most popular chap in the nudist colony?
The chap who can carry a cup of coffee in each hand and a dozen doughnuts.

Then who, you may ask, is the most popular girl in the nudist colony?
Ah. Now, that's the girl who can eat the last doughnut!

So! "Strictly" ended last Saturday. I must confess I was glad that Chris Hollins and little Ola Chops won. Their personalities shone through. Aware as I am that Ricky Whittle's dancing ability was much stronger, I do feel that anyone charged with any offence faces an uphill struggle to win over the public. As always, throughout the series, everyone was "amazed" on a weekly basis, though the "journeys" of previous series were conspicuous by their absence. Perhaps someone in the production team has had a word with them. Still, we will no doubt be subjected to more "amazing journeys" once again when that partnership of words is used to the "nth" degree during "Dancing on Ice". Its return in January will sate my reality TV fix for a while, although doubtless I will give "So You Think You Can Dance" a chance. I really am a sucker, but then we are sorely short of variety programmes and these dance shows are the closest we have.

I've just returned from yet another appointment at the Health Centre. There is a notice board, among several, that relates to the activities of the Citizen's Advice Bureau, or CAB for short. I used to think that it was the working man or underdog's sanctuary, somewhere where advice could be sought on a range of subjects, somewhere where volunteers with no axe to grind, no company to represent, could impart information in your quest for fairness. They could help you through that myriad of forms designed by government and local council departments to force you into submission. They represented the sword of David against the shield of the dragon. Naïve, I suppose, to assume that the friendly face of honest help would not become sullied by courses, issues and political correctness. On this notice board is a range of leaflets, one of which invites the reader to seek advice for compensation, should they be involved in an accident. I'm not convinced that encouraging would-be claimants to seek advice is really what the basic premise of CAB help should be. Everything evolves, I know, but there is a part of me that questions the motives of those that get themselves into positions of power in these sorts of organisations. Earlier this year "someone", you never read a name or see a hand being raised, thus admitting responsibility, decided that the term "blacklist" should no longer be used by volunteers at the CAB on the spurious grounds that it "spreads racial prejudice". I just wish for once that the sad proll, or prolls if it is a committee, who advocated or invoked this dictat would come clean and show their face or faces. Only those obsessed with the ridiculous come up with rules such as this. It's a form of subconscious bullying where everyone has to share the same views for fear of being out of the politically correct loop. Everyone must sing from the same pc textbook, where individuality of thought is lost and control is all. If I were a volunteer I would tell the mindless hierarchy where to stuff their dictat. But then, painful as it would undoubtedly be, I wouldn't and couldn't sit in front of people looking to gain on a personal basis at the taxpayers' expense, or claim their rights. I remain to be convinced that it's not a breeding ground for benefit claimants to acquire even more unearned income.

I gave a talk last year at a hospital in Bedfordshire. The speaker's secretary was to meet me at Reception. As I waited for a minute or so until she arrived, I perused the leaflets on a nearby carousel. They contained advice on compensation, benefits, rights, immigration and translation. You name it, there was advice on it. Talk about feeding the hand that bites.....

Just to finish on a more uplifting note, I saw today that there was an armed raid on a bookmaker's in the market town of Wallingford in Oxfordshire. The robbers apparently escaped with a large amount of cash and were "last seen heading towards Waitrose". So much more tasteful than last being seen heading towards Lidl.

It's twenty years since I wrote my first book, "From Where I Sit". The Tories were still in power and I was pretty peeved about the way our country was heading. Margaret Thatcher had sold our silver – gas, electricity, water, public services and playing fields! Parts of our post office, telephone service and the NHS had all been opened up to private money. I've never understood the principle of inviting an injection of private money. There is no such thing as a free lunch and there is always payback time. With a public/private partnership there are always shareholders and directors whose sole intent is to gain financially. When our utilities were sold off Britain became a mass of small shareholders. The small sold to the large and the large made profits by selling on again. The same has happened to building societies. Many demutualised and we were all given shares, which we then sold for a windfall profit. They then became banks and most have been swallowed up.

Tony Blair offered prospects for a fairer Britain. Everything was in his favour. Sadly, Iraq and Afghanistan were to be worn as a ball and chain around his ankles in a manner than Northern Ireland had been with previous incumbents. Ironically, it was Ulster that was unshackled during Tony Blair's premiership. The part he played and the relative success that has come from the peace process has sadly been overshadowed. I looked for the humility and compassion that I thought he would bring to our society. Sadly, his leadership was an extension of Mrs. Thatcher's government. You could hardly separate their policies. More private money into our once hallowed public services coincided with the selling off of more playing fields, which coincided with the signing away of yet more of our independence to Europe. He then resigned for what seems to be no good reason, other than it was convenient to him. He went on to be a Catholic, a Middle East spokesman and an after-dinner speaker, although he did oversee the ban on hunting.

His successor, Gordon Brown, who had raided the pension pot as Chancellor and sold off our gold at rock-bottom prices, continued in the same vein, by attempting to sell off the Royal Mail. Rail franchises with new names and colours and corporate logos have been and gone. All the operators have increased their fares above the rate of inflation, yet their top dogs seem to be doing remarkably well, but when something goes wrong the taxpayer still ends up subsidising either the franchise concerned or Network Rail. It's a strange concept that a few make a fortune out of something we once all owned and yet we all still subsidise through direct taxation.

Gas, electricity and water, commodities that are essential to the basis of life and the society in which we live, have all seen price rises at the drop of a hat, yet it seems to be beyond them to reduce in the same manner when the wholesale prices have contracted. Many are foreign owned and I find it strange that abroad their services are cheaper than they are in this country. The petrol companies seem to work on much the same principle. Up goes the price of crude oil and overnight the pump price rises by 10p, plus VAT. Down comes the price of crude oil and a marginal drop is seen some months later, usually just in time for another price rise, plus the fuel escalator, plus VAT.

Gordon Brown's obsession with Middle England continued where Tony Blair's left off. Free laptops to poor families, apparently so they can track the school records and results of their offspring. What a joke! These are the very people who cannot afford the children they've bred and come under the heading of those who should have been sterilised at birth. And you know darn well that in most cases the offspring will be following the progress of their drug dealing and other nefarious activities through which they will earn their dishonest lucre.

As Chancellor and PM, Mr. Brown has increased the scope of VAT and taxation in general and overseen the expansion of the work-shy, the benefited and the cosseted, embracing those from the indigenous population and those from an expanded EU, as well as those from the Third World. I understand that the Whitehall mandarins are now looking to find a way to tax car boot sales. Incapacity benefit fraudsters are costing £11 billion a year. There are jobless families with umpteen children who are bringing in £37,000 a year. Where is their incentive to work?

What alternatives are there? David Cameron looks like the marketing man he is and frankly, sounds like the marketing man he is. He's never managed to convince me that in him we have a political world leader in our midst. Actually, I would be pressed to be inspired if he were chairman of the local town council. He's missed the biggest trick of all by shying away from the aspects of life that would have Middle England voting for him. I don't trust him on immigration, justice, public services or the scaling back of benefits. I distinctly distrust him on fox hunting and the future of the BBC. He has made no secret of his admiration for Margaret Thatcher. I remember him praising the Iron Lady's "awe-inspiring achievements". He gushed that the nation owed her a "huge debt". I think you'll find it's a debt the nation is still paying off. The true ramifications of her legacy to this nation will be determined over the years to come as history continues to unfold, but for me her legacy was one of selling off everything we collectively owned and the spiteful way she dealt with the coal miners and industry in general. This has led to the corporate and individual greed that has permeated throughout our society. David Cameron has aspirations of creating all-women shortlists for prospective members of parliament. Does he not understand that by promoting women, ethnic minorities, the disabled, anyone, he stops someone else from applying. By promoting one group you automatically disadvantage another. Should it not be on the basis of the best person for the job, irrespective of – well – everything? All these parliamentary wanabees seem to start life with sincerity, thrust and a desire to get things done, but seem to get bogged down by political niceties promoted by the few at the expense of the many.

I wouldn't be surprised if he is elected, but with a small majority, we may even end up with a hung parliament.

And what of the others? The Lib Dems picked the wrong leader. Vince Cable is by far and away their most consistent and down-to-earth speaker. He comes over as an eloquent and forthright MP and one who shares old-fashioned values with a good dose of common sense.

UKIP remains a leaderless, rudderless enterprise, which should be romping through the polls, but alas, shows little direction. I have no doubt the BNP will continue to rise slowly but surely, and less slowly if nothing is done to stem immigration.

Surely, any fool who leads this country – and it seems to be a job which attracts them – can see that immigration is the most pressing area to control. This is the basis of how our society, our values, our heritage and our culture survive. We firstly need to tighten up our border agencies. Our lax system is allowing thousands to exploit loopholes in visa control, plus passport, multiple and extra wives and arranged marriages. One birth in five in this country is to a foreign woman. This has an enormous impact on our NHS, an NHS they have contributed nothing towards. It impacts on our benefits system, a benefits system they have contributed nothing towards. It impacts on our housing stock and our workplace and that's before our culture and social order have been considered. I remember last June when cheap Eastern European labour was being brought into Lincolnshire. At the time local unemployment was rising fast. A Boston resident remarked, "I am not against foreign workers coming over here but how many more can the town take? We are bursting at the seams. I'm getting to the stage where I don't like going into town because I never hear anyone speaking English. It's very intimidating".

That most ineffective of Immigration Ministers, Phil Woolas, stated, "We've got it wrong on immigration". Patricia Hodge, Labour Minister, commented that, "Indigenous families are being marginalized". Judge Trigger said, "Britain's immigration policy is desperate" and these are the ones whose comments have made the headlines. Millions of us feel the same. In Newham, London, 74.8% of all babies born are to immigrants. London's overall figure is 55%. Out of interest, Torfaen in South Wales is 3%, but it's mixed blessings! You are either surrounded by burkhas or drowning in a sea of phlegm as the locals sing their way down the valleys to watch Wales playing rugby – there's lovely! Eighty per cent of Somalis, 49% of Turks and 41% of Bangladeshis are all in social housing. All this at a time when there is political pressure from the EU to take in yet more African refugees – great for Wimpey and Barratts, not so great for the countryside and wildlife.

Do those in power not understand the indigenous white population's frustration when we see our fairness and tolerance stretched to breaking point? The taxpayer has paid a fortune sending illegal immigrants back to their country of origin. In many cases those concerned have not been allowed back and we're left funding their return flight, where they slip nicely through the statistics and into the benefits system. A foreign attacker carries out one rape in six. Eight million pounds has been spent by the UK Border Agency on public relations. Twenty-five million pounds has been spent on translations for immigrants. Twenty million pounds per annum has been paid in benefits to immigrant children. Last year, 220,000 were given British passports, that's 57% up from the previous year. It is estimated that it will cost the UK £130 billion if we were to give an amnesty and allow those awaiting deportation to stay. And for what?

Kent County Council has been handing out envelopes of cash containing up to £25 per week to immigrant youths in order for them to "learn to use our money". I'm sure they don't need any help on that score. When are the good people of Kent going to rise up and protest against this and many other misuses of their hard-earned money? The Muslim population of this country is now 2.4 million – that's a hell of a lot and worrying when you consider that one in four, worldwide, are Muslim. Many have said they have chosen Britain because of our tolerance to their dress and religion. Alan Johnson, the Home Secretary, has publicly stated that Britain can cope with the flooding of new arrivals and he is happy for a population of 70 million in this country. Well, he would be – they will never be living next to him or his cronies. Those in power are never exposed to the living and working conditions of the ordinary man.

I used to have a modicum of respect for Mr. Johnson, but his assumption that Britain can "cope" with 70 million because "we are a civilised society" beggars belief. All respect vanished at that point. What does he expect the population to do? Just stop? The children of the children will be reproducing, especially with the child benefit, child trust fund, housing benefit, incapacity benefit..... The number of immigrant offspring will have repopulated to the point that the likes of Bradford and Oldham will be seen in what were traditionally more leafy areas. Britain is not made up of racists, it's made up of ordinary taxpaying people who are sick and tired of being politically bullied and made to feel unequal in their own country for fear of accusations of racial intolerance. If anyone has been tolerant, it has been the indigenous population, but I really do feel time is running out. Only a nation as tolerant as this would put up with a fire service that designs a new uniform for Muslim workers. In Boris Johnson we have a Mayor of London who encouraged everyone to "become a Muslim for a day". Interesting that he didn't urge Muslims to integrate with us for a day to see how we live in our country. Oh, no. T'is always the other way round.

Only this country would install special toilets with footbaths so that Muslim prisoners can wash their feet before prayers. This has happened in Canterbury jail – and the cost? A mere £17,000. And that's when they've decided to be tried through our courts. There has been an enormous rise in the number of Sharia courts, at the expense of our own legal system. And when they are put in our jails we're now giving them free compasses so that they can pray to Mecca. In some cells the compasses have been painted. If it was down to me, I'd have them facing Merthyr, just for the heck of it! We've seen photographs of three Afghans holding aloft a banner proclaiming "We want our human rights" whilst another held aloft a placard stating, "We want political asylum". So do we and we're the poor buggers who live here!

What other country would put up with immigrants being allowed to protest against our troops overseas the way we do?

I really wouldn't be surprised if there is a very costly amnesty for all and sundry, and if there is, the announcement will be on a day when there is a major disorder somewhere else so that the effect of that announcement is dissipated. Never believe any figures regarding immigration or policies. Take everything as a lie and work back from there. Last year, 395,000 people left our shores. I wonder just how many were white and middle-class. I'd ask the race equality lot, but I don't suppose they would keep or reveal those sorts of statistics – might not look too good on Middle England.

Last summer we watched our televisions as "breaking news" (another irritating phrase) informed us that Romanian immigrants were not receiving the welcome they had expected to find in Belfast. So lacking was the hospitality that they were forced to take flight, literally, back from whence they came. Catholics and Protestants may still hate each other, but they seem to have found a common ground in their dislike of "Johnny Eastern European". You've got to give it to the Ulstermen, they certainly know how to nip a problem in the bud.

Something also has to be done about the corporate and individual greed that has marched steadily across our country over the past twenty years. The BBC, whom I love dearly, must start to draw in the financial excesses that start with those at the top and end with those who are not far from the top! When you read that many of their "executives" earn more than the Prime Minister it tells you something. We have dentists on £300,000 a year. Despite the appalling crash in the financial services industry, bankers' salaries are still rising above the level of inflation. Chief executives of FTSE 100 companies are paid on average salaries of £800,000, plus bonuses of £720,000 and still they don't understand. That new non-job, the EU presidency, is worth £320,000. MPs are making upwards of £200,000 from "work" outside of their parliamentary remit. Border Agency staff received bonuses. Please tell me for what. Network Rail bosses received bonuses when the work was behind schedule. Police chiefs are not only on terrific salaries, some are also receiving bonuses bringing their annual pay to £200,000. Not bad when you consider that the sighting of a policeman on foot patrol is as likely as an albatross at the recycling centre. Police Chief Ian Blair took home a salary, plus bonus, of £580,000. This is not to mention his pension of £160,000 – give or take a quid or two, and that's every year for life. The Kinnocks – you remember them, not a great deal of success in this country, but didn't they do awfully well "over there". It's not been many months since Gordon the Gopher made Glenys Kinnock the Minister for Europe. She and her ex-leader of the Labour Party husband have spent twenty-five years working in Europe, Glenys, as an MEP for fifteen and Neil as an EU commissioner for ten. I wonder if they could honestly tell you of any achievement they have made throughout their tenures that has benefited a single soul in the UK? They may have done, but once again, I must have been in the loo contemplating my navel when it happened. An organisation called "Open Europe" estimates that the couple has made some £10 million between them in salaries and bonuses. Each has a nice little earner in the form of a Euro pension. Glenys will receive a pension from her present job when she retires. She already has a teacher's pension and another UK pension with regard to her old job as an MEP. Neil receives £83,000 pension from Europe and another £29,000 a year for his twenty-five years as an MP in this country. Son, Stephen, has worked for the British Council in Brussels for many years and now works in St. Petersburg, while Rachel, their daughter, was a researcher for Glenys. So they've all done awfully well out of the European taxpayers, whether at home or abroad – very socialist and very "Old Labour".

MPs, and many of those in the House of Lords spent the year stating that they were so sorry for the expenses scandal in which they had become so embroiled and discredited. Sadly, it seems that they were only sorry for being caught. Their greed was universal. Some monies may well have been paid back, but their arrogance is such that you could almost be forgiven for thinking they were German. The Labour peer, Clive Soley, who received £45,000 in expenses said that members of the House of Lords are surviving on "little more than the minimum wage". Health Minister, Ann Keen, whose salary is £96,167 per annum, said she would have been better off "sticking with my job as a nurse". How ungrateful. No-one asked her to go into politics. From duck ponds to moats, from bell towers to flowers, you name it, they claimed for it. Then, we had the flag bearer for all of those who grunted their way through the trough. Mr. Michael Martin, the Speaker – he doesn't seem to have done too badly for himself and his missus. They appear to have milked every conceivable cow put in front of them. In retirement, this smug ex-steelworker will receive an annual pension of £38,000 for his former role as Speaker. He will also receive an ex-MP's pension of £80,000 and as a peer, up to £25,000 in allowances – this for staying overnight when attending the House of Lords. Probably not enough in his eyes, but ever so slightly more than the man deserves. Didn't he do well! Never forget, those who get too big for their breeches, will be exposed in the end!

Here's an interesting little statistic – guess the odd man out.

Lord Stevenson: former chairman HBOS
Fred Goodwin: former chief executive RBS
Andy Hornby: former chief executive HBOS
Tom McKillop: former chairman RBS
John McFall, MP: chairman of the Treasury Select Committee
Alastair Darling: soon to be former Chancellor of the Exchequer
Gordon Brown: soon to be former Prime Minister and former Chancellor
Terry Wogan: former presenter and interviewer

You are probably thinking that the answer is Terry Wogan – and you're not wrong. Terry Wogan is the only one out of this gathering of minds who actually holds any formal banking qualifications! It's this sort of information that you can use at dinner when conversation dries up and you wish to impress your guests.

I remember a certain Conservative prime minister who only seemed to come alive as a spitting image puppet stating, "We will be tough on crime and tough on the causes of crime". John Major would and possibly does make a very good uncle. Sadly, as with many in politics, he was promoted above his level of ability. He wasn't tough on crime, but then neither were his successors, Messrs. Blair and Brown. You know, looking back, I think one of the major causes of despair in this country is the lack of legal guidance as to what measures the ordinary man and woman in the street can take in order to defend themselves. The lack of justice which is meted out and the apathy and misguided logic of the police and judiciary leave us all in a state of continued perplexity.

I recall a judge who allowed a killer to have his tag removed so that he could jet off to Prague for his 21st birthday. Another judge freed two thugs after just one day's imprisonment because he "changed his mind". Judge Adrian Smith decided not to jail a 16-year-old rapist who went on, just days later, to rape a 6-year-old. I suspect society was more to blame than the 16-year-old, it usually is. There was the case of a 73-year-old man and his neighbours driven to despair by vandals. He spent £610 on an advert in an effort to catch the yobs, such was his frustration by the lack of effort made by the police. A disabled pensioner was left pleading with vandals not to damage her car because the police were so ineffective in stopping them. Warwickshire police, who advised a lady who had been assaulted "not to summon officers as it might make matters worse", showed a classic case of arrogance.

Local authorities are no better. A man who suffered years of abuse by yobs pleaded with his council for them to act. They suggested "mediation". The police, councils and housing chiefs collectively stated that they "acknowledged the problems". Gutless, absolutely gutless! The lack of desire to tackle this disease runs from agency to agency. Everyone is involved and collectively absolved from responsibility. No-where was this highlighted more brutally than the deaths of Fiona Pilkington and her daughter. They died after Ms Pilkington set fire to the car they were in. One can only begin to imagine the despair and hopelessness they must have felt, having been let down so badly by both the police and various agencies over so long a period. It was Superintendent Steve Harrod who, when speaking or giving evidence at the inquest into their deaths, uttered the comment that sums up modern policing. He said, "Low-level anti-social behaviour is mainly the responsibility of the council". Says it all really.

If it were not so serious, it would be laughable, but the situation arose a few months ago concerning prisoners who had escaped from jail. These two were both killers who walked out of Sudbury jail in Derbyshire. Derbyshire police refused to release photographs of the two prisoners as it would "breach their human rights". One was later re-arrested in Rochdale after a two months' search, the other was held whilst shopping in Asda. What a very common criminal!

I have come to the conclusion that the number of MPs one could have respect for is probably to be counted on the fingers of one hand. Top of my list would be Frank Field, with Vince Cable second. Actually, I'm now struggling to find a third. Those who run and have run our country have been unfit for purpose, unfit to govern. We have been led by fools. By signing away our freedom, heritage and future to Europe they have reduced their powers, though not their salary. How do these people, so lacking in quality, manage the ascent to such positions of power and control? They lack leadership, courage, guile and most importantly, honesty. Their vision is short term with investment to match. It seems that whichever party is in office, any real change and power lie within the hands of the backroom boys, lobbyists and big business.

Irrespective of recession and whatever decreases are made within vital services that we all pay for; overseas aid remains immune from any cutbacks. Charity should begin at home and until you can afford it, stay there. I have no doubt that climate change is happening. Ask any polar bear. But it has opened up a whole new area for taxation. How much money have we, the taxpayer, spent on advertising the fact that by reducing your car journey by five miles per week you will be saving the planet. Oh, spare me! It's people we need to reduce, numbers that is, not size, although if the world were full of midgets it would surely save space. Blocks of flats could be fitted with mezzanines, whilst the counter tills are already in place at Barclays Bank in Frimley!

Well, time has come to line up the latest group of miscreants, misfits and mishaps. In previous books we've had them stood against the wall and shot. This time we'll try something a little different. The first batch to be rounded up is all those MPs and lords and ladies who snaffled anything more than a paper clip from their office or expense account. Following on behind them are the football agents, estate agents and solicitors who have profited from no-win, no-fee claims cases. Next in line and sprinting into position are the lycra-clad arses who pedal faster than most residential speed limits allow for and who totally ignore all traffic lights. I can see the road is blocked as close on their heels are thousands of caravan owners, driving like lemmings to their fate. Trying to overtake them and hooting raucously are those in their four-wheel drive vehicles with personalised plates who can't even wait to seal their own demise. Walking behind, looking very concerned, are those involved in health and safety, inter-agency partnerships, twinning committees and all others who have cost a fortune and given so little in return. But wait! What is that I hear? Ah, t'is the bells. Every Morris dancer in the land is gathering for one final dance before they become that extinct specie I have dreamt about for yonks.

Now the horns are sounding. It's the last hurrah for the fox and hound brigade. It's nice to see that they're leaving their hounds at the door to be cared for by someone who..... well, cares. They'll all be going down the ladder into the pit of foxes after which the ladder will be retrieved. It's filling up nicely. I've just spotted Jonathan Ross and Russell Brand. They're talking to Gordon Ramsay whose cooking a last supper, but please don't get any closer, the language is as spicy as his chilli. There's a group over there I don't recognise – I'll just go and enquire who they are. Just found out. They are the committee who introduced the costly and pointless Home Improvement Packs. They should have listened to Kirstie Allsopp and Phil Spencer. Talking of Phils, just over there is Phil Woolas, the Immigration Minister, and his friend, the equally pointless Alan Johnson. They're busy, they've been given the task of rounding up all illegal immigrants. Similarly, Jack Straw's demise has been put back until he's finally brought to justice all the thugs, rapists and murderers who were given sentences not commensurate with their crime. The benefit agency staff is spending their last few days accompanying all the benefit claimants, the long-term unemployed and the disability benefits scroungers.

Once rounded up and shot, more money will be available for the genuinely disabled. You see, all's fair in life and death. The gates will remain open for new admissions for the next two months, so please feel free to bring along your very own choices. The final departures will be painfully slow as they will be forced to watch a giant screen. This will show that picture of Fred Goodwin smiling as he was driven off into retirement and an extremely healthy bank balance – or so he thought. He will be with the rest of those in the city who brought down our country so dramatically. They will all be put into a pit of vipers. They should feel at home with other snakes. Two well known faces will be kept back for a final dinner. Harriet Harman and Trevor Phillips will join me one evening soon. Over this dinner I will ask Ms Harman if looking back over her career there is anything she actually and genuinely thinks she has done that has benefited the public who have paid so much for her salary. I will ask her if she doesn't think in hindsight it would have been more beneficial for her and us to have gone into a life of domestic servitude, been a housewife, borne children and made sure dinner was on the table for hubby when he returned from a shift at a factory near Accrington. I will also ask her if she really thought it was worthwhile giving women the vote when one sees pictures of scantily clad chapesses throwing up in Cardiff city centre at 2 am. Whilst she muses over the answers I will turn to Trevor Phillips and ask him if he really feels it was a good thing abolishing slavery, as the moment this happened inflation took off. You knew where you were with slavery, everyone knew their place, labour was cheap – all right, you had to feed it – and okay, you had to invest in shackles and chains, but for the slaves it was a cheap and effective introduction into a lifetime of bondage, which as you know is quite an expensive proposition these days in the West End, or even Eastleigh!

I think the following little gag will be proven truer than at first it may appear. President Obama and Gordon Brown are both shown a time machine which can see twenty years into the future. They decide to test it out by asking one question each. President Obama goes first. He asks, "What will the USA be like in twenty years' time?" The machine whirrs and beeps and goes into action before giving a printout. "This is good", he says, "it states that our country is in good hands, crime is non-existent, there is no conflict, the Taliban are beaten, North Korea is a democracy, inflation is low and our economy is healthy". Gordon Brown thinks, "It's not bad, this time machine, I'll give it a go". So he asks, "What will Britain be like in twenty years' time?" The machine once again whirrs and beeps, goes into action and gives him a printout. He just stares at it. "Come on, Gordon", says Obama at length, "what does it say?" "I can't tell you", says Gordon, "it's all in Arabic".

When all's said and done, and push has come to shove, nothing changes. I really would like to witness greater depths in speech patterns and word usage. I object to "'n' stuff", which seems to be the "stuff" of all and sundry under twenty-five years of age. I object greatly to the insidious rise in Americanisms, "upcoming", for "forthcoming", "train station" instead of "railway station", "garbage" for "rubbish", "rubbishing" for "criticising". Another one is "downplayed" instead of "played down", "upbeat" – what was wrong with being optimistic? "Skedule", "no brainer", "It's a big ask", "It's a given" can all be added to the incinerator in Room 101. Another phrase liked by women is, "So", as in "I'm so not into dairy products" or "I'm so not liking my work", etc. etc. And if it's not Americanisms, it's that dreadful antipodean trait where the voice goes up at the end of a sentence in the manner of someone asking a question.

Another irritation is when saying "thank you" to someone who has helped you or given service, they respond with "no worries" or "no problems". Once again, I assume these two phrases are products of our reliance on Australian soaps to augment our English vocabulary. I always retort, "I wasn't worried to begin with", or "I never saw it as a problem in the first place". These phrases have to be said in a slightly dismissive manner, but then I'm sure you understood that anyway, what with you being a proper person!

T'is New Year's Eve and Maureen, Ben and I will be spending the night indoors. It used to be with wine, nibbles and possibly neighbours. Latterly it's been with cocoa, in bed before midnight and a Victor Meldrew DVD playing loudly enough to drown out the endless rounds of fireworks being detonated by common people on estates. What with Ben and his phobia, I can't see us getting any sleep before 1am. Televisions are on in four rooms in an effort to minimise his stress. We watched the final episode of "Gavin and Stacey" and wished we hadn't. Sadly, it was a series too far. Jules Holland's "Hootenanny" is underway and is a marginal improvement on Andy Stewart and Moira Somebody who, in the days of my childhood, made whoopee with a Scottish accent. So before I write these last lines, I'll just mention that Maureen has looked through various brochures (I've looked through various pub guides) in an effort to pin down a destination for our, well Maureen's, weekend away. You do remember, don't you? It's part of my Christmas present to her. Anyway, we're off for three days to Essex. I know, but it sounds like a very nice pub on Mersea Island. Then again, it sounded like a very nice pub in the Peak District last year. There are lots of wetlands to walk round, watching wading birds and maybe the odd Vauxhall Corsa from a hide. Well, at least it's a break. Don't ever tell me that I don't treat that woman like a queen!

One final joke:

This concerns an elderly couple who were both widowed. They had been going out with each other for some time and having been urged on by their friends, decided it was time to get married. Before the wedding they went out to dinner and had a long conversation regarding how their marriage might work. They discussed finances, living arrangements and so on. At length the old gentleman decided it was time to broach the subject of any physical relationship. "And how", he asked rather tentatively, "Do you feel about sex?" The lady paused, before replying, "I would like it infrequently". The old gentleman sat quietly for a moment, adjusted his glasses, then leaned across the table towards her and whispered, "So, just to clarify the situation, is that one word of two?"

Messrs. Biggs and Al Megrahi have both beaten expectations and the system by making it into the New Year – and possibly the Honours List. I have no idea as to whether Sainsbury's regularly stock Gala pie as we now tend to shop at Morrisons in Fleet, although I did see a sign advertising a Persian rug sale close to Godalming (GU7). Our larder is stocked with Branston pickle and a fine selection of Wilkin of Tiptree jams, marmalades and lemon curd. So, all's well on the domestic front, though I'm still receiving counselling as I've never quite been able to come to terms with Jif being rebranded as Cif.

Can you hang on a mo? I'd better go and lock the front door before I forget. You never know, I could be radished in my bed. No, you're right – not with my diabetes. Tomorrow morning I shall contact the printers and get this show on the road. With the march of sycophancy towards everything minority, one wonders just how long it will be before freedom of speech and writing are banned under counter-terrorism laws and books such as this are burned on a funeral pyre of rights and retribution. Given the similarities between Neville Chamberlain's appeasement to Hitler and our government's lamentable surrender to all things Muslim, it probably won't be long.

As Boy George treads his way to the mike once more and the clock ticks menacingly towards midnight, it's time to say one's goodbyes. So, to those of you who have illegally chosen to stay in our once beloved country, I wish you a speedy despatch and a Crappy New Year. To proper people everywhere, I wish you all the best in fortitude, knowing that whatever the New Year brings, it will be the same as last year, but only more costly. It's also goodbye to Abbey (National, as was) and the Bradford & Bingley, now swallowed by that Spanish giant, Santander. Goodbye also to Norwich Union, now under the branding of Aviva, which sounds awfully like a transport franchise. For me, whenever I awake, which is often a disappointment in itself and I think of the misery that each day will bring, I comfort myself in the knowledge that despite being top cat of all she surveys, head of an inbred, dysfunctional, multi-cultural family whose ancestry can be traced back to Scotland, Germany, Greece, Denmark and most of the civilised and uncivilised world and probably Merthyr Tydfil, the Queen may well reside in Windsor Castle, but she still possesses a Slough postcode – and that helps me through the day!

So a Happy New Year, and in the words I feel sure Dave Allen would have uttered had he been lysdexic – "Goodnight, and may your Dog go with you".

AFTERTHOUGHT

Millions of men and women died so that these islands remained free. Free from rule by outside forces. Free for citizens to voice their opinions. Free for our culture and values to flourish. Our manners, our ability to "turn the other cheek", our ability to "queue" have been admired universally. So why, when the Scots, Irish and Welsh are encouraged to feel a sense of nationality, is England's being eroded.

Successive governments, aided, abetted, actively encouraged and legislated by the E.U. have reduced England to a "region", bereft of identity, individuality of thought and pride.

The worm must turneth, so that the shackles of foreign rule may be released and an Englishman's pride restored, with his head held high, knowing who he is and what he stands for...

You might like to read the reviews and comments regarding other books and CDs published by Trouser Press.

All books are available direct from Trouser Press, PO Box 139, Aldershot, Hants, GU12 5XR, P & P £1.50 per book, £1.00 per talking book (CD)

FROM WHERE I SIT
by Anthony Mann
ISBN: 978-0-9516501-0-3
Price: £6.99 (second re-print)

What the critics say:
"Set to become a humour classic..... the find of the year"
  - WH Smith's Bookcase Magazine

"Liberals with a heart condition beware" - Croydon Advertiser

"An amusing collection of personal experiences, anecdotes and memories" - Surrey Mirror

"The book earns the author full marks for humour, determination and street-wise common sense" - Aldershot News & Mail

AS I WAS SAYING
by Anthony Mann
ISBN: 978-0-9516501-1-0
Price: £5.50

"Courageous enough to write what most of us think....."
  - Surrey Advertiser

"A humorous look at life as it really is" - Croydon Advertiser

"Rude, insensitive, arrogant, self-opinionated, sexist – he is also very, very funny" - Wandsworth Borough News (author's note: I particularly warmed to that review!)

THE FURTHER THOUGHTS
OF CHAIR MANN
by Anthony Mann
ISBN: 978-0-9516501-7-2
Price: £5.99

"The book for all Millenniums, not just this one" - Author

"Lively reading for your holiday? Commuter train? Outside toilet? – this is the book for you!" - Author again

"I don't know why he doesn't get a proper job!" - Author's mother

And when he's not A. Mann

THE CLUB –
An Everyday Story of Trainspotters
By Mel Rees
ISBN: 978-0-9516501-2-7
Price: £4.99

"There is humour found a-plenty in Mel Rees's novel, The Club - Sunday Express

"There is an honesty about the characters that is refreshing ...the story is highly entertaining, I struggled to put it down" - Railway Magazine

"The author has discovered a rich vein of comic drama, a highly readable story unfolds ...David Shepherd's appearance adds a further touch of authenticity to a believable story" - British Railway Modelling

"Light-hearted, barbed but not vicious and entertaining – don't blame me if you find yourself in the pages" - Railway World

The following are talking books, each lasting 2 ½ hours
(two discs per CD)

A MANN AT LAST
by Anthony Mann
ISBN: 978-0-9516501-4-1
Price: £11.99

Equality! Political correctness! Tolerance – you'll find none
of it here News, views and comments on life's little problems
– like life itself.

From the over-stated, to the under-staffed, the over-blown, to
the under-estimated – all human life is here. Compensation,
asylum, minority rights, fox-hunting, no turn is left unstoned.

"Thought provoking", "Wonderfully entertaining"
"Hilarious", "Like a breath of fresh air"
(These comments were uttered by friends of the author, or those
accustomed to taking backhanders.)

A MANN FOR ALL REASONS
by Anthony Mann
ISBN: 978-0-9516501-5-8
Price: £11.99

Enjoy listening as the CD unfolds and all human frailties
are exposed. From the under-stated to the over-staffed, the
under-blown to the over-estimated – all human life is dissected
and reassembled.

"Refreshingly thought-provoking", "A cynical view of the
Septic Isles"
(These comments were uttered by the same friends who listened
to above CD. Trainspotters don't have many friends.....)